WOMEN IN GERMAN YEARBOOK

11

EDITORIAL BOARD

Leslie A. Adelson, Ohio State University, 1992–2000
Angelika Bammer, Emory University, 1992–2000
Barbara Becker-Cantarino, Ohio State University, 1992–2000
Jeannine Blackwell, University of Kentucky, 1992–97
Gisela Brinker-Gabler, State University of New York, Binghamton, 1992–97
Helen L. Cafferty, Bowdoin College, 1992–97
Jeanette Clausen, Indiana University–Purdue University Fort Wayne, 1995–2000
Susan L. Cocalis, University of Massachusetts, Amherst, 1992–97
Gisela Ecker, Universität-Gesamthochschule-Paderborn, 1992–97
Ruth-Ellen B. Joeres, University of Minnesota, Minneapolis, 1992–97
Anna K. Kuhn, University of California, Davis, 1992–97
Sara Lennox, University of Massachusetts, Amherst, 1992–2000
Ricarda Schmidt, University of Sheffield, England, 1992–2000
Inge Stephan, Humboldt-Universität zu Berlin, 1995–2000
Arlene Teraoka, University of Minnesota, Minneapolis, 1995–2000
Susanne Zantop, Dartmouth College, 1995–2000

PAST EDITORS

Marianne Burkhard, 1984–88
Edith Waldstein, 1984–87
Jeanette Clausen, 1987–94
Helen Cafferty, 1988–90

WOMEN IN

Feminist Studies in German Literature & Culture

GERMAN

Edited by Sara Friedrichsmeyer & Patricia Herminghouse

YEARBOOK

11

University of Nebraska Press, Lincoln and London

© 1995 by the University of Nebraska Press. All rights reserved. Manufactured in the United States of America. Published by arrangement with the Coalition of Women in German.
♾ The paper in this book meets the minimum requirements of American National Standard for Information Sciences – Permanence of Paper for Printed Library Materials, ANSI Z39.48-1984.
ISBN 0-8032-4781-8 (cloth)
ISBN 0-8032-9785-8 (paper)
ISSN 1058-7446

CONTENTS

Acknowledgments vii
Preface ix

Jutta Brückner 1
On Autobiographical Filmmaking

Margaret McCarthy 13
Consolidating, Consuming, and Annulling Identity
in Jutta Brückner's *Hungerjahre*

Janice Mouton 35
Margarethe von Trotta's Sisters: "Brides Under a Different Law"

Jenifer K. Ward 49
Enacting the Different Voice: *Christa Klages* and Feminist History

Renate Möhrmann 67
"Germany, Pale Mother": On the Mother Figures in New German Women's Film

Barbara Becker-Cantarino 81
"Gender Censorship":
On Literary Production in German Romanticism

Dagmar von Hoff 99
Aspects of Censorship in the Work of Karoline von Günderrode

Lewis Call 113
Woman as Will and Representation:
Nietzsche's Contribution to Postmodern Feminism

Alyth F. Grant 131
From "Halbtier" to "Übermensch":
Helene Böhlau's Iconoclastic Reversal of Cultural Images

Lynda J. King 151
Vicki Baum and the "Making" of Popular Success:
"Mass" Culture or "Popular" Culture?

Katharina von Ankum 171
Motherhood and the "New Woman": Vicki Baum's *stud. chem. Helene Willfüer*
and Irmgard Keun's *Gilgi—eine von uns*

Friederike Eigler 189
Feminist Criticism and Bakhtin's Dialogic Principle:
Making the Transition from Theory to Textual Analysis

Imke Lode 205
The Body in the Discourses of Colonial Savage
and European Woman during the Enlightenment

Sara Friedrichsmeyer and Patricia Herminghouse 223
The Generational Compact: Graduate Students and Germanics

About the Authors 229
Notice to Contributors 233
Contents of Previous Volumes 235

ACKNOWLEDGMENTS

In addition to members of the Editorial Board, the following individuals reviewed manuscripts received during the preparation of volume 11.

We gratefully acknowledge their assistance.

Sigrid Bauschinger, University of Massachusetts, Amherst
Ute Brandes, Amherst College
Barton Byg, University of Massachusetts, Amherst
Sandra Frieden, University of Houston
Marjorie Gelus, California State University, Sacramento
Eva Geulen, University of Rochester
Anke Gleber, Princeton University
Willi Goetschel, Columbia University
Marjanne Goozé, University of Georgia
Atina Grossman, Columbia University
Susan Gustafson, University of Rochester
Sabine Hake, University of Pittsburgh
Beatrice Hanssen, Harvard University
Ritta Jo Horsley, University of Massachusetts, Boston
Sheila Johnson, University of Texas, San Antonio
Lynda King, Oregon State University
Barbara Kosta, University of Arizona
Erika Kluesener, Clarion University
Alice Kuzniar, University of North Carolina, Chapel Hill
Nancy Lukens, University of New Hampshire
Janet Lungstrom, University of Colorado
Claudia Mayer-Iswandy, Université de Montréal
Richard McCormick, University of Minnesota, Minneapolis
Heidy Margrit Müller, Universiteit Gent
Vibeke Petersen, Drake University
Simon Richter, University of Maryland, College Park
Lisa Roetzel, Eastman School of Music, University of Rochester
Azade Seyhan, Bryn Mawr College–Haverford College
Monika Shafi, University of Delaware
Patricia Simpson, University of Michigan
Katie Trumpener, University of Chicago

Special thanks to Victoria Hoelzer-Maddox for manuscript preparation.

PREFACE

With this volume, the *Women in German Yearbook* enters its second decade, marked, we hope, more by continuity with its tradition of excellent and innovative feminist scholarship in all areas of German literature and culture than by dramatic change for the sake of change. But change there has been, too.

New, for example, is a recent decision by the Editorial Board that seeks to broaden the extent to which work published in the *Yearbook* is read and discussed by scholars in other disciplines, such as feminist studies, film studies, other literatures, and history. To this end, a policy of publishing all articles in English has been established, the result of which can be evaluated in the present volume. Implementation, as many of our contributors can attest, has not been easy, particularly in the case of our wish to increase contributions by feminist Germanists in the Federal Republic and other countries abroad. While encouraging readers to tell us their responses to the new policy, we will continue to receive and review submissions in English or German and pursue the question of translation only after a manuscript has been accepted for publication.

With thirteen contributions from three continents, authors from all ranks of the profession, topics ranging from the eighteenth century to recent years, and attention to philosophy, film, drama, popular literature, and theory, Volume 11 reflects the diversity of interests and talents on which the *Yearbook* has thrived. While our contributors hardly speak as one, the collection of their voices offers considerably more than cacophony: Articles that are significant in themselves, enter, when clustered together in ways unforseen by their authors, into engrossing dialogue with one another. The volume opens with a contribution from filmmaker Jutta Brückner, one of our special guests at the Nineteenth Annual Women in German Conference in October 1994, at St. Augustine, Florida. Her essay traces her attempts at expressing her own female subjectivity and documents her discovery that autobiography is inextricably grounded in the biography—and the body—of the mother. "The body," she asserts, "had to be reconstructed before language could be won back." Brückner's analysis of the development that led to her stunning 1980 film, *Years of Hunger* (*Hungerjahre*), is followed by Maggie McCarthy's commentary on that film. Mc Carthy develops a detailed analysis of how experiences that evade language in the struggle for subjectivity are given expression through the images of the film.

While McCarthy's ability to read Brückner's film is grounded in the psychoanalytic theories of thinkers such as Jacques Lacan and Julia Kristeva, Janice Mouton moves beyond Freudian models and draws upon D.W. Winnicott's insights on "play" and the "relational space" between the sisters in two of Margarethe von

Trotta's best-known films. Employing yet another critical lens, Jennifer K. Ward examines von Trotta's first film within the historical context of feminist thought in the 1970s and the gendered moral code that Carol Gilligan explicated in her early work. The attention to early critical reception in Ward's analysis also serves as the point of departure for Renate Möhrmann's spirited critique of filmic representations of motherhood. Moving from *Germany, Pale Mother* (*Deutschland, bleiche Mutter*) to larger questions of the depiction of motherhood in the international history of film, Möhrmann locates the subversive potential of German women's film in its resistance to the narrative pattern that E. Ann Kaplan has categorized as the classic maternal melodrama: the sacrifice of the mother so that the child, who is almost inevitably male, can be integrated into the world of the fathers. Möhrmann concludes her arguments about the paradigm shift in German feminist film—and our film cluster, as well—with a provocative reference to the work of Brückner.

Refocusing our attention on an earlier period, two articles assess the role of gender in censorship. Barbara Becker-Cantarino's essay on "gender censorship" examines the impact of Fichte's philosophy in establishing male tutelage over the intellectual and literary activities of women. Reference to women Romantic writers, such as Caroline Schlegel, Dorothea Schlegel, Therese Huber, and Sophie Mereau, demonstrates the extent to which women adjusted their literary activities to patriarchal norms. The workings of such "gendered censorship" are further explored by Dagmar von Hoff. Invoking Freudian paradigms, von Hoff argues that elements of external and internal censorship explain not only Günderrode's suicide and the attempts to cover it up, but also distinctive features of her attempts at self-expression: her use of authorial pseudonyms and her decision to leave some of her dramas unfinished.

In yet another look at a philosopher whom feminists have often dismissed as misogynist, Lewis Call examines the possibilities offered by Nietzsche's thought for a contemporary feminist position that recognizes "woman" as multiple and as representation. In their resistance to modernist feminism, he suggests, Nietzsche's texts attempt to construct a new metaphor of woman that contains possibilities for post-modern feminist politics. Nietzsche's penchant for referring to women with images of wild beasts recurs in the following article. Alyth Grant shows how Helene Böhlau's novel *Halbtier!* resists the oppressive ethos of self-sacrifice examined in some of the preceding articles of this volume, both drawing upon and subverting key concepts of Nietzschean philosophy, such as the notion of *Übermensch*, to develop new possibilities for female subjectivity.

The emancipatory tendencies detected by Grant in Böhlau's 1899 novel come to the fore in the Weimar period and are examined in two quite different approaches to popular literature of this period. Lynda King discusses the marketing of Vicki Baum and her serialized novel *stud. chem. Helene Willfüer* in terms of its appeal to the ideology of the "New Woman," but then argues, using recent theories about the power of readers to make their own meanings from artifacts of popular culture, that the novel ought not be dismissed according to the conventional critique of "mass culture." While King does not deny evidence that Baum's novel can also work to "tame" and contain women within the political system, Katharina von Ankum takes a more critical stance toward the configuration of the "New Woman" and the "New Mother" in novels by Baum as well as by Irmgard Keun. Von Ankum contends that these novels ultimately adapt a kind of essentialist femininity and cult of rationality that prepared the ground for the National-Socialist backlash against women.

The two final articles are specifically concerned with feminist applications of theory. Friederike Eigler reviews feminist appropriations of Bakhtin's theories and suggests the usefulness of terms such as "the dialogic," "voice," and "heteroglossia" for feminist criticism. Turning to Lou Andreas-Salomé's story "Eine Ausschweifung," she illustrates how Bakhtin's linguistic categories "facilitate the exploration and identification of women's multiple and often contradictory subject positions." Taking as her point of departure a 1987 article by Sigrid Weigel, Imke Lode demonstrates the difficulty feminist critics encounter in the attempt to rethink issues of race and ethnicity, gender and sexuality. She posits the need for integrating these issues discursively and materially into discourses of the body, thereby enabling women to challenge patriarchal constructions of history and knowledge. Although spatially separated from the opening articles of the volume by some two hundred pages and chronologically by some two hundred years, Lode's text is linked to them thematically in ways that we hope will stimulate and delight.

The volume concludes with the editors' ruminations on the "generational compact" that defines the relationship between graduate students and faculty in Germanics. While asking tough questions of ourselves and our discipline is nothing new for Women in German, the actual issues are perennially new; we hope that this issue of the *Yearbook* reflects them in sufficiently provocative form.

In producing this first all-English volume, the editors are grateful for the assistance of Jeannine Blackwell, Barton Byg, Esther Fritsch, Marjanne Goozé, and, most especially, Jeanette Clausen. Jeanette concluded her official duties as coeditor with volume 10, but has not withdrawn her commitment and support, to say nothing of her superb talents in the art of translation. The University of Cincinnati and the University of Rochester have generously supported the work of editing the *Yearbook* with significant financial and human resources.

Sara Friedrichsmeyer
Patricia Herminghouse
August 1995

On Autobiographical Filmmaking

Jutta Brückner

Jutta Brückner's autobiographical essay traces her own development from early attempts to write the text of her "female subjectivity" in the language of prose to her discovery of how much more suited the medium of film was for establishing an immediate relationship to her material. Arguing that autobiography is a desire, not an accomplishment, she locates the beginning of that desire in the mother, whose images have to be reconstructed in order to free the self. The dialectic of history and biography, loss of language and loss of body, is played out in the struggle between mother and daughter in the films of the body-less author. Losses that cannot be recovered via the written word can be shown in the images of film. In trying to locate the place that women can actually occupy in the cultural scripting of history and identity, Brückner traces two lines of autobiographic approach: a semiotic one in which the daughter separates from the body of the mother and a symbolic one that concentrates on the language and culture defining the autobiographical line of the father. (PH)

I began filmmaking as an autodidact after giving up writing, which I had worked at for some time. No matter what I wrote, it was never what I wanted to write. It was not a question of good or bad, nor of true or false, but rather that I never reached the center of my desire to write, the center from which legitimation must come. I wrote in the third person; it was impossible for me to say "I," but this third person remained a phantom. I noticed that the closer I came to myself while writing, the stronger were the tones that overwhelmed the few traces of the external world present in my texts. In the 1970s, under the influence of the women's movement and the escape to a different life that it provoked in many women, my desire to write grew out of a longing for "female subjectivity." But the many prose descriptions of breaking away (*Aufbrüche*) that were produced at the time had nothing in common with what I wanted to do. My concern was not with movement literature but with creating a mark of my existence in poetic language. Apparently I had no talent for writing. I found my texts deficient, tore them up, threw them away, burned them. I grew silent.

Through a biographical accident, I met some filmmakers and immediately seized upon this new medium with the vague expectation that the film image would help me succeed in crossing that threshold at which words had forsaken me. As for film: It was the period of German "auteur film," which approached image-making almost as a cottage industry, like something preindustrial. In German television at the time there was a very important department for beginners. It produced films that were intended to be as spontaneous and personal as notes written in pencil. This filmmaking was closely related to writing; it was like working at the kitchen table, hungering for new views of reality. It had much to do with the intensive relationship to one's material that is well-known from the other arts, and very little to do with the specialized professionalism that characterizes film as a business in which money and the laws of a consciousness industry dominate. At the time, film as a medium was more open to questions than at almost any other time in its history. I very soon realized that it would certainly release me from my realism problem. For no matter what approach you take in film, the photographic image portrays external reality without fail—before the question of what you want to say about this reality has even been asked.

In film I took up the thread at the point where it had broken off in writing. My first film project was just as autobiographical as my writing had been. It was named after the segment of my life in which I planned it: *Aufbrüche* (Breaking Away). It is the story of a woman who sets out, though it is not clear where from or where to. At the time, breaking away was the movement that led women out of the isolation of a feminine-domestic existence into a community of other feminists and on to political action. In my script there is constant talk of such a breaking away. Only it doesn't take place. Yet the farthest thing from my mind was to demonstrate that such a breaking away was impossible. Nor could it simply be blamed on a beginner's ineptness—scriptwriting is an art that must be learned, after all—for the obvious scenario would have had the protagonist break away and escape into political activism, as was constantly happening around me in those very politicized feminist times. The remarkable thing was that "breaking away" and "immobility" had to be reconciled for my protagonist, and I realized that solving her life-problem would require more than a society that was more equitable to women. The breaking away depicted in the film did not lead to a political utopia, but to a life in which the mark of the protagonist's existence found expression in her becoming a filmmaker. This released the film's author, the filmmaker, both from her desires for expression and her existential fears. Critics could then jeer that it was a self-referential loop, an empty form; that the author was lacking a theme and that I was concerned only with using poetic language to create for myself a social space in the symbolic order that I wanted my protagonist to enter. I did not spare myself such reproaches. But something else was happening here. In a perfect and therefore self-destructive way, this project revealed the truth of the statement: *autobiography is a desire, not an accomplishment.*

This statement, still important today, was never more true than at this historical moment, when feminism was functioning as a mirror in which women "jubilantly," as Lacan says of small children, discovered their image as a perfect one, and their jubilation concealed the knowledge that they are not who they think they are. For me, the jubilation also contained proof that individuality begins with the felt need for autobiography, and that autobiography no longer is the sum of a lived life, the artifact of a heart-script grown cold, but rather the longing that sets the process of "identity" in motion. And that is precisely why my planned film *Aufbrüche* was so lifeless. It depicted the zero point of desire, the longing for identity circling within itself on a quest for material, a longing like in the eye of the hurricane, where deadly stillness prevails. This film could not be made for reasons that had to do with the topic's law of motion. Reasons having to do with the German funding situation saved me from having to learn this while making it. I grew silent again.

This failing on the second try, after those inexplicable difficulties with writing, showed me that something very basic was missing. Nonetheless, I had learned something important: the fascination of film images in which the external world—past and present, persons and objects—could be rescued and reconstructed. The arsenal of images, that veritable cemetery of modernity, became the key. In a bookstore one day I discovered a book with the photographs of August Sander. In the 1920s, Sander had photographed people as if for ancestral tables of a great pictorial sociology of the classes of German society. These people, usually in their work clothes, facing the camera attentively, are a piece of history of a world in which the individual and the archetypal had not yet diverged. Self-confidently they bear witness to themselves and in like manner to their world without the rupture that is one of the characteristics of modernity. These photos had a very strong attraction for me, and a possible project began to form around the tension between individual and archetype.

And so my first film was not *Aufbrüche*, a film about the zero point of an autobiographical desire that could show only an imaginary I, but *Do Right and Fear Nobody* (*Tue recht und scheue niemand*), a film inspired by the materiality of August Sander's photos about the real life of a woman in the last sixty years of German history. This woman, a true child of her petty bourgeois class, was to narrate her life, which had run its course prototypically in the metaphysical unreality that this period of history had prescribed for women, with all the demands and obstacles to which women had to bow, with their hidden struggles and their often silent revenge, with the unredeemed hopes of a too well-behaved, because eternally childlike, life and the possibility of rebellion. I wanted to show a female view of society and of German history, for during this time every life was marked by the German catastrophes and had to respond to them by conforming or resisting. Through this woman's life it would become clear how difficult it was to distance oneself from collective expectations and assumptions—and how necessary it was nonetheless. I had to find an older woman who would narrate her life to me that way, and I would take this narrative as a model for many other lives, archetypal and personal at the same time. At least, that was my wish.

I had long since found this narrative and the woman who would tell it. She was my mother. Searching for the point where the empty movement of autobiographical desire could finally begin, I had approached her some time earlier and recorded our long conversations on tape. There they had rested as disembodied language and voice until August Sander's photos could be inserted as the bodies that belonged to them. My mother's private stories would have probably continued to rest if the fiction of a historical and sociological paradigm had not lessened the horror that lay in a confrontation with the mother. I imagined that she would deliver the female view of history; I proclaimed her the model for "women and Germany," prototypical in her masochistic compulsion to pursue real life, and I declared her passion for consumption and her hectic urge to make up for missed opportunities to be a generational and class problem. As the reception of the film showed me, this was correct, and it uncovered an unknown view of history. But for me it fulfilled a different purpose. In reality, I was using history to hide the image of my mother.

The devaluation involved in my turning her into a social paradigm came from my fear of confronting the uniqueness of what a mother is for her daughter. When, after my first two failed attempts to look into the (autobiographical) mirror, I was finally able to see something, I saw my mother. The image horrified me, and my horror frightened me even more. I was forced to understand that there was no way around it, that my autobiography did not begin with me, but with my mother. Before the generational chain could be disavowed or severed by awakenings (*Aufbrüche*), it first had to be reconstructed, along with the image of the mother within it. That image had to be freed from the internalized depths of the daughter's life so that the daughter could free herself. My generation was the first one that, with the help of the pill, could make a clear decision not to become mothers and thus to renounce a generational contract that obligated women over and over again to make their bodies the mirror of the maternal one. But if it is really true that having one's own child is the best means for the daughter to resist her tendency to dissolve into the mother—and up to the time when Freud wrote this, no other social rituals were known that could fulfill the same purpose—then the first generation of feminists had to find a surrogate ritual if they didn't want to battle the problem of mother-daughter fusion their whole life long. I found the surrogate in my reconstruction of my mother's image in the medium that, more than any other, keeps the processes of the unconscious in motion. And this movement of reconstruction, which is also the psychoanalytical model, and which long remained characteristic for my filmic method, made me the creator of a maternal object that was different from me and separate from me. It turned the relationship between me and my mother around and at the same time shifted it from the semiotic level, where the bodies are in play, to the symbolic, where the signs reign.

Of course, if all this hadn't remained completely unconscious, it wouldn't have worked. I had to cling to the notion that my mother's life was a model for something more general in which German history, the great trauma for me and an entire generation, plays the main role. The process of making the film was a gradual coming closer to the fact that the woman who was narrating her life and also being photographed was not just anyone. For my self-deception was shared by my rather shy and insecure mother, who would have found it presumptuous to see herself as important enough for a film to be made about her life. While having her photographed in little scenes, so that the individual images could be grouped into photo sequences, my justification—for it was no longer possible to deny that it was her image and no other—became: "It doesn't work as well with others as with her." That was a flat-out lie, for she had resisted a long time and it had taken a lot of convincing before she acquiesced. Step by step, inventing one excuse after another for myself, I drew nearer to my mother in order to wrest from her the image that she wouldn't have given me voluntarily. Her own cooperation sprang from the argument: "I must see to it that it turns out right." For meanwhile, she had accepted herself as the sociological paradigm I had put into her head; my self-deceptions had become hers as well. This masked an unmistakable secret and slowly growing pleasure in herself. When I would ask her to repeat, under better technical conditions and in condensed form, what she had already spoken onto tape for me, she would initially refuse on the grounds that it would then become "a film about me." I went to her cousin and gave her the impossible task of telling me my mother's life as if it were her own. Theoretically that would have been a brilliant justification of my method. But of course it didn't work. The cousin couldn't think of much to say about my mother's life that she was asked to tell as her own. And so, outwardly distressed but inwardly pleased, I could go back to my mother and tell her the experiment had failed. She capitulated a second time. And both times the practical-maternal background to these capitulations was that she suddenly felt responsible for making the venture commercially successful. My new "profession" as filmmaker and producer was suspect, and she feared that I would be held accountable for the production budget if the film failed.

The small sum that the television company had provided me seemed an infinitely large amount to her, as indicated by the sentence she repeated several times in a threatening undertone: "I'm only doing this because you're my daughter." However, that statement also struck at the heart of the project's unconscious history: a mother-daughter system of unconscious mutual agreement and unconscious self-deception.

The film is *Do Right and Fear Nobody,* and it turned into her film, as she told me to my great relief the first time she saw it on the cutting table. It consists entirely of photos. Photos of social and political situations, many photos of unidentified private individuals, photo sequences of my mother and of a series of August Sander's photos. Her person cannot be recognized in the many historical photos; she disappears in the documents. Only in the last third, when she begins to rebel against her prior ideas, does the identical image appear, the picture of *one* face and *one* body, both of which are hers. At this point the photo sequences begin in which the images, all of them snapshots of a situation, try to move away abruptly across their own borders, as if they were trying to learn to walk and yet persist in their immobility. At the end she is sitting with her husband on the sofa and both are looking full-face into the camera, just like the people photographed by Sander fifty years ago. The pose is the same, but the past cannot be recovered. This time the pictures were only made by an employee of Sander's company, an organization that still exists. For August Sander is long since dead. The picture is the flat, badly lighted product of a gray white-collar workers' culture. My mother's commentary is: "I can't do it the old way any more, and I don't know if the new way will work."

History can only be experienced as biography, and biography is formed under the pressure of history. That which I saw as the difficulty, in part also as the failure of her life—the fact that she continually referred to herself in the neutral third person: "that's what one does," "one mustn't do that"—was simultaneously what enabled me even to make the film in this aesthetic form. For photos allowed me to mediate visually her flight from individuality, which also means responsibility. Her voice is unmistakable and concrete because she narrates her life herself. In counterpoint to this, the photos narrate the same story as anonymous, archetypal moments, and in these concrete images she conceals herself, makes herself invisible and anonymous. Through long segments of the film her body is concealed in the anonymous bodies of the many unknown people who make up the collective corpus of the film. Photos show the image that an individual or a class makes of itself as the history of that which is private. The overlapping of biography and history gives the film two protagonists. Next to my mother, the subject of the film is history itself. In the studio, staged after the fact, it would inevitably have become a mere backdrop. Photos are themselves history; they narrate history in an autobiographical way.

The overlapping of biography and history is only one of several overlappings in the film. Another is that of hearing and seeing and the related one of body and not-body. In English this has a secondary meaning that German lacks: body/nobody; one who has no body is a nobody. History is also the history of bodies. For this reason I could not imagine the film with actors, and for this reason, despite all my attempts at self-deception, my mother's image and body ultimately prevailed, late in the process of filming and late in the film as well. I follow the traces of this woman by following her voice, this voice without a body, disembodied voice. My mother speaks. Mother-tongue. Learning to speak means learning one's mother-tongue. In my first film I am mute, listening to my mother-tongue. To learn to speak in images as a filmmaker, I borrow my mother's voice. Learning film language meant for me conquering, together with my mother, the realm of images that, like all elements of the symbolic, is controlled, administered, and passed on by men. I took her with me on this path, and I couldn't have done it without her. The process in which my mother becomes aware of herself as an unmistakable individual is simultaneously the process of my own artistic coming-to-consciousness and my conquest of the artistic technique I had chosen. It became a film of many beginnings. Here the historical beginnings of the aesthetic of the photographic image are reconstructed from the static image to the moment where the image (almost) stumblingly learns to walk in the photo sequences and then stops again.

My mother's biography is the beginning of my autobiography, not only in the sense that without her I simply would not exist, but in another sense as well. She was the matter that I fed on during my breaking away into the symbolic order. The empty autobiographical desire circling within itself had finally found its matter. If I had not been able to make this film, I probably never would have made one. The fundamental thing I had lacked until then, that which I had sought and never found, was there in the form of a female genealogy of art. Another result was that the matter in which the autobiographical desire could now circle does not vanish into thin air by being consumed in the unconscious, as has always been the fate of female matter in Western history. The biography I had made of my mother, in which she is so unmistakably present that she creates her own autobiography, is the beginning of my autobiographical work in progress, the unavoidable foundation stone: matrix, not matter.

And for that very reason I am absent in the film. She narrates the birth of her daughter and the dreams she had for this daughter, but then the daughter completely disappears. The moment this woman becomes a mother, her being-a-mother becomes unimportant. What counts in the film after this is her own process of coming-to-consciousness as a woman and a human being. Had I described her as my mother, I couldn't have left out myself as the daughter. At the time, I was not yet capable of this confrontation. In *Do Right and Fear Nobody*, I am present as a voice that functions like a social authority, speaking the texts that confront and comment on her life. Coming to terms with the daughter's so thoroughly ignored body required a separate film, *Years of Hunger* (*Hungerjahre*), that I was not able to make until five years later. And the autobiographical spiral I had entered with *Do Right and Fear Nobody* required an intermediate station so that I could venture a step closer to myself, a film about my best friend, in which I myself had a powerful role, played by an actress, to be sure, but unmistakably authentic. This film is *A Fully Demoralized Girl* (*Ein ganz und gar verwahrlostes Mädchen,* also translated as *How Low Can a Girl Sink?* and as *A Totally Degenerate Girl*). Making it was like taking a deep breath before the great test of courage that was *Years of Hunger*, a film that fits *Do Right and Fear Nobody* like the always-hidden other half of a medallion.

Years of Hunger tells the story that was left out in *Do Right and Fear Nobody*: the difficult story of my mother and me that led to the silence I had tried to overcome years later through writing. *Years of Hunger* shows the struggle of two bodies for separation, the daughter's dreamed-of beginning of freedom and the mother's insistence on fusion as validation of her own existence. The mother's body is the barrier that blocks the way to the open spaces. Slowly the silencing of the daughter's speech sets in, the destruction of her own body through attempted suicide. And only after I had made this film did it become clear why that which had been impossible in writing was possible in the film image. The autobiography I had struggled so hard to describe was the story of a double loss: loss of the body and loss of language, the one caused by the other. The body had to be reconstructed before language could be won back. Female identities are bound differently and more dramatically to the body than male identities. In autobiographical writing, however, in the stringing together of words, the body is unreachable.

The very young actress, a non-professional, who plays me in *Years of Hunger* and who in appearance and actions was so very different from me, became the guarantee that the film could actually be made. Just as the photographic-documentary gesture in *Do Right and Fear Nobody* had been the condition enabling me to create the image of my mother, this fiction was the condition for my own image. Reconstructing my lost body as that of the young actress created it not as my own, but as "the other," more other than my mother's and more other than that of the "I" speaking off-screen, my own voice, which sets the process of remembering in motion. The author herself is body-less, her body is not on the screen but behind or before it. In this relationship of ego and image the fiction permitted me, in a specific form of stylistic gradation, to find an autobiographical "I." It came about as in Rimbaud's formulation a hundred years ago: "Je est un autre."

This double step was intended to suspend the symbiosis, not only with my mother but also with myself. The fusion of "je" and "moi," of "I" and "me," is a fusion too; it closes a gap I wanted to keep open. The symbiotic resting in one's self would have stopped the movement that had only just begun and needed to be reflexively impelled forward. Its end in the film itself comes about not through an "identity" achieved by cathartic remembering, but by destroying the image in a fire. The image, a picture of the actress, was so much like me that my editor was painfully moved to comment that this was taking narcissism too far. I convinced her that it was not my picture. But if it had been, it would have been clearer that autobiographical desire under the conditions I had experienced is also a circling around a narcissistic blank space.

Years of Hunger makes visible what my longing as well as my difficulty was at the time and then again ten or fifteen years later: writing. The silencing of the words in language and the attempt to regain possession of them by writing go together. The silenced young woman sits at the table trying to write. The result of her self-tormenting struggle is an empty page with the words "Short Story" at the top, and then we hear the sentence ". . . they still spoke not a word." In the fantasy that follows she sees the bodies of dummies torn apart by atom bomb experiments in the Nevada desert, the image of her own internal catastrophe. If the body is lost, language is lost too, and cannot be recovered via the written word. And this loss can be shown in an image because the image can live with the muteness of the flesh. Word and flesh in Western-Christian mythology only come together as God's act of creation. Autobiography as construction of the body's identity in an image is an attempted act of self-creation grounded in the logic of Western individualism. No woman today escapes it, even though it assumes different forms for women than those handed down by the traditional culture for men. The quest for the word is suspended, but not brought to a stop, in the image.

Only then, after my third film, could I regard filmmaking as my profession, to the extent that this is even possible under German conditions. The autobiographical movement that had led from "expression," which came from "confession," to "profession" seemed to be exhausted. I began making other films, which my public did not at first condone because it had the effect of a farewell to "authenticity." My next films were, among others, *Colossal Love* (*Kolossale Liebe*), which is about Rahel Varnhagen, a woman writer of the eighteenth century, and *Do You Like Brecht?* (*Lieben Sie Brecht?*), a film about Margarete Steffin, a woman writer of the twentieth century. I planned two others, about Marieluise Fleisser and Ingeborg Bachmann, that I haven't yet been able to make. I was really not aware that nothing interested me so much as the complex "women and writing," the contradictions and obstacles contained in it, the relation between life, the desire for expression, and social representation. Always present is the question of what is left, the question of the non-ascetic writing practices in which life refuses to be absorbed in the writing, the body refuses to be consumed in the word. The most intensive word for "what's left over" is love. The binary relation of love and body that I had investigated so far becomes a triad of love/body/script, as is clear from the very titles of the films. In the context of a discussion of my most recent project, a film about Bertolt Brecht and his three women, I was asked whether I didn't want to make a film about my father after making one about my mother. I was surprised myself that I'd never had the desire to do this. The woman who had asked answered her own question in a way that temporarily silenced me: "You're doing it though, by planning a film about Brecht." Sometimes one such statement is enough to open up a new association. That was the case here.

But it is not a question of a fantasized family novel in which a magnificent figure becomes the longed-for ancestor and thus authenticates one's own existence. The figure of Brecht the playwright stands for a necessary altercation with the father as cultural authority. This had played no role for me up to that time because I had been working on a female genealogy of art in confrontation with my mother. The altercation with my father is, for me, not one of bodies, but takes place on the symbolic level, at the point where he both promises and blocks access to the realm of culture, holds it open and simultaneously denies admission. Culture and one's own female body are two different worlds, impossible to bring together. The rupture I experienced between them plays no role in the autobiographies we know, those of men. For the male, culture functions as the great mirror, replacing the small private mirror that the mother had been. In the sum of cultural products it recognizes itself again and again as "that which is identical." The body only becomes a major player in illness or death, when it no longer functions. Until then it can continue as a source of the unknown and as a receptacle for the spirit. The mother also remains in the half-twilight of an "uncultural" private attachment; the revolt takes place in the interior space of culture and against its paternal authority figures in competition for the most advanced post of the "avant garde." The new is not new but only a contrast to the old, which had the same assumptions, and not to the other possibility, which comes out of a critique of those assumptions.

I was interested neither in private therapy nor in a film-diary blown up to the size of a film screen, but in art forms connected to life "by the umbilical cord" and not simply self-referentially; therefore, I couldn't avoid grappling with the symbolic system of the father. But what form can it assume when women do not see themselves reflected in the symbolic system, since revolt presupposes such a mirroring? As a woman filmmaker who was gaining ground in cultural production, my experience has been that my female autobiography must pursue the autobiographical project on two different levels: the semiotic level when dealing with the mother, the symbolic level when dealing with the father. One strand is the autobiography of the body, a second is that of the written word, for me the most important part of the paternal culture of law and symbol. For this reason biographical films about women writers from the eighteenth to the twentieth centuries are the other part of my autobiography, and the inclusion of their language and of their attempts to write is part of my own language. In the films about Rahel Varnhagen and Margarete Steffin I have repeated what I had done in the films about my mother and my friend: I incorporated the words of those others as a part of my own filmic language. Over eighty percent of the sound track of each of these films consists of the female protagonists' own language. For Steffin and Rahel it is quotations from their works, letters, and diaries. Thus equipped I enter the confrontation with the symbolic father.

In modernity the subject is not simply there, it must be constructed. How does the female subject construct itself? The questions that emerge from identity crises and intrude on autobiographical processes can only be approached reflexively. Biography is produced in reflection; it is not reproduced according to the pattern of life. But if it is no longer a question of life as a model and autobiography as the likeness of this model, then the likeness can also become a model and identity can consist of the sum total of passages through real and fictional bodies. Art forms can become the horizon of autobiographical sketches without leading to loss of life or dandyism. Over and over again, as in waves of fever, the question of the relationship between art and life arises in modern art, and has been answered again and again by artists in their own individual ways. When autobiography is no longer a literary genre but rather an event mediating as work in progress between art and life, it can become a foundation of identity, if identity is not falsely conceptualized as a thing that one tries to achieve and then possesses. This does not mean, as the dandy would have it, understanding life as a work of art, nor does it mean understanding art as an instruction sheet for life, as feminist movement literature would have it. For me, autobiography, which I can now conceptualize only as "autobiography in progress," is still in search of the place that women can actually occupy in this culture, beyond the fact that they are meanwhile allowed to exhibit their works here and there, that one can see their films and buy their books—all these things still marginally.

The subject from which everything proceeds, even when it doesn't have itself, and the subject toward which everything flows, is the same thing and yet always other, a subject continually in motion and constantly oscillating. This movement can, in the logic of Western development, also be the movement between image and word. With the explosion of new technologies, we are just now entering a new phase of this development. It is necessary for women to intervene here so that the splitting of body and spirit is not perpetuated once more in the splitting of image and word.

Identity and biography are objects of desire, not something that results necessarily from the sum of what has been lived. They are connected to an undisturbed exchange between the individual and the place where the individual lives. This exchange was not available to women, and that is why women's autobiographical urges were so great when the women's movement began. The fact that this need does not exist to the same extent today shows only that a younger generation has a strong desire for "normality"; it does not mean that the underlying questions have been definitively answered.

Translated by Jeanette Clausen

Consolidating, Consuming, and Annulling Identity in Jutta Brückner's *Hungerjahre*

Margaret McCarthy

Situated within German feminist practices of the 1970s, Jutta Brückner's *Hungerjahre* attempts not only to represent the director's youth during the years of the Economic Miracle, but also to find expressive forms to articulate experiences that evade language. While the voice-over searches for such a language, it is hindered, I argue, by its very embeddedness in the structures that produce such stunted subjectivities as Ursula's, the protagonist of the film. More compelling is the voice that Ursula herself constructs through the repressive mechanisms of socialization that shape her subjectivity. By examining how she speaks through the contradictions that characterize her socialization—the double bind of consumption and denial—I emphasize her ability to speak through such contradictions, to create her own language and unique voice through the very oppressive terms that otherwise deform her identity. Although her "language" is ultimately self-defeating and self-destructive, it still manifests the strands of a unique self emerging within the fabric of social, cultural, and historical conditions woven into her subjectivity. (MM)

Autobiographical criticism has undergone radical revision in recent years, having absorbed evolving theories of subjectivity to continually redefine autobiographical selves. No longer beholden to models of self-made men as the prototypical autobiographical subject, critics have been able to locate other kinds of voices and to redefine "self-made" as precisely the project of autobiographers who create, rather than merely reflect, the self in textual form. Ironically, as poststructuralist theory insisted that "real" subjects were irretrievably eclipsed by textual ones, critics were nevertheless able to identify new kinds of subjectivities articulated in autobiographical form. In *Recasting Autobiography,* Barbara Kosta departs from this irony to examine the boom of autobiographical texts and films by women in Germany during the 1970s. By carefully reconstructing the historical conditions in which these texts emerged, Kosta makes it clear that autobiographical selves are inextricably linked to the lives of real women of a particular place and time. She offers a wealth of compelling reasons for autobiography's reemergence in Germany, albeit in significantly altered form. Concerns about fragmented selves in a postmodern world, the disappearance of historical consciousness, the need to work through the past to gain a vision of the future and to examine the "metanarratives that imprint culture and understanding" (6), she argues, spurred autobiographical production. Additionally, women in particular were compelled by even more basic imperatives: the need to find a voice and to articulate publicly, for the first time, "repressed knowledges" previously beyond the purview of cultural consciousness. Kosta identifies two major themes that emerged in women's personal histories: the repression and devaluation of female sexuality and the confrontation with Germany's fascist past (7). Long before autobiography critics began resuscitating the "bios" in autobiography, the real lives to which poststructuralism barred access, German women brought their lives into sharp focus via textual and filmic creations very firmly anchored in German history, past and present.

The nature of the link between textual and real selves, between language and subjectivity in these texts demands, however, closer analysis. German women's autobiographies often lagged behind some of poststructuralism's basic claims and were more the product of other discourses of German feminism as it evolved in the 1970s. Sigrid Weigel wrote two extended articles in the mid-1980s that critiqued many texts written by women for their unproblematized assumptions about language as a presumably transparent medium that could transcribe experience into textual form.[1] As Leigh Gilmore argues, generalizations about how "daily life 'produces,' or even 'causes,' autobiographical forms depend on a kind of formalist gender logic that transcribes lived experience onto textual production and then presumes to read textual *effects* as experiential *cause*" (x). Missing in such logic is an awareness of the extent to which such effects *produce*, rather than reflect, categories of experience. Recent critical theory emphasizes that any process of self-discovery cannot escape the confines of language, which constitutes its very terms from the outset. As Judith Butler writes of women in particular, "representation set[s] out in advance the criterion by which subjects themselves are formed ..." (1). Thus recourse to language to render women "visible" or viable as subjects cannot help but be "self-defeating" (2).

It thus becomes critical to examine carefully the links between textual and real lives in German women's autobiographical works of the 1970s and the assumptions at work there. This is particularly true when such projects are motivated by an attempt to reveal "repressed knowledges" of women's experiences. Such "repressed knowledges" were often located in the process of gendered socialization and were often the focus of filmic productions in particular.[2] Jutta Brückner's *Hungerjahre* specifically aligns itself with this project of speaking unspoken knowledges and expressing experiences that evade language. More specifically, as Kosta argues, the film documents the production of a "self-destructive, self-hating female subjectivity" (153) firmly anchored in the historical conditions of the Economic Miracle years of the 1950s. Kosta pays particular attention to the voice-over, Brückner's own voice, in fact, and the manner in which it attempts to reconstruct a former self with a language "based on personal knowledge and interpretations of her own experiences as a girl and as a woman outside linguistically sanctioned discourses" (154). Kosta emphasizes the ways in which Brückner's voice-over departs from traditional autobiographical practices and assumptions. By engaging in a dialogue with the spectator, Brückner's voice-over encourages active participation in the film's meanings and cultivates distance between spectator and image. Additionally, Brückner in no way assumes a position of sovereignty or mastery over her former self, as autobiographers have traditionally done. At the same time, by naming her former self Ursula, Brückner underscores the inevitable split between autobiographer and autobiographical subject (159–62).[3]

But if language itself, as Judith Butler argues, remains trapped in the very structures that produce such stunted subjectivities as Ursula's, the extent to which Brückner can locate and/or create linguistic forms to capture experience is limited. Much contemporary autobiographical criticism has begun to focus on forms of resistance that challenge, even while they remain implicated and located in, the structures that shape subjectivity. While Brückner's film clearly participates in the earlier feminist project of attempting to articulate a new language, it also represents a young woman who constructs a unique identity and voice *through* precisely the cultural forms and structures that hinder this revised autobiographical aim. To understand this process, however, one must move away from the voice-over to the voice of the film's protagonist. By focusing on the protagonist's own voice, it becomes possible to understand more fully how she participates in the process of socialization that shapes her, how she situates herself within the fabric of social, cultural, and historical conditions woven into her subjectivity, and to glimpse whatever forms of agency emerge, or how the strands of a unique self emerge within this fabric. My analysis thus moves away from the retroactive creations of self located in the voice-over to those created by the film's protagonist. This shift makes it possible to locate a unique voice, a self created within, not seemingly over and above, the repressive mechanisms of socialization.

Hungerjahre reconstructs a former self expunged from memory and almost from life itself. Brückner literally fleshes out the black and white image of her filmic self that burns at the film's conclusion, revealing this self in all its materiality. Ursula, the film's protagonist, slurps soda loudly through straws, menstruates reluctantly, and, above all, articulates her own myriad desires for psychic and corporeal sustenance. Both her own and her mother's body, the latter often graphically represented, loom large throughout the film. Traditionally, the autobiographical subject has taken its cues from the Cartesian subject and enacted a process of separating the body from the mind, the presumed locus of symbolic activity and identity.[4] At first glance, Ursula seems to engage in a similar struggle, as practices of disciplining the body, passed from mother to daughter, structure her "coming of age." Such actions, however, mark Ursula's body with diverse symbolic forms and practices that divide, subdue, and repress—often brutally—her desires. In this sense, it becomes clear that her body, like her mind, squarely inhabits the domain of culture as well. At the same time, however, cultural forces also work to instigate Ursula's desires: throughout the film, she dreams of exotic objects, fashionable clothing, and free-wheeling pirate adventures, fantasies that the immediate cultural surroundings of a working-class family can never fully satisfy. Consequently, Ursula's needs and appetites perpetually threaten to exceed forces that would both produce and contain them.

This process of socialization, with its contradictory demands that Ursula both desire consumer goods, yet also regulate such desires, may have served the larger needs of Germany during the Economic Miracle years. In order to revive the economy, Germans needed to embrace what Susan Bordo identifies as the "double bind" of subjects in consumer culture, or the "contradictory requirement that [they] embody both the spiritual discipline of the work ethic and the capacity for continual, mindless consumption of goods (*Unbearable Weight* 15). The gendered aspects of this socialization further the range of contradictions. For a character like Ursula, the question becomes how to gain independence and a voice in a world where femininity is both put on display, as in the documentary footage of beauty pageants from the 1950s, and then objectified, if not brutalized. Even as Ursula play acts before the mirror with a beret and cigarette, demands nicer clothes and dancing lessons, she is also taunted, harassed, and eventually forced into an unwanted sexual encounter by some of the men she encounters in the film. This socialization situates Ursula at the heart of irreconcilable contradictions of a particular historical moment: women as consumers, partaking of the newly available goods—like fashionable clothes—that ironically consolidate their position as objects to be "consumed" or exploited, and women denying and/or regulating the very desires—for pleasure, for prosperity and an improved economic situation—that such consumer goods instilled in them.[5]

In the midst of these contradictory forces, Ursula searches for a voice and an identity that would enable her to escape the structures that contain her. One could argue, following Foucault, that Ursula's containment within larger social structures renders her a "docile" body,[6] or a body habituated to the cultural forms of femininity at a particular historical moment. The voice that emerges, in fact, does articulate many internalized, conventional desires. Clearly marked by the world that shapes these desires, Ursula avidly reads romantic fiction, dreams of dancing lessons and fashionable clothing. These desires arise in an economy of consumption, fueled by the post-war economy, and are filtered through her parents' working-class desires.

If Ursula does, in fact, inhabit a "docile" body, what space remains in *Hungerjahre* for that vaunted self of traditional autobiographers—that autonomous being who speaks in a unique and singular voice? Can Foucault's "docile bodies" speak?[7] By what means does this voice articulate the unfulfilled desire that permeates *Hungerjahre*? Trapped within competing discourses that promote both consumption of material goods and stringent self-regulation and denial, Ursula longs for escape, autonomy, and differentiation from her parents. Significantly, she dreams not only of exotic items, but of speaking a language that only she and an imagined lover can understand.[8] The conventional nature of her fantasies, however—their very foundation in consumer culture—belie the possibility of this unique and separate language. Even when Ursula imagines exotic goods, lifestyles, and adventures—an obvious bid to differentiate herself from her parents' more conventional tastes—she articulates desires only a few steps removed from her mother's dreams of Persian rugs and Chippendale furniture. To speak her own language and construct that unique autobiographical self, Ursula must make the forms she has internalized to construct her identity *signify* differently.

While escape remains an impossibility for Ursula, she nevertheless constructs a unique voice *through* the competing discourses, especially the logic of consumption, which stamp her subjectivity. While culture, in its myriad, contradictory forms, inscribes itself on both mind and body, the first-person-singular "I" may create an alternative narrative that paradoxically both affirms and thwarts the larger cultural narratives in which it is embedded. A unique self emerges in the *narrative* autonomy with which the "I" articulates its embodiment of cultural forces otherwise wholly inimical to the notion of a core, essential self. If consumption remains the only language available for Ursula to articulate her identity, she uses it in ways that both affirm and thwart its intended effect—to consolidate her position within the family. Within this logic, Ursula initially tries to differentiate herself by dreaming of exotic objects, a form of consumption that again merely affirms her ties to the mother's dreams of improved material wealth. However, Ursula asserts a more radical form of difference when her consumption practices articulate a whole range of other meanings. Rather than "consolidate" herself with such practices, she instead expresses the breakdown of subjective boundaries. They also enable her to articulate a sense of "otherness" not just from her parents, but also from herself, ultimately providing her with the means to annul, rather than to reinforce her identity.

As the film begins, boats bob on water in a park entirely devoid of human presence, a space later marked by Ursula's acute longing and its frustration in an awkward, violent sexual encounter. This opening scene offers a visual representation of a dramatic erasure, of a self wholly stricken from consciousness. The narrator's voice speaks of fleeing a banished earlier self who nevertheless asserts her continued presence in the form of illness, of "mortifying paralysis." Material traces of the thirteen-year-old remain trapped in the thirty-year-old who speaks these words. This insistence bespeaks the continual pull of unfulfilled desire and reveals a suppressed autobiographical imperative articulated by the body. As Juliet Mitchell writes in *Psychoanalysis and Feminism*, "...at every moment of a person's existence, he is living and telling in word, deed, or symptom the story of his life..." (14). *Hungerjahre* manifests that repressed material self, graphically represented in all its bodily functions and desires. Indeed, throughout the film, we see soiled menstrual pads and female genitals being angrily scrubbed free of semen—traces of stubbornly material bodies that exceed and bleed out around the edges of cultural influence and containment.

After the opening, the scene abruptly shifts when the camera slowly pans a long row of uniform windows in a modern-style apartment building. At the same time, a female voice catalogs a list of goods found by an adventurous young boy who makes his way out into the world. The voice speaks of ivory chests, violins, shawls, chess figures, wine glasses: objects which are thoroughly at odds with the uniformity of the windows and which contrast with the modest possessions piled before Ursula and her father on the threshold of the apartment. Ursula herself stands poised on the threshold of puberty, of improved material conditions promised by the Economic Miracle years, and increased access to the larger world. Father and daughter, however, move inwardly into the repressive confines of the family's working-class apartment. As the next shot reveals, this movement takes them into a communal bed as well, where mother, father, and daughter lie together. Here Ursula encounters her mother's efforts to repress the dubious means by which the apartment was acquired, namely through the eviction of an unmarried woman. Throughout the film, Ursula's imagined outward flight, fueled as it is by her parents' aspirations of upward mobility, will repeatedly confront the repressive structures and centripetal force of a nuclear family that both kindle her desires for a better life, but also inhibit these desires through repression and denial.

Initially, mother, father, and daughter are held together by their pursuit of material items. The film's earliest scenes depict them driving and washing their first car and examining supermarket goods piled high on the kitchen table. At the same time, however, such consumption instigates individual desires that alienate mother, father, and daughter from each other. Even if the family collectively bows to the logic of consumption, they all, in fact, long for very different kinds of lives. The mother's dreams of washing machines and new carpets are most clearly inspired by the promises of the postwar years. The father, by contrast, aligns himself with Communists, resistance movements, and workers' unions, situating himself both within and in opposition to the family's consumption practices. Ursula's imagined exotic adventures carry her far beyond the parameters of either working- or middle-class lives. At the same time, though, she comes to embody her parents' contradictory positions; even as she dreams of acquiring material possessions, Ursula's pirate fantasies suggest an anarchic form of resistance. But despite the disparities evident in the family, mother, father, and daughter articulate their individual desires and differences in relation to the consumer practices of a given historical moment.

Tenuous connections among family members are nowhere more obvious than in the small community of women that surrounds Ursula—her mother, grandmother, and aunt. The film most often represents them together as one solid mass, even though physically they do not resemble one another, and their words reveal profoundly different life experiences as well. Ursula's mother often mourns her lost youth and stringent upbringing, while the grandmother waxes nostalgic over her youthful popularity as a talented dancer. Ursula's aunt sits silently and recites the Bible under her breath. While the rituals of consuming coffee work to unite these women and repress their differences, an even stronger form of repression is needed to hold them together—one that veils and contains the materiality of the female body. This veiling occurs throughout the film on many levels—through appropriate dress, by stemming menstrual flow with sanitary napkins, and by using opaque words to describe bodily functions. Such veiling not only covers the particularities of physical difference, but also provides these women with a specious sense of mastery over bodily functions that only partially submit to regulation and containment. For Ursula to join the fold, she must ignore individual differences and unite with these women in rituals of coffee consumption and pedicures, regulating her appetites and grooming her body in similar ways.

Hungerjahre strives everywhere to lift the veil with graphic representations of the female body. When Ursula first begins menstruating, the film depicts her sitting on the toilet surveying the blood in her underwear. Soon thereafter, her mother straps her into a menstrual belt and pad, a gesture that veils and contains those graphic material traces of the female body which the film often exposes. It also demonstrates precisely the mother's sphere of influence: discipline of the female body—both her own and her daughter's—by continually maintaining boundaries in the face of the body's abject traces.[9] Explaining to Ursula that a menstruating woman is "d.u." (*Dienstunfähig,* or "not fit for service," a military designation), the mother uses words that further veil the female body. She also tells the father that Ursula ate too much cake and has a stomach ache, repressing knowledge of the event and linking it to a bodily process out of control.[10] Her explanation suggests an individual unable to regulate basic bodily functions and appetites, or a body that controls the individual, not the other way around. By consuming foods in the proper proportions, veiling and removing the abject traces of her body, the mother demonstrates to Ursula her own way of constructing a cohesive identity.

Female complicity in repression surrounds Ursula as she is brought into the larger female fold of women that her mother, grandmother, and aunt represent. Holding up a dress in front of Ursula, the mother cloaks her in a sign of femininity that also veils her difference from these other women. Later "unveiling" scenes will enable Ursula to establish her difference, specifically from the mother. Lifting the veil not only manifests physical difference (and indeed, Ursula and her mother do not look at all alike), but more importantly allows Ursula to recognize and partially distance herself from the symbolic meanings tied to her mother's body. She often visualizes this body lying prone and naked in the garden, where it seems subject to injury and penetration. As the father's shadow passes over it, children's voices recite "once in, once out."[11] Ironically, the boundaries of her mother's imagined body are extremely vulnerable and contrast sharply with the self that manifests its agency in the bathroom by cleansing and maintaining bodily boundaries. Ursula continually strives to establish her own separate identity by lifting the veil and moving beyond superficial similarity. Leaving the veil in place covers over her difference, keeps her within the family, firmly placed along that traditional female trajectory that ensures an ultimate destination as wife and mother.

Ursula's immediate response to her first menstrual period is to engage in some roughhousing with a neighborhood boy. As she wrestles with him, a voice-over reinvokes the earlier pirate poems, which, however, end abruptly as the boy walks away and Ursula lies alone, immobile, and corpse-like, much as she imagined her mother. In the next shot the camera shifts 180 degrees to reveal an entirely different perspective: Ursula, still lying prone, but now with a table full of food behind her. Trapped between two contradictory points of identification here, Ursula can choose either the mobility associated with those exotic adventures and her contact with the boy or the passive consumption of material goods upon which the family dynamic relies. By removing her sanitary pad and riding on the boy's shoulders, she refuses containment both within the familial community of women and by the devices that would harness her body. Such mobility may distance Ursula from the mother's passivity, but it also denies the reality of a menstruating body, graphically represented by the soiled sanitary napkin that she discards and upon which the camera lingers. Beneath the veil lurks a body that produces a variety of bodily fluids and substances that are not so easily eradicated.

But for women, maintaining bodily bounds in the face of abject bodily traces has traditionally assumed paramount importance. Such practices not only establish a cohesive identity, but also provide a sense of agency within the patriarchal structures that constitute femininity. Following Foucault, Bordo writes of the "direct grip" that culture has on our bodies through the practices and habits of everyday life:

> Through routine, habitual activity, our bodies learn what is "inner" and what is "outer," which gestures are forbidden and which required, how violable or inviolable are the boundaries of our bodies, how much space around the body may be claimed and so on. These are often far more powerful lessons than those we learn consciously, through explicit instruction concerning the appropriate behavior for our gender, race, and social class (*Unbearable Weight* 16).

Bordo also asserts that within a Foucauldian framework, the power that is inscribed on the body through everyday, habitual practices does not cancel the pleasure that subjects experience in performing such rituals. While culture may train the female body in "docility and obedience to cultural demands," such demands may be "*experienced* by female subjects in terms of power and control" (27). Far from being "dupes" for pursuing particular normative regimens, Bordo argues, women quickly realize that these are the routes to success in patriarchal cultures. One of the main lessons of femininity that Ursula must learn is the basic maintenance of her body, i.e., consuming the proper foods in the proper portions, cleansing her body, taming her unkempt hair, and containing her menstrual flow. According to this logic, some form of autonomy should emerge precisely from tending to and veiling her body.

Yet in Ursula's mind, such activities are too firmly aligned with the family's repressive structures and the manner in which the mother keeps her veiled within the apartment. As Ursula gazes out the window one night at couples strolling in the dark, the mother also appears beside her for a glance, but soon draws her half of the curtain before the scene. Her subsequent attempts to suppress Ursula's emerging sexuality suggest that the mother would like to draw the curtain before her daughter as well, a goal she partially achieves by carefully mediating her daughter's knowledge of the outside world. One scene depicts the two of them before the radio listening to news of the riots of 17 June 1953. The film represents the chaos of this historical moment with visual stills and overlapping voices, fragmentary pieces that resonate with implications for the chaos in their family. Division exists, in fact, within a presumably unified state—be it East Germany or the nuclear family. The last words heard on the radio before Ursula's mother switches it off are about two very different worlds existing so close together, words that speak directly to the tenuous but enforced unity that exists not only within East Germany, but within the family as well.

If the historical and the personal resonate together here, then Ursula's mother reveals the ways in which the historical is always mediated through the personal. Probing for more information, Ursula asks her mother what freedom is. She responds: "It is when we're doing well and don't need to be afraid." Larger historical circumstances can only be accounted for in terms of their direct bearing on the family, and external chaos must be disavowed so as not to disrupt the family's fragile stability. The mother turns away from Ursula as she speaks, addressing her words to a group of small figurines on a shelf. This movement away from her daughter towards the figurines suggests that acquiring material goods and turning away from individual difference, dissatisfaction, and rebellion ensure the family's well-being. In fact, a later classroom scene suggests that the way to unite all of Germany is by the transferal of material goods and foodstuffs from West to East. As the students diligently take notes, a teacher instructs them on what articles of food to send to East Germany, while a voice-over talks of not resting until all of Germany is united. In both the family and the classroom, practices of consumption are linked to unity and consolidation, attenuated states that also demand denial and the suppression of information. This classroom scene ends as Ursula is summarily censured by her teacher for asking about Nazi war criminals presently active in the government.

More threatening to family unity is the father's ambiguous relationship with another woman. Ursula meets this woman face to face after she herself has just been rehearsing the role of the *femme fatale*—complete with beret and cigarette—before the mirror. Ironically, her head is reflected in one mirror, separated from her body reflected in another, an image that suggests fragmentation and an ill-fitting role. The father's lover then appears at the door, perhaps as a living embodiment of the role Ursula has momentarily adopted. Particularly confusing to Ursula is not only this woman's alliance with her father, but also that this "*femme fatale*" inhabits a deformed body. Shouting derogatory epithets after her, Ursula watches the woman depart, rendered less mobile, less alluring, less sexual by her clubfoot. This scene links autonomous sexuality to a bodily deformity, a symbolic marker that has profound implications for Ursula, and a very confused identification ensues.

When her father proffers a cake to subdue Ursula's anger and heal the gap that opens between them, she initially rejects his offering, but later engages in her first eating binge. If food here is meant to subdue Ursula and consolidate her position within the family, it also provides her with the means to articulate frustrated desires normally held in check. The manner in which she retrieves the cake, which she had tossed into the garbage, is highly sexual: she squats with the pail between her legs, running her hands up and down her thighs before reaching in to salvage it. Ursula becomes here, like her father's lover, a deviant body whose unchecked eating signals sexual excess and bodily needs that will not be met. The epithets she mutters while eating—"Whore, dirty broad"—could be directed at either the other woman or at herself, since Ursula becomes here the deviant, undisciplined body that her parents fear. More significant is that consumption here *does not* consolidate her identity or solidify her position within the family; rather, Ursula uses it to articulate a confused identification with someone outside the family and the breakdown of her own subjective boundaries. While I would emphasize the alternative meanings Ursula articulates here, it is also important to point out their double-edged nature. The forms of resistance she cultivates here and elsewhere in the film are ultimately self-defeating.

Even as Ursula attempts in this manner to construct an alternative narrative from the family's consumption practices, she comes up against her mother's efforts to insert her into the pre-existing script that charts "normative" heterosexual femininity for women. In a brief moment of empathy with her mother, Ursula attempts, however, to reconfigure the nuclear family to exclude the father, proposing that she live with and take care of the mother after she has grown up. In doing so, she articulates a strong preoedipal bond that affirms the mother's position as first love object for both male and female subjects. According to the Freudian script of femininity, however, female subjects are obliged to renounce their first object choice, the mother, and displace their desire onto the father.[12] Despite the difficulty the mother confronts in giving up her own mother and submitting to her husband's sexual demands, she pushes her daughter away and along the socially sanctioned path for women, rejecting Ursula's proposal as long as the father is alive. Visually separated from her daughter by a pair of the father's pajamas on the clothesline, the mother promises to buy her her first bra, thereby placing Ursula in one of the "foundational" forms that rein in the female body. Her response not only pushes Ursula towards the father as desired object, but also towards the differentiation—which sometimes occurs in the form of violent rejection—that inevitably occurs between mothers and daughters. In Freudian terms, preoedipal bonds are not merely broken by the daughter's ability to differentiate herself from the mother; she must also come to see the mother as being entirely deficient, and by extension, the cause of the daughter's own deficiencies as well. Ursula will ultimately follow this narrative to the letter, effecting an even more violent rejection by using the very terms she learns from her mother to establish her own separate identity.

Ursula witnesses firsthand the brute reality of heterosexual relations between her parents in the following scene as she stands before the keyhole to their bedroom and watches them engaged in sex. Her subsequent response—running to the bathroom and repeatedly flushing the toilet—ostensibly drowns out the sound of her father's increasingly high-pitched moans. Yet it also links Ursula to her mother's attempts in the bathroom to wash away the material traces of sex—the semen that runs down the mother's legs following intercourse. A later scene graphically depicts the mother squatting in the tub, angrily scrubbing her genitals and muttering to herself, "One should rip out one's ovaries." Her words reveal not only frustration over the female lot, but also the potential invasiveness of both sexual relations and possible unwanted pregnancies. The bodily mutilation invoked here undermines the agency and the mastery the mother asserts in reestablishing her boundaries. Even her benign acts of regulating bodily bounds—like washing herself in the tub—barely compensate for potential violence against the female body, as in the form of unwanted coitus. More significantly, her own acts to reassert her boundaries become bound up with this violence to constitute a form of self-destructiveness. Disciplinary measures imposed on the body thus exist on a continuum of potentially violent external forces that not only regulate, but also perpetually fragment the body. The unspoken narrative here is one of alienation from the body, a sense of "otherness" to the self, a legacy traditionally passed from mothers to daughters.

Ironically, the bathroom becomes the space where Ursula chooses to lay down boundaries between herself and her mother. As the mother washes her naked upper torso at the tub, Ursula suddenly appears to survey her, simultaneously conjuring the image of her mother's body prone, naked, and passive in the garden. These contradictory images render her mother vulnerable, subject to violence, yet in control of her body insomuch as she attempts to reassert her own boundaries by removing the body's abject traces. As they mutually survey each other in the mirror, Ursula triumphantly proclaims, "We're not alike at all." Having laid her mother's body bare, Ursula rejects it, its relation to her own, and its symbolic sphere of action, both passive and active. Rather than articulate her solidarity by performing similar rituals, Ursula attempts to rewrite the script by using her mother's logic not only to differentiate herself from, but also to "abject" the mother.[13]

In doing so, Ursula rewrites one of the formative moments of identity formation. According to Lacanian psychoanalysis, the mirror scene enables children to establish their identity. Through an imaginary transaction with its mirror reflection, an infant comes to recognize itself as "other" in its idealized, cohesive reflection. The mother participates in this process both by initially mirroring the child with her own face and voice, then by orchestrating the mirror scene itself, joining the infant to its reflection. But the Lacanian model, based as it is on the internalization of external, idealized imagoes like the mother's face or the subject's own reflection, breaks down here. Ursula orchestrates an entirely different kind of "mirror scene," and it is one that revolves not around imaginary identification, but active distancing from the mother. Ursula manifests herself not only as "other," but, more specifically, as "other" from the mother. Recalling the Freudian paradigm, however, Ursula can only achieve a normative femininity by rejecting her mother *and* by reifying the father. In *Hungerjahre*, however, *both* parental imagoes prove to be deficient; when Ursula discovers the spurious nature of her father's war narratives, she is no longer able to accept his patriarchal authority. The question that remains is what kinds of external forms Ursula will find to internalize and construct another kind of identity.

Her attempts to pursue sexual desires on her own terms invariably result in awkward or violent encounters with men. Confronted with the sexist remarks of an accordion instructor, harassed by a stranger as she walks home one night, and forced by a group of boys to consume a bottle of alcohol, Ursula discovers that any display of femininity can lead to sexism, objectification, and potential violence. In a particularly painful scene in a cafe, Ursula makes halting conversation with an equally awkward male. After her parents arrive and forcibly remove their daughter from the scene, the mother tucks her beneath the bedcovers and carefully removes her hands. Ursula responds by beating the covers and then running to the kitchen for food. As she eats in bed, she mentally recites a poem about a pirate captain, a fantasy which, of course, is completely undercut by her enforced containment within this bed and within the logic of consumption that locks her within the familial unit.[14] As it did following her encounter with the father's lover, Ursula's consumption here signals desires that will never be satisfied by the food, and more generally, by the family dynamic of consumption and denial. Yet once again, in eating, she renders herself a deviant, rebellious body like the pirate captain, even if this rebelliousness still asserts itself within the framework her parents provide. Problematic, however, is that by articulating her desire through the terms her parents provide—terms that will never allow for satisfaction—Ursula will eventually become "other" not just to her parents, but to herself as well. In placing the girl's hands above the bedcovers, the mother also splits Ursula's body up into separate spheres, ensuring that she will never experience either knowledge of or pleasure in her own body. Consumption and veiling work here to contain and control, but also to fragment the body.

Fragmenting forces continue to take a toll on Ursula's body. She complains to her paternal grandmother of terrible, recurring dreams where she stands on a sinking globe and both grows into space and is torn apart. "It pulls and tears me in the middle," she says. Her grandmother puts food in front of her in a familiar gesture intended to pull Ursula back together, to consolidate these disparate pieces. Ursula complains that she lacks a center, which is not surprising, given that she has no unifying image of femininity to internalize. Despite the film's representation of her mother, grandmother, and aunt as one unit, they in fact represent very different kinds of femininity. In one scene where the aunt recites from the Bible, the mother gives the grandmother a pedicure and complains of Ursula. "She isn't at all nice to me," she observes, criticizing Ursula's apparent greed. When she mentions their inability to send Ursula to dancing lessons, the grandmother reminisces about her youthful days as a renowned dancer, when she was envied for her small feet. Sending the aunt for a cup of coffee, the grandmother complains that she is getting younger and smaller, as if she represented a stunted form of femininity. These women alternatively embody asceticism, vanity, and the weight of maternal duty, none of which provides Ursula with a consistent means to construct and sustain her own identity.

Ursula's fragmentation is also abetted by the fact that her schoolmates steal the voice with which she attempts to articulate her self-alienation by reading one of her poems aloud while Ursula is presumably out of earshot. The fact that her voice is articulated outside of her body here is significant, since Ursula's poem speaks of bodily effects: "My innards are screaming, and my mouth speaks of grammar." Ursula's poem highlights the disjuncture between the body and the words that would represent it. Not only is her voice articulated by schoolmates, thoroughly disconnected from her own body, but the very "grammar" of language—which divides and represses needs and desires—remains stubbornly external and alien to her body as well. There are no words for unifying and healing her fragmented body, no means to fully articulate or satisfy its desires. Lacking this language, the body, as the site of a violent symbolic inscription, begins to dissolve, and Ursula imagines herself growing increasingly wrinkled, transparent, and without resistance.

Yet Ursula does find another means to articulate her self-alienation, again by identifying with and appropriating that position of "otherness" about which she so often fantasizes. Her manner of doing this, however, is both an exotic appropriation meant to shore up her own alienated identity and a means to articulate her "otherness" to herself.[15] This process is played out in a scene where Ursula is mistaken for a foreigner and simply goes along with the misperception. In an exchange in a small grocery store, Ursula uses very basic German, stripping her needs down to the bare essentials to request: "a pound of the white, sweet stuff...."

This disjointed means of communicating suggests an increasing lack of voice, or at least a voice that struggles to articulate even the most basic needs. When the two other women present assume that she is French, Ursula feigns the appropriate accent. Speaking from the position of the "other" renders language an opaque, material medium and manifests the wide gap between words and the desires they are meant to convey. Nevertheless Ursula's voice here struggles to reconnect itself to her body, to the needs of the screaming "innards" for which her poem could not find words. At the same time she hears voices in her head telling her to stand up straight and act normally. Posing as a foreigner separates Ursula from these voices, their language, and allows her to choose the lure of sweets over the exigencies of disciplining the body.

Yet the voices that populate Ursula's mind with a litany of self-disciplinary measures will not recede and soon speak to her with destructive injunctions. Destroying external forces, as the voices admonish her to do, necessitates damaging the self, the site where these forces are inscribed. With the voices resonating in her head, Ursula takes a compass and begins etching into her wrist. If language appears to completely usurp and destroy the body here, the body, however, refuses to recede. Ursula finally retreats to her bedroom, shuts the curtains, and begins clutching her belly. Her adult voice speaks in hindsight, revealing that she simply began floating like a cork on the water, foregoing any efforts at being "in order." Imagining herself as a cork suggests her sense of superfluousness, but clutching her belly bespeaks just the opposite—the heavy drag of a body whose needs continually exceed the self-disciplinary measures imposed on it. The body rears up here, refusing to be contained. Ursula is reduced to her most basic needs, as she lies in bed sucking from a tube of some presumably sweet concentrate. She becomes pure body here, her head the cork that floats, disconnected from and unable to manage her body.

In the film's final scenes, Ursula looks beyond the family to find a living embodiment of the "otherness" with which she has so strongly identified. The "other" that she finds may threaten Ursula's protected position in the family, but he also offers her—briefly—the possibility of speaking another language. Lying in the park one day, Ursula drops a lit match and sets her skirt on fire, then runs to a fountain where a man from Mali helps her to extinguish the flames. They strike up a conversation, and Ursula soon discovers that certain cultural concepts signify completely different things to him. Germany and other first-world countries, for example, describe the strife in Algeria, where he has fought, as a conflict, not a war. War or not, his scarred body bears its visible inscriptions and offers Ursula, whose own internal war goes unacknowledged by her parents, strong points of identification. By unveiling his violently inscribed body, the Malian offers Ursula the mirror she never found in her mother's body. This battered body represents a self rendered "other" both to its surrounding community and to itself. Lacking "positive" images to internalize, Ursula finds here a mirror of her alienation from her family and herself.

What she finds in him may offer strong points of identification—relying on both "positive" and "negative" representations of otherness—but the Malian nevertheless remains stubbornly other. Ursula follows him towards the boats and enters a completely different cultural frame of reference, where her sexual knowledge and willingness are taken for granted. Despite their different frames of reference, they manage to form a tenuous connection. However, in the forced sexual encounter that follows, no meaningful communication occurs, and Ursula lies passively beneath him, much as her own mother does during intercourse. In describing this encounter, it is impossible to detangle the confusing web of gender- and race-based, first- and third-world relations that inform it. On the one hand, even a working-class female teenager enjoys enough first-world privileges to project fantasies onto the Malian that enable her to sustain her own identity, even if these projections enable her to find a mirror of her own self-alienation. But at the same time, he also offers her an image that mitigates this self-alienation. After forcing himself on Ursula, for instance, the Malian wades out into the water to cleanse himself. Unlike the mother's angry scrubbing after sex, this gesture offers Ursula an image of a less alienated relationship to the body. Although this representation may reflect romanticized notions of third-world men,[16] it is important to remember how this image serves a working-class teenager alienated from her own body. On the other hand, however, the Malian, like first-world men, retains power and the potential for violence in their gender relations. If this representation seems to reflect racist notions of third-world men as would-be rapists, it is important to realize that his "otherness" in this respect manifests the impossibility of finding an identity or some form of connection at her fantasized site of "otherness." By positioning Ursula beneath him—just as the mother lays motionless beneath the father—the film aligns their encounter with the other violent and potentially violent heterosexual encounters that Ursula experiences. They spend the night together and form a brief, intimate bond, which is abruptly severed the following day. Communication breaks down as Ursula grows increasingly frustrated over his deficient German. When the Malian is unable to offer Ursula a fixed address, she further severs their ties by insisting that she is "a lazy pen pal." Her irritation mounts as she must repeat this expression three times, due to the Malian's look of incomprehension. Ultimately, this particular form of "otherness," useful as it may be in some ways for constituting Ursula's identity, remains inassimilable.

Her encounter with the Malian sends Ursula fleeing back to the confinement of home, with all its passivity and repressive silences. Looking out the window, she sees in the other windows of the apartment building a possible vision of her own future. Framed in various windows are a dog, a child, an old woman with binoculars, and a plant—none of which exhibit any trace of agency or mobility. Ursula retreats entirely now, drawing the curtains to shut herself in, withdrawing completely into the world that confines her. Ultimately the only exotic items available here to construct her identity are to be found in her mother's kitchen. Ursula imagines making the perfect cake with an exotic array of ingredients. Conspicuously missing from these ingredients, however, is flour: her cake, like her subjectivity, lacks the means to cohere, despite the presence of material plenty and variety. Ursula then consumes all these ingredients, together with a random assortment of pills, thereby rendering consumption an act of annulling, rather than sustaining and consolidating, identity. The final shot shows a black and white image of Ursula burned from all sides by fire, at once consumed and annihilated. Her mother speaks in a voice-over, posing the ironic question: "Child, why didn't you say anything?" As elsewhere in the film, Ursula's final nihilistic gesture speaks powerfully through the very terms she has internalized and in which she is embedded, yet it also simultaneously thwarts them by creating an alternative meaning. Ursula forcefully articulates the impossible position of wresting a voice—a unique and singular voice—from the very structures that ultimately consume and annul her identity.

Notes

[1] Weigel faults many German women's texts of the 1970s for their focus on representing undocumented female experiences and attempts to overturn external causes of women's oppression. Such texts failed to thematize the construction of the self through language and the manner in which the structures of the male order have "engraved themselves on the female psyche, into her very desires," rendering "liberation...only possible through the transformation of internalized structures" (64). Weigel's critique of Vera Stefan's autobiographical text *Häutungen* exemplifies these problems. Many critics, in fact, faulted Stefan for her attempts to create a new language that would capture female experiences, when the nature metaphors she chose remained trapped in a long (patriarchal) tradition of cultural tropes that link women with nature.

[2] The editors of *Gender and German Film: Feminist Interventions* point out in their foreword that the "products and processes of cinematic production provide an illustrated study of gendered socialization." Feminist film critics, in turn, have found in film analysis "the opportunity for a graphic accounting of existing social structures," meaning not just the "historical representations of

values and experience," but also the "workings of contradictions and associations revealed in content, internal structure, and layers of social relations" (xii).

[3] The voice-over plays a significant role in many German women's films of the same time period. Helka Sanders' feminist version of modernist cinema also emphasizes the importance of voice-over text. In "She Says, He Says: The Power of the Narrator in Modernist Film Politics," B. Ruby Rich identifies similar aims in Sanders' film *REDUPERS*. Here again the voice-over engages in a dialogue with the spectator and assumes a benign, rather than controlling relation to the characters in the film, while also problematizing the power structures in the viewing process (161). Kosta links Rich's notion of a "cinema of correspondence" to Brückner's film, where the engagement between the narrator and the characters she reflects on resembles a conversation.

[4] Writing of the "universal self" that emerged from the Renaissance to serve as the foundation for the Western autobiographical "I," Sidonie Smith writes that this "unique, unitary, unencumbered" self "escapes all forms of embodiment" (6). According to Francis Barker, the body became a mere object disassociated from the mind, situated elsewhere: "Neither wholly present, nor wholly absent, the body is confined, ignored, exscribed from discourse and yet remains at the edge of visibility, troubling the space from which it has been banished" (quoted in Smith 6).

[5] Another gender-based contradiction emerges in Helma Sanders-Brahms' *Deutschland, bleiche Mutter*. The Economic Miracle years instigated a return to traditional gender roles and the nuclear family. After women gained independence during the war years by working in factories, clearing away rubble, and simply by surviving, they were then expected to resume more narrowly defined roles as wives and mothers. For Lene, the heroine of *Deutschland, bleiche Mutter*, this imposition of traditional gender roles led to facial paralysis, loss of voice, and an aborted suicide attempt.

[6] Paraphrasing Foucault, Susan Bordo describes the manner in which bodies are "trained, shaped, and impressed with the stamp of prevailing historical forms of selfhood, desire, masculinity, femininity." In pursuing an "ever-changing, homogenizing, elusive ideal of femininity," Bordo writes, female bodies become "docile," or "bodies whose forces and energies are habituated to external regulation, subjection, transformation, 'improvement'" (*Gender/Body/Knowledge* 14).

[7] Contemporary theories about the link between corporeality and subjectivity begin with and increasingly depart from Foucault. At first glance, his conceptions of subjectivities so thoroughly inscribed by larger power structures hardly seem compatible with the notion of a self that can speak and articulate some form of agency. Feminist critiques of Foucault take him to task for ignoring the specificity of the power structures shaping female specificity. More importantly, such critiques chart possibilities of resistance only hinted at but never fully elaborated by Foucault, who speaks of marginalized discourses as sites of resistance, but rarely elaborates on them. In questioning why women did not simply slip away behind the power structures imprinted on their bodies, Lois

McNay argues that within oppressive constraints, contradictions and instabilities often "provided women with a space from which to undermine the very system that constructs them" (135). The extent to which Ursula is able to speak through contradictions—the consumption/denial bind that characterizes her process of socialization—and articulate her own unique subject position is the object of this analysis.

[8] Ironically, after Ursula articulates this desire, the following scene shows her and fellow classmates being drilled in school to learn their lessons by rote. Given such circumstances, it seems unlikely that Ursula will develop the means to cultivate her own language.

[9] According to Kristeva, this process of "abjection" forms the basis of identity by establishing bodily bounds through the opposition of self and other. Paraphrasing Kristeva, Elizabeth Gross writes that the abject is "a necessary condition of the subject, and what must be expelled or repressed by the subject in order to attain identity and a place within the symbolic" (88-89). At the same time, "the abject demonstrates the impossibility of clear-cut borders, lines of demarcation, divisions between the clean and the unclean, the proper and the improper, order and disorder" (89). Particularly in the case of menstrual blood, the boundaries become even more tenuous, since it marks the subject's corporeal link to the mother. Menstrual blood separates the subject's existence from the mother via a substance that initially constitutes its very existence.

[10] This reference to a stomach ache also recalls Ursula's parents eating a pound of candy together when they first met and the mother's subsequent need to teach the father self-control. "I had to teach him right off," she states. Food is thus linked to uncontrollable sexuality, which renders modest eating habits a sign of a disciplined body within one's control.

[11] Although the father may seem menacing here, the film reveals that his presence is, in fact, no more threatening than a shadow. Repeatedly, he fails to live up to idealized notions of the patriarchal position. In a sense, however, this deficiency matters little. His authority need only be invoked by an article of clothing—his pajamas or boxer shorts, for instance—for the heterosexual power dynamic to function.

[12] My invocation here of a psychoanalytic model may be inevitable, since psychoanalysis has long offered one of the most prevalent narratives of socialization. Yet as much as psychoanalysis asserts itself as an objective model of subject formation, it also demands a Foucauldian analysis if we are to understand its discursive, as opposed to scientific, status. While the Foucauldian and Freudian subject are both ruled by the internalization of external structures, largely experienced unconsciously, Foucault makes it possible to understand who or what these structures serve. More specifically, a Foucauldian analysis reveals how psychoanalysis is implicated within power structures that produce as much as they observe particular forms of subjectivity. Feminists of all kinds have long debated the extent to which psychoanalysis has served as a "normalizing" discourse of femininity. More importantly, feminism has made it possible to

understand how women have both inhabited and resisted the psychoanalytic paradigms that define femininity. Again, the point of my analysis is precisely to examine how Ursula constructs herself in relation to the structures that she internalizes.

[13] According to Kristeva, abjection is, in fact, bound up with the maternal, specifically "with our earliest attempt to release the hold of the *maternal* entity even before existing outside of her, thanks to the autonomy of language. It is a violent, clumsy breaking away, with the constant risk of falling back under the sway of a power as securing as it is stifling" (13). This process turns what was once the mother into the abject.

Elsewhere Ursula performs another kind of abjection to challenge her mother. When the forms of oppression she must "consume" turn increasingly violent—as, for example, in a scene where a bottle of alcohol is shoved down her throat—Ursula's only form of agency is to purge what she consumes. Whereas the mother reestablishes her boundaries in the tub, Ursula achieves the same ends by taking laxatives, which enable her to retroactively reclaim her boundaries. Her mother, however, challenges this form of agency by taking away the laxatives and insisting that Ursula eat with the family.

[14] Eventually Ursula's fantasies shift away from escape, pirate adventures, and exotic objects to reflect her containment here. In a later scene she envisions herself going through a meadow, climbing over a viaduct to find shelter in a house where she is safe from a man pursuing her. As in her life, a movement outward culminates in the threat of violence and then renewed containment.

[15] In "Eating the Other," bell hooks writes of the dependence of first-world consumer practices on marginalized groups, whose exoticism spices up available commodities. Describing the position of such groups, hooks writes: "The over-riding fear is that cultural, ethnic, and racial differences will be continually commodified and offered up as new dishes to enhance the white palate—that the Other will be eaten, consumed, and forgotten" (39). Ursula's appropriation of the position of the other could be understood, on one level, as yet another form of consumption present in the film.

[16] Quoting Torgovnick, bell hooks writes that a critical element in Western fascination with primitivism is its focus on "overcoming alienation from the body, restoring the body, and hence the self, to a relation of full and easy harmony with nature and the cosmos" (32). Ursula's identification with the Malian cannot escape a problematic exoticism; she assumes that he is one with his body, despite the scars.

Works Cited

Bordo, Susan. "The Body and the Reproduction of Femininity: A Feminist Appropriation of Foucault." *Gender/Body/Knowledge: Feminist Reconstructions of Being and Knowing*. Ed. Susan Bordo and Alison Jaggar. New Jersey: Rutgers UP, 1992. 13-33.

———. *Unbearable Weight: Feminism, Western Culture, and the Body*. Berkeley: U of California P, 1993.

Brückner, Jutta. *Hungerjahre in einem reichen Land* (*Years of Hunger*). Basis-Film, 1980.

Butler, Judith. *Gender Trouble: Feminism and the Subversion of Identity*. New York: Routledge, 1990.

Foucault, Michel. *Discipline and Punish: The Birth of the Prison*. Trans. Alan Sheridan. New York: Vintage, 1979.

Freud, Sigmund. *The Standard Edition of the Complete Psychological Works*, Trans. James Strachey. Vol. 19. London: Hogarth, 1953.

Gender and German Cinema: Feminist Interventions. Ed. Sandra Frieden, et al. 2 vols. Providence: Berg, 1993.

Gilmore, Leigh. *Autobiographics: A Feminist Theory of Women's Self-Representation*. Ithaca: Cornell UP, 1994.

Gross, Elizabeth. "The Body of Signification." *Abjection, Melancholia and Love: The Work of Julia Kristeva*. New York: Routledge, 1990.

hooks, bell. "Eating the Other." *Black Looks: Race and Representation*. Boston: South End, 1992. 21-39.

Kosta, Barbara. *Recasting Autobiography: Women's Counterfiction in Contemporary German Film and Literature*. Ithaca: Cornell UP, 1994.

Kristeva, Julia. *Powers of Horror: An Essay on Abjection*. Trans. Leon S. Roudiez. Ithaca: Cornell UP, 1982.

Lacan, Jacques. *Ecrits: A Selection*. Trans. Alan Sheridan. New York: Norton, 1977.

McNay, Lois. "The Foucauldian Body and the Exclusion of Experience." *Hypatia* 6:3 (1991): 125-39.

Mitchell, Juliet. *Psychoanalysis and Feminism: Freud, Reich, Laing and Women*. New York: Vintage, 1975.

Rich, B. Ruby. "She Says, He Says: The Power of the Narrator in Modernist Film Politics." *Gender and German Cinema: Feminist Interventions*. Vol. 1. 143-61.

Smith, Sidonie. *Subjectivity, Identity, and the Body: Women's Autobiographical Practices in the Twentieth Century*. Bloomington: Indiana UP, 1993.

Torgovnick, Marianna. *Gone Primitive: Savage Intellects, Modern Lives*. Chicago: U of Chicago P, 1990.

Weigel, Sigrid. "Overcoming Absence: Contemporary Women's Literature (Part Two)." *New German Critique* 32 (1984): 3-22.

———. "'Women Begins Relating to Herself': Contemporary German Women's Literature (Part One)." *New German Critique* 31 (1984): 53-94.

Margarethe von Trotta's Sisters: "Brides Under a Different Law"

Janice Mouton

Margarethe von Trotta's representation of the sister relationship suggests new ways of envisioning personal identity and personal relationships. Her telling of the female identity-formation story moves beyond the Freudian model and the traditional masculine and feminine positionings in narrative. It focuses on the sister attachment itself and on the relational "space between" the sisters, since it is here that the two subjectivities are formed and where the possibilities for a relationship of creative mutuality and independence are played out. (JMM)

The joyous flashback scene of two little sisters reflected in their mother's vanity mirror, caught up in a fantasy world of beautiful red lips and mirror kisses, and the later nightmare scene where blood flows from the slashed wrists of one of those sisters frame the story development in Margarethe von Trotta's *Sisters, or the Balance of Happiness* (*Schwestern, oder die Balance des Glücks* [1979]). Von Trotta uses a similar frame in *Marianne and Juliane* (*Die bleierne Zeit* [1981]) where, in an early flashback, two little girls in short skirts and long pigtails play together in the courtyard and, in a later scene, one sister stands in mourning at the side of the other's coffin. These stories which begin with kisses and end with death, stories which portray love and loss, recall the traditional romantic love narrative. Yet the characters here are sisters, not traditional heterosexual lovers. What difference does this make? What possibilities does this open up for the representation of relationships in narrative?

Film has from the beginning specialized in stories of heterosexual romance; male buddy scenarios have also always comprised the normal fare at the movies. Recently women's friendships, mother/daughter ties, and gay relationships have been given occasional filmic treatment but, oddly enough, sister relationships, some of the most intense, entangling, and intimate of relationships, have remained virtually untouched as cinematic subjects.[1] In the face of this, Margarethe von Trotta's *Sisters* and *Marianne and Juliane* stand as striking exceptions and expressions of a truly rare vision.[2] Although in both movies the sisters' mother is present, that relationship is treated as secondary; throughout it is the sister-sister connection that is primary. There are fathers, lovers, an occasional friend or colleague, but never is the interest deflected from the sisters themselves. Although the sisters' lives are complicated by other considerations such as political events and professional concerns, first and last the the films are about the two sisters and their relationships with each other.

What is there in the sister relationship, and in particular the sister relationships portrayed in these films, that could suggest new ways of envisioning personal identity and personal relationships? Which would move us beyond the Freudian model with its pre-oedipal and oedipal attachments onto a new ground of sister attachments? Away from the same old story of the masculine narrative position as desiring, creative subject and the feminine as desired and passive object? One text that envisions a sister relationship under a "different law" is Adrienne Rich's "Sibling Mysteries," a poem dedicated to her own sister. Here she speaks of the sister tie as paramount:

The daughters never were
true brides of the father

the daughters were to begin with
brides of the mother

then brides of each other
under a different law (52).

The sisters represented in von Trotta's films are daughters of authoritarian fathers, preoccupied with their public worlds, and of traditionally powerless and self-sacrificing mothers, passively present in the privacy of the family home. Within this constellation the sisters move away from the early mother bond and become attached to each other, "brides...under a different law." Rich sees words themselves as both constituting and describing the mysteries of the sister relationship:

words flash from you I never thought of
we are translations into different dialects

of a text still being written
in the original (51).

The still-being-written text in von Trotta's films that begins to take shape during the girls' childhoods—when they write "what they don't know they know" (Rich)—is revealed in the flashback sequences. In the present time of both film narratives it is this material, the common experiences of the two little girls, that enables the adult sisters to continue writing the text.

In this paper I look at the sisters model and the possibilities it offers for representing the constitution of two independent subjectivities in a relationship of mutuality and creativity. Since von Trotta chooses to work within the traditions of film realism, she has been criticized by those who believe that this in effect undermines the feminist meanings she wishes to express. According to my reading, such criticism is a failure to recognize that in her use of the sister model itself von Trotta is breaking with the Oedipal narrative form; she is seeking—and invites her audience to seek—alternative ways of envisioning the construction of identity, the representation of relationships, and the sources of viewing pleasure. In her new telling of the female identity-formation story, von Trotta attempts to create a new structure centered on sisterhood under a "different law." Of course, as Rich says, the sisters' "lives were driven down the same dark canal," so that the mother's role cannot be dismissed. Neither would one wish to ignore the influence of the broader family constellation, nor the community in which it is embedded. Nevertheless, it is clear that what interests Margarethe von Trotta in her film is the sisters and their relationship, and this is also what interests me.

In examining the Maria/Anna relationship in *Sisters*—and attempting to understand why the relationship developed as it did—I would like to fasten on the image of the little girls playing before the mirror. This is quite notably the most joyous and vital scene in the entire film and it represents the kind of connection and communication that was once present between the sisters. Why were they unable to maintain and build upon this early state of creative mutuality? Why did they allow themselves to sink into the stifling and destructive entanglement that tortured their adult lives? Why were they incapable of nurturing and caring for each other—even incapable of helping one another survive?

In interpreting this scene of play against the later absence of any sense of "play" between the sisters, I will be drawing upon some of D.W. Winnicott's original insights on the subject. In contrast to Freud, Lacan, and Chodorow, for example, whose ideas have provided the theoretical ground for so much feminist writing, Winnicott is concerned less exclusively with the parent/child relationship, focusing instead on the child in relationship to its whole inner and outer world. Winnicott's approach thus seems an especially productive one in seeking to understand the sister-relationship model as suggested by von Trotta's films. Basic to his understanding of what goes on in play is its spatial dimensions:

> This area of playing is not inner psychic reality. It is outside the individual, but it is not the external world. Into this play area the child gathers objects or phenomena from external reality and uses these in the service of some sample derived from inner or personal reality. Without hallucinating the child puts out a sample of dream potential and lives with this sample in a chosen setting of fragments from external reality (51).

The lipstick game takes place in a space that is neither the inner psychic world of either girl nor the world of external reality but rather in a space between, which the two discover, create, and inhabit together. The "objects from external reality" are their mother's lipstick and their mother's mirror, and the "sample of dream" that they "put out" and "live" is that they are beautiful grow-up women, perhaps mothers as well, fond of each other and pleased with themselves.

In *Playing and Reality* Winnicott presents his theories regarding an individual's development in relation to objects, beginning with a transitional object (the first "not-me" attachment), such as a teddy bear or a blanket, and moving on to subsequent attachments. What is crucial in respect to the teddy bear—just as it is later in the activity of playing—is that the child must in a sense "create, think up, devise, originate, produce [the] object" (2). Recognizing and accepting this paradox, that the object exists in the exterior world and is also created by the child, enables one to understand what is involved in the later on-going task of keeping inner and outer reality separate yet interrelated. This intermediate experience area is precisely that area where, in adult life, all kinds of imaginative, creative activity occurs and where relationships are played out.

In Anna's case there is some evidence of this kind of activity: her photography, her writing, her appreciation of music, her interest in the Druids and their notions about trees, her connection to the childhood playing scenes (all flashbacks are her focalizations), her creation of her personal space in the apartment that incorporates her animals' habitat—all these can be seen as evidence of Anna's moving out of the strict confines of her inner psychic world into another world that is not simply external reality either. In other words, Anna (Gudrun Gabriel) continues after childhood to inhabit that intermediate area of creative experience posited by Winnicott, but she inhabits it alone. That there is no longer the opportunity for "shared playing" as in childhood or for "shared cultural experiences" as the adult extension of playing is partially due to the fact that her sister Maria (Jutta Lampe), the primary person in her life, appears incapable of play, cultural experience, or creative activity. Her apparent loss of this capacity means that she cannot meet Anna in the intermediate space. In the face of this sisterly absence Anna withdraws more and more into herself, developing a narcissistic inwardness and inaccessibility. The scene where—in a gesture reminiscent of Garbo—she enfolds her body in a self-embrace presents a perfect visualization of her inner state, and repeatedly in her responses to others and in her solitary musings we see this narcissistic self-attachment. The forms taken by her creative activities, self-focused diary writing and her self-portraits, are also narcissistic expressions. The self-portraits, of course, are reminiscent of the mirror-pool reflection gazed upon by the mythical Narcissus, and like him, Anna gazes upon her own photo images. Other indications of

Anna's narcissism are readily apparent: for example, her close association—even identification—with her animals. When she and her animals are framed together in what is in effect a common habitat, the scene functions as a visual image of that association Freud made between the narcissistic woman—because of her inaccessibility and indifference—and cats and large beasts of prey (Freud 89). Furthermore, that Anna should interpret as a personal betrayal any inclination on Maria's part to become romantically involved with a man clearly marks her as a narcissistic personality, just as her childlikeness does. When she shrinks from moving out of her sheltered student life into the "real world," when she allows Maria to take care of her, or when she rejects male overtures even of the most innocent sort (a fellow student who wants to sit beside her over a cup of coffee), all these point to that self-centeredness and self-involvement characteristic of the child. Here is a narcissistic concept of self that senses every outside influence or stimulus as constituting a danger rather than an opportunity for maturation, growth, or change.

It seems altogether possible that for Anna, who having been deprived of—and having deprived herself of—anyone with whom she can relate in that "space-between," the ability to play and to create has become blocked and she retreats ever more into her own inner world. As she becomes increasingly self-focused and self-involved, she demands that Maria be totally dedicated to her. However, unlike traditional heterosexual lovers who desire fusion, she resents and denies her dependency on Maria, perceiving it as a threat to her sense of a unified self.

But what of Maria? What accounts for her disastrous development from a little girl, able to share play space with her sister and participate in mutual dreaming and creative communication, to a duty-bound, self-sacrificing woman, markedly lacking in spontaneity, self-expression, and creativity—the traditional feminine position in the heterosexual relationship? In particular, how has Maria's relationship to external reality become one of compliance, or how has she, in Winnicott's words, come to recognize "the world and its details...only as something to be fitted in with or demanding adaptation" (65)? At one point the film gives us the mother's perspective on how such attitudes and behavior on Maria's part may have begun to develop. In a conversation with Maria's friend Miriam (Jessica Früh) shortly after Anna's suicide, the mother (Agnes Fink) expresses the opinion that "Maria is like my late husband, she was always his favorite. She knew from early on what she wanted" (Baer 74). Why does the mother think that Maria "knew what she wanted?" Later we hear Maria telling her friend Maurice that she did "what her mother wanted." Both mother and daughter have internalized a value system that makes the socially acceptable role the one to be desired and enacted. Neither is capable of inventing new models or envisaging a "different law." For Maria this "knowing what one wanted" comes to mean *not* playing and *not* dreaming, but simply pursuing a goal. A failure to play or to dream is what brings one to acceptance, compliance, and "fitting in," the gradual result of which is a dying off of a person's vital, creative dimensions. This is what Maria has allowed to happen as she goes about her day serving her boss at work and serving her sister at home. Seeing the world as "ready-made" (Marcuse), Maria can only conform to it; the creative imagination of her girlhood has been stifled and she allows herself to be positioned as both breadwinner and selfless server of others. This positioning is of course reinforced by those who benefit from it. Her boss sees her only as someone to serve him and gives her the "opportunity" to serve him in more and more ways, always praising her as his "angel." Anna desires and demands that Maria be dedicated exclusively to her and, by escalating those desires and demands, renders her sister incapable of releasing herself from this tyranny or of acquiring any autonomy. Maria's lack of autonomy evidences itself in a failure to claim her own words, her own story, or her own dream. She takes dictation from her boss, types Maurice's dissertation, and helps her friend Miriam practice her vocabulary words; she tells Maurice Anna's story but not her own; she transcribes Fritz's dreams but does not dream herself. Nor does she write her story in a journal as does her sister.

Another scene, the film's opening—and later recurring—fairy-tale flashback, offers the viewer another glimpse into the early sister relationship. The tale is told in a child's voice-over as the accompaniment to a striking long-take of a "deep, dark forest," its slim, pale gray trunks standing in a thick growth against the dark gray space of the background: "And then they came to a deep, dark forest," says the voice. "It was a pitch black night and the only sound was the hoo, hoo, hoo of the owl...." Next we see onscreen the two little girls, Anna, the frightened four-year-old clinging to the six-year-old Maria, who continues telling the fairy tale:

> They held each other's hands tightly as they walked through the darkness. But after a while their feet began to grow tired. "Oh, Sister," said the little sister, "I'm tired, let's stop and rest." But the big sister said, "If we stop to rest the wild animals will devour us in our sleep and we'll never again find our way home."

Thus we see mirrored in the shared space of play the same patterns that are present in the actual world of the family. Maria as big sister is the wise protector of Anna, who as little sister is her trusting companion. The pair thus becomes bonded—not through rivalry and mimetic desire as in traditional masculine versions of this story—but rather through mutual support and mutual need. This mutuality, which is fundamental to the "different law," implies movement beyond the binaries that characterize that relational structure that passes for law itself: desiring subject /

desired object; and activity, creativity, power / passivity, sacrifice, powerlessness. When Maria and Anna are children, this mutuality functions to the benefit and pleasure of both sisters. Why are they unable to maintain the relationship in its productive, mutual form? Why do they turn their backs on the magic mirror? Why leave the enchanted forest?

From Winnicott we know that the child's playing and occupying the "play space" is equivalent to the adult's creativity in actual artistic production, in the creative use of language, and simply in a creative apperception that colors one's whole attitude to the external world. As he says, more than anything else this makes the individual feel that life is worth living (65). In her filmmaking von Trotta refuses to concede to a world in which there is only one possible law, one possible structure, one possible dream. Precisely in that "space between" can we see the possibility for representing relationships differently. Anna expresses the situation in the negative when, shortly before her suicide, she writes in her diary, "The dream I have of life robs me of that life." Indeed, it is necessary to create a new narrative, to let the imagination reach beyond the conventions, if one is to remain alive.

On two occasions when Anna and Maria speak of their relationship and their situations we recognize that, although they have some insight and awareness, they are incapable of envisioning alternatives to the models available. One evening when Maria comes home from work—late as usual, exhausted as usual—and begins cooking dinner for Anna, she complains, "If I didn't work so much, you couldn't keep on studying so long." Anna's response to this is, "You accuse me of being the cause of your working so much since you have to support me. But as a matter of fact you need me to need you—that's how it is." Instead of envisioning a new structure, the familiar structure is re-enacted; instead of dreaming a new dream, the old dream is allowed to rob one of life. On another occasion Anna expresses the opinion that Maria is irreplaceable at work, an opinion that Maria disputes. "Everyone is replaceable," she says. If Maria feels replaceable in the marketplace world where she has so fully dedicated herself, perhaps she needs to be needed at home for a sense of place and security, her identity as a person dependent upon her sister's needs, she herself someone because she is needed by someone. After Anna's death when Maria attempts to replace her with her friend Miriam, putting Miriam in the position of needing her and being dependent on her, we see the fuller implications of the truth of what Maria was claiming to Anna about "replaceability." For her it is not the person *per se* whom she must bind to herself; it is the relationship with someone who needs her that she must have in order to maintain a hold on her identity.

While Anna is right in believing that Maria needs her in order to feel needed (and this because she feels so replaceable in the work-world), it is also true that Anna herself needs Maria to enable her to stay in the dependent position, to keep on supporting her and taking care of her, so that she can avoid entering into and fitting into that work-world, which she fears as destructive of the individual and of humane values. Both sisters imitate the old models instead of seeking to envision and enact new ones. Each sister is creating her own and the other's enslavement. Each sister diminishes the other and blames her for her own diminishment. Anna's diary references to the frightful topic of vampirism are well taken: indeed each sister *is* sucking the life out of the other.[3]

After Anna's death, when Maria finds the diary with its ghoulish death imagery (photos of medieval gargoyles and stone sculptures), she discovers the line, directed to her, "I took my life in opposition to you. Beware of me; I will return to haunt you...." At first Maria dismisses this, claiming that Anna always thought only of herself and that her suicide was simply an escalation of her self-absorption. Soon, however, Anna does return to haunt her. In a mirror, reminiscent of her mother's mirror of long ago, Maria sees Anna's reflection instead of her own looking out at her. This confronts her with the need to see through the other's eyes and moves her to re-enter that creative realm she once abandoned.

The film concludes with Maria writing in her own diary, for the first time using her own words to tell her own story. "I will learn to dream in the course of my life," she says, "I will try to become Maria and Anna." As she writes she comes to the awareness that the Anna persona is not replaceable. Nor, to be sure, is the Maria persona. Through dreaming, through writing, she is, once again, attempting to "put out a sample of dream potential and live with this sample in a chosen setting of fragments from external reality" (Winnicott). "Becoming Anna" will mean that Maria, like the sister in "Sibling Mysteries," will call on Anna in her absence:

> I call you from another planet
>
> to tell a dream
> Light-years away, you weep with me (52).

Like that sister, living under the mystery of a different law, writing for herself and for the other, she will say:

> I know, I remember, but
> hold me, remind me
>
> Tell me again because I need to hear (49).

And the presence of the other will also enable her to say:

> Let me hold and tell you (52).

The difficulty of living under a "different law" has been made apparent in this movie. Even though the sisters were "brides of each other," they had no models to follow toward realizing what that might mean. In the struggle against the conventions, the dark side has been revealed in this sister story. Clearly it would be a mistake to see Anna as having sacrificed herself so Maria might live on as "Maria-Anna," writing their common story. The mystery remains. The relationship of creative mutuality and independence has yet to be represented. There is no happy ending.

In *Marianne and Juliane,* made two years after *Sisters,* von Trotta continues to explore issues and possibilities presented by the sister relationship.[4] Although this sister relationship is not as troubled as that of Maria and Anna, it raises issues similar to the ones I have elaborated in regard to the earlier film. By bringing *Marianne and Juliane* into the discussion at this point, we can recognize a continuity in von Trotta's work as she again attempts to open up possibilities for the representation of relationships in narrative. The need for a "different law" is confirmed in the second film where the sisters do inhabit to a degree Winnicott's "space between," yet, like Maria, Juliane (played by the same actress) is unable to save her sister's life. Furthermore, the need for continued searching is affirmed since the film's resolution—the surviving sister becomes the writer of the still-being-written text—again points to a dilemma.

In flashback scenes reminiscent of Maria's and Anna's lipstick mirror game, we see Marianne and Juliane as little girls with their cups of cocoa at the breakfast table or racing each other across the courtyard. The major difference between the sisters' relationships as adults is that in the Marianne/Juliane story each woman has her own independent life; each has her own involvement with work, her dedication to a cause, her attachment to other people. At the same time, the relationship they have with each other retains its central importance, its intensity, and its difficulty. While Marianne is alive, even though she is at first "underground" and then in prison, she and Juliane manage to meet and talk as well as communicate in writing so the "space between" is maintained. Their connection weathers outbursts of anger and expressions of rejection. Visually, through the sweater exchange or the final face-merge in the reflecting glass, and again and again through what they say (for example, the dream Juliane relates to Marianne when she visits her in prison: "I dreamed I freed you"), the viewer recognizes the extent to which each of the sisters has her identity bound up with being related to the other. Each *is* who she is because of her connection with her sister. Each is enabled, because of her involvement in the shared space of the relationship, to expand her definition of who she is.[5]

Whereas in the case of Maria and Anna we noted a failure even to imagine a relationship of both independence and mutuality, for Marianne and Juliane this becomes, at times at least, a possibility they realize. They are able to envision and act upon the idea of a relationship in which they can "care for, respond to, or attend to the well-being and development of the other. Moreover, they [can] care for and take care of the relationship between them" (Surrey 56).[6] We are given an example of this in one of the prison conversations when Marianne recalls how, as little girls, even if they were feeling like deadly enemies, they always helped each other button up their undershirts. As adults they frequently evidence a similar concern for the relationship. However, the situation changes radically when Juliane, the feminist journalist, attempts to write the story of her sister, the political terrorist. Marianne rejects this in a fury, refusing to speak to her sister, refusing even to see her. It is acceptable for Juliane to bring things to Marianne in prison: socks, make-up, tea, her cello. It is important for both to talk about their childhood, their parents, their daily affairs—even if they disagree. But for one to tell the other's story? This seems not to be possible. It is only later, in the space of loss, that Juliane writes. Though we have glimpsed the promise of Rich's "different law," and have envisioned the possibility of two subjectivities constituted in a relationship of mutuality and independence, we cannot fail to see the precariousness of the structures thus represented.

Neither Maria nor Juliane is able to save her sister's life. This is the tragic aspect of both stories and an illustration of the limitedness of human relationships. Yet in both cases the living sister discovers the presence of the other within herself, hearing the other's voice, seeing the other's image. The final scenes of both films portray the Jutta Lampe character sitting alone at her desk writing and thinking of the sister from whom she is now separated by death. As Maria, she is writing in her diary, telling her own story for the first time—a story that from now on is to include her sister's story ("I will seek to become both Maria and Anna"). As Juliane, she looks up and sees Jan, once her sister's son and now her son. She promises him that she will tell him the story of his mother—or as much of it as she knows. In telling the sister's story she speaks for the sister, enabling her, though she is no longer present, to continue to speak and to continue to live. Von Trotta has been successful in working against the conventions in envisioning a sister relationship under the "different law." But the ending is open. What remains to be imagined, even beyond the relationship of mutuality and independence we have seen, is a structure that enables both figures to occupy the creative position, the position of the writer. Why must one sister die for the other to tell the story? To rephrase the plea Luce Irigaray makes in "And the One Doesn't Stir Without the Other," "What I wanted from you, Sister, was this: that in giving me life, you still remain alive" (67).

To the memory of Eleanor Risteen Gordon, 1935-1994

Notes

[1] Jane Campion's *Sweetie* and Bill Forsyth's *Housekeeping* are outstanding counter-examples, as is Michele Citron's *Daughter Rite,* although in none of these cases is the sister relationship so exclusively the focus of the film as it is in von Trotta's films. Still, these movies are actually about sisters (along with mothers and others) in contrast to—the titles not withstanding—Woody Allen's *Hannah and Her Sisters* or Brian de Palma's *Sisters,* to cite a pair of relatively recent examples, or the "sister exploitation" movies made in Hollywood in the forties, including *Cobra Woman, The Dark Mirror,* and *A Stolen Life.* Lucy Fischer has discussed these latter films in connection with von Trotta's sisters (172–215).

[2] In the 1970s sisterhood served as a dominant model for feminist relationships, though that sisterhood was as much a metaphor or an ideal as it was an experience. As Jessica Benjamin said regarding that sisterhood, "We have known it in the inspiration and appreciation we give one another, in the mirroring and challenging of our own autonomy—choosing ourselves. It is the relationship in which we are able to identify and take pleasure in each other's growth without the aspects of merging and dependency which characterize the maternal relationship" (158).

[3] Interestingly, von Trotta also includes in the film an elderly sister pair, grotesque doubles, locked together in a conflicted relationship, suggesting another sister-scenario that could have played itself out for Anna and Maria: the inward-looking sister position now occupied by a blind woman, the serving-sister role taken by a woman frozen in masochistic duty-boundness.

[4] *Marianne and Juliane* has been the more widely discussed of the two sister films, most often with primary interest focused on the politics of terrorism and reform feminism in the context of West Germany in the 1970s. See, for example, Barton Byg, Lisa DiCaprio, Sheila Johnson, E. Ann Kaplan, and Ellen Seiter. Kaplan dismisses *Sisters or the Balance of Happiness* as being "morbid" (and thus a poor choice for use in the classroom) ("Discourses"). Anna Kuhn has written on this film, raising the personal/political question ("Sisters"), and Roswitha Mueller has considered the sisters and their relationship from a psychological perspective.

[5] This is not, as Byg would have it, a matter of interwoven images carrying on "a long German tradition which was prominent in Romantic literature as well as in Expressionist film: the image of the *Doppelgänger.*" According to this interpretation, Marianne would "represent the forbidden other self of Juliane; her transgressions reveal Juliane's shallowness or point to her real (repressed) desires" (267). As Kaplan shows, the doubling functions on "an altogether more complex level [than an externalization of an inner split], revealing first, the strong attraction that women feel for qualities in other women that they themselves do not possess; second, the difficulty women have in establishing boundaries between self and Other; and finally, the jealousy and competition among

women that socialization in patriarchy makes inevitable" (*Women and Film* 107). Also, as Kuhn mentions in discussing von Trotta's *Rosa Luxemburg,* "Luxemburg's symbiotic relationship with Leo Jogiches must have fascinated von Trotta. Emotional symbiosis is a theme she has explored in depth in *Sisters or the Balance of Happiness, Sheer Madness,* and to a lesser degree in *Marianne and Juliane*" ("A Heroine" 174, note).

[6] Surrey figures the relationship itself as a third term, something located between the two individuals, to be cared for as they care for each other. Like the creative "space between" theorized by Winnicott, Surrey's conception of the relationship is also a specifically spatial one. She sees this space as the ground for developing a "dynamic of mutual empowerment" (56).

Works Cited

Baer, Willi, and Hans Jürgen Weber, eds. *"Schwestern oder die Balance des Glücks": Ein Film von Margarethe von Trotta.* Frankfurt a.M.: Fischer, 1979.

Benjamin, Jessica. "Shame and Sexual Politics." *New German Critique* 27 (Fall 1982): 151–59.

Byg, Barton. "German History and Cinematic Convention Harmonized in Margarethe von Trotta's *Marianne and Juliane.*" *Gender and German Cinema.* Vol. 2. 259–71.

Di Caprio, Lisa. *"Marianne and Juliane / The German Sisters:* Baader-Meinhof Fictionalized." *Jump Cut* 29 (1984): 56–59.

Fischer, Lucy. "Sisters: the Divided Self." *Shot/Countershot.* Princeton: Princeton UP, 1989. 172–215.

Freud, Sigmund. "On Narcissism: An Introduction." *The Standard Edition of the Complete Psychological Works of Sigmund Freud.* Ed. James Strachey. 24 vols. London: Hogarth Press, 1953–74. Vol. 14. 69–102.

Gender and German Cinema: Feminist Interventions. Ed. Sandra Frieden, et al. 2 vols. Providence: Berg, 1993.

Irigaray, Luce. "And the One Doesn't Stir Without the Other." Trans. Helene Vivienne Wenzel. *Signs* 7.1 (1981): 60–67.

Johnson, Sheila, *"The German Sisters." Films & Filming* 334 (July 1982): 25–26.

Kaplan, E. Ann. "Discourses of Terrorism, Feminism, and the Family in von Trotta's *Marianne and Juliane.*" *Women and Film.* Ed. Janet Todd. New York: Holmes & Meier, 1988. 258–70.

———. *Women and Film: Both Sides of the Camera.* New York: Metheun, 1983.

Kuhn, Anna. "Margarethe von Trotta's *Sisters*: Interiority or Engagement?" *Women in German Yearbook 1.* Ed. Marianne Burkhard and Edith Waldstein. Lanham, MD: UP of America, 1985. 77–84.

———. "A Heroine for Our Time: Margarethe von Trotta's *Rosa Luxemburg.*" *Gender and German Cinema.* Vol. 2. 163–84.

Mueller, Roswitha. "Images in Balance." *Gender and German Cinema.* Vol. 1. 59–71.

Rich, Adrienne. "Sibling Mysteries." *The Dream of a Common Language: Poems 1974–1977.* New York: Norton, 1978. 51–52.

Seiter, Ellen. "The Political is Personal: Margarethe von Trotta's *Marianne and Juliane.*" *Journal of Film and Video* 37 (Spring 1985): 41–46.

Surrey, Janet. "The 'Self-in-Relation': A Theory of Women's Development." *Women's Growth in Connection: Writings from the Stone Center.* Ed. Judith V. Jordan, et al. New York: Guilford, 1991. 51–66.

Trotta, Margarethe von, dir. *Die bleierne Zeit* [*Marianne and Juliane*]. New Yorker Films, 1981.

———, dir. *Schwestern, oder die Balance des Glücks* [*Sisters, or the Balance of Happiness*]. Krypton c/o Almi, 1979.

Winnicott, D.W. *Playing and Reality.* 1971. New York: Routledge, 1989.

Enacting the Different Voice:
Christa Klages and Feminist History

Jenifer K. Ward

This article examines Margarethe von Trotta's first film, *The Second Awakening of Christa Klages* (1977), as an exemplary document of late 1970s feminist thought. It asserts that von Trotta's narrative can be understood in light of the early work of Carol Gilligan on gender and moral development, and goes on to argue that von Trotta uses this notion of a gendered moral code to critique and recuperate a Christian ethical stance through her characterizations. The article also re-evaluates the (German) reception of von Trotta and her film. (JKW)

The "myth of Germany"—as it was articulated in West German cinema of the 1970s and early 1980s—has been the subject of a number of recent contributions to the rich field of criticism surrounding cultural attempts at *Vergangenheitsbewältigung*.[1] The early 1990s also saw the appearance of long overdue books that treated the works of German women filmmakers in a sustained way.[2] It is in the intersection of these two trends that I wish to situate this essay, which treats Margarethe von Trotta's first independent film, *The Second Awakening of Christa Klages* (1977), as a different evocation of that myth of Germany.

Christa Klages appeared almost twenty years ago, in a time of great political turmoil. It was released at approximately the same time as one of the watershed films in the history of New German Cinema, *Germany in Autumn* (Filmverlag der Autoren, 1978), which responded to the events of fall 1977 in the form of a collaborative work by several filmmakers. *Germany in Autumn* was completed in an intense few weeks and consisted of individual episodes created by many of the major players in New German Cinema, among them Rainer Werner Fassbinder, Edgar Reitz, Alexander Kluge, and Volker Schlöndorff. The episodes varied greatly from documentary and quasi-documentary to autobiographical to allegorical to fictional, but all of them responded to events of the fall. In short, those events were the following: after the kidnapping and murder by terrorists of Hans Martin Schleyer, the head of the West German Confederation of

Industry, an act which also involved the hijacking of a Lufthansa jet and its subsequent liberation by special German "stormtrooper" units, three members of the Red Army Faction were found dead in the maximum-security Stammheim prison.

The political backdrop against which these events were played out was marked by the remnants of the past and the fears associated with those memories, both for the Right and the Left. According to Richard McCormick, the 1967 murder of Benno Ohnesorg during the height of the student movement and the subsequent speech given by Gudrun Ensslin denouncing that murder—a speech that contributed to the founding of the RAF—still had great resonance for the Left. As the state cracked down on the RAF in 1977, those memories of ten years ago were stirred. On the Right, memories of the revolutionary activity after World War I were evoked. McCormick rightly perceives the circular nature of the fears:

> Why such tremendous fears—on both the right and the left—should have been prevalent is at first glance not clear to the foreigner. The answer has to do with the relation of the events in 1977 to what are undoubtedly the greatest (German) crimes of the century: the scuttling of German democracy by National Socialism, the resultant persecution of political dissidents and Jews; and the eventual mass extermination of Jews, gypsies, homosexuals, and others. The fears of the Right go back at least to the revolutionary unrest after World War I in Germany; these fears contributed to the ultimate success of the Nazis. That success in turn explains the fears of the German Left (179-80).

As rumors circulated about the Schleyer murder and the cause of death of the RAF prisoners—suicide or murder, depending on which end of the ideological spectrum one was located—West Germany seemed close to an ideologically motivated civil war.[3] These deaths serve as the structural glue for the disparate episodes of *Germany in Autumn*, which were framed by documentary footage of the funerals of Schleyer at the outset and the members of the Red Army Faction at the end.

Christa Klages serves as a good companion document to *Germany in Autumn*; whereas the latter provides an immediate—in part, documentary—collaborative response to political events, *Christa Klages* represents a narrativized and fictional—some would say melodramatic—one. Attention to the reception of von Trotta's film affords us yet another glimpse into the culture of this period, both in terms of the public discourse surrounding the events of that fall and in terms of how opinions about this film would come to shape and reflect later attention to her work.[4] While her film also deals with the political climate of Germany at this time, it does so from a perspective that takes seriously the promise of feminism for the betterment of society. Von Trotta's film enacts—through a fictionalized narrative—the transformative potential of feminist theories about the "nature" of women's ethical and moral decision-making in the late 1970s in Germany and the U.S., particularly theories developed by Carol Gilligan and Margarete Mitscherlich. While both authors' major works appear after *Christa Klages,* and cannot, therefore, have influenced Von Trotta's thinking directly, the theories contained in them were already fermenting, indeed on both sides of the Atlantic. Thus, von Trotta's film can be seen as a document of feminist history grounded in a specific historical, national context, but also in a context of international theorizing about women's morality.

In *Christa Klages,* von Trotta presents the utopianism of the feminist movement as a way of intervening into what she saw as a calcified political culture. She constructs in the character of Christa Klages a kind of vigilante messiah (her name also embodies the accusatory,[5] yet ultimately Christ-like nature of her character), whose actions represent the "female" approach to the solution of problems posited by Gilligan and Mitscherlich. This approach is then depicted in contrast to the "male" approach embodied by the character of Hans and the various bureaucrats in the film narrative.

This essay will begin, then, with a summary of the reception of *Christa Klages* in the German popular press, will go on to outline Gilligan's theory of gendered moral development, and then offer a reading of the film based on the links between that theory and the Biblical parallels found in the film text. What von Trotta ultimately does with *Christa Klages* is to construct a world in which two seemingly separate threads are intertwined—feminist psychology on the one hand and Christian ethics on the other. By weaving the two together, von Trotta is able to create a utopian vision in which "female" ways of being in the world unfetter the notion of Christian *salvation* from its patriarchal base.

Von Trotta was inspired to make *Christa Klages* by a real incident concerning a day-care worker who had robbed a bank to save her financially troubled day-care center. Von Trotta stated:

> The point of departure is the case of the Munich bank robber Margit Czenki. I simply couldn't get this character out of my head. Ultimately, though, I approached the story in a different way: I don't depict the developments up to the bank robbery, but those that come after. And all of that is purely fictional (Naefe).

As in most of her later films, von Trotta makes clear in the case of *Christa Klages* that she is less interested in depicting real historical events than in depicting the effects of those events on people, particularly women. Even as von Trotta concerns herself with the "personal" aspects of German history, however, the backdrop of larger events is always present. What concerns her is the way in which "history"—be it political, social, personal, or cultural—moves characters beyond themselves in catalytic fashion, enabling them to perform actions, adopt new visions of themselves and their place in the world, or come to new understandings, which had been impossible or unattainable at the beginning of their filmic journeys.

An equally important message is that these transformations occur when women learn from each other. In *Christa Klages* the three central women characters move in and out of each other's lives as the film progresses. Although they may not be in constant contact with each other, the imprints they leave on each other are indelible, and while the ultimate moment of "awakening" for each of them may occur in isolation from the other women, it is clear that the process leading up to that moment is a result of solidarity or mutual influence.

Aside from the events specific to fall 1977, the more general atmosphere pervading Germany in the mid- to late 1970s, including the "Radikalenerlaß"[6] of 1972 and the prevalent labeling of perceived leftists as "sympathizers," made the subject matter of *Christa Klages* quite provocative. Indeed, the bank robbery itself is not the central point of the film. Far more important are Christa's motives for this deed, which are portrayed as honorable; her attempts to implicate others in her scheme and the degree to which the others appear cowardly or hopelessly bourgeois for not recognizing the honor of the deed; and the negative portrayal of the State. Perhaps most important of all is the extent to which Christa ultimately "radicalizes" those around her, a process that is represented sympathetically by von Trotta.

Reception

The provocative nature of the film is reflected in reviews in the German popular press. Positive reviews generally fell into two categories: those that praised von Trotta's sensitive rendering of the complexity of the German political atmosphere, and those that avoided discussions of history and politics altogether, seeing the film instead in terms of its humanist/utopian message.[7] Negative critiques (of which there were few) also fell into two camps: those that called into question von Trotta's refusal to "take sides" or otherwise make explicit a moral position and, similarly, those that criticized the film for its refusal to take a more pointed stand against what Hans C. Blumenberg calls "decent society":

...It is true that *The Second Awakening of Christa Klages,* which was warmly received at its premiere at the Berlin Film Festival, is based on the real-life case of kindergarten teacher Margit Czenki, whom the tabloids have nicknamed "Bank Lady" and for whom decent society has made it virtually impossible to get on with a "normal" life. Nevertheless, this did not turn out to be a political film: rather a friendly, all-too-friendly leftist fairy tale, which fails to really offend anyone, not even its state-supported co-producer WDR.

Blumenberg goes on to criticize what he sees as cliché-ridden plot construction, calling it "naive cops-and-robbers stuff" even as he admits von Trotta's remarkable technical and stylistic facility in her first independent effort. The most striking aspect of Blumenberg's article, however, is that it prefigures a common trend in subsequent reviews of von Trotta's films, especially those that draw on real historical events and personalities for their subject matter, namely a use of the subjunctive to describe the film that would have been more historically "true" or somehow more appropriate. His review begins: "This could have become a bitter, angry film...." This tendency is much stronger in reviews of von Trotta's later films *Marianne and Juliane* and *Rosa Luxemburg*, since Margit Czenki did not command the same attention as figures like Gudrun Ensslin (upon whose life *Marianne and Juliane* was based) or Rosa Luxemburg. More importantly, Czenki certainly did not occupy the role of hero or anti-hero for segments of the German population as Ensslin and Luxemburg still do. Nevertheless, even here we begin to see some of the contested nature of von Trotta's characterizations.

Just as Blumenberg sees *Christa Klages* as cliché-ridden, other reviewers—the overwhelming majority—praise the degree to which it is *not* formulaic.[8] Most reviewers laud the film for avoiding an ideological heavy-handedness, especially in its portrayal of feminist issues. In fact, most reviewers use quite a bit of space in their articles to embrace the feminist content on the one hand, and to distance themselves and the film from the women's movement on the other:

> Although the feminine perspective (including its irrationality) dominates in this film, we are not dealing with a brittle "women's lib" sermon. Because: even with all the awkward unhappiness and painful realizations, the dialogue does not suffer from a lack of humor, exactitude, charm, and—this is a rarity in German films—lightness. No stiffness, no excess, no incessant digging in old wounds, rather a gentle touch and a quiet turning of the pages (Auffermann).

This article is quite typical and speaks not only to *Christa Klages*, but also to common assumptions about the nature of feminist cinema: it is perceived to be irrational, rigid, pedantic, humorless, and vague, and its methods are perceived to include persistent opening up of old wounds. It is important to keep in mind that these are the earliest discussions of von Trotta's films in a public arena. The fact that they also contain negative appraisals of women's cinema in general and that von Trotta's film is being lifted, more or less, above such ideologically "tainted" cinema by its reviewers in the mainstream press helps to explain the later ambivalence of feminists toward von Trotta. If the terms of the discourse around these films are being defined by the mainstream press, in other words, and if these terms set up a dichotomy with non-feminist cinema (and von Trotta) on one side and feminist cinema on the other, then it appears that von Trotta has been co-opted by the mainstream.

If von Trotta's intention was to remain in solidarity with other feminist filmmakers, she made a crucial miscalculation early on. In two separate interviews she refused the designation "woman's film" for her work. In response to a direct question as to whether *Christa Klages* was a "woman's film" or not, she replied simply: "One cannot distinguish between the woman's point of view and politics, just as one cannot separate the private and the public!" (Naefe). In another interview, she described women's cinema as a "thought ghetto" (Mudrich). Even though she was offering statements that reflected positions articulated by the women's movement, she did so in a troubling context. First, she clearly wanted to redeem her work for mainstream viewers, knowing the implications of the label "feminist" and thus wishing to avoid the term. Second, by avoiding the term, she gave the appearance of disavowing her alignment with the goals of women's cinema. Confronted with the necessity of "choosing" between mainstream audience support and vocal solidarity with other feminist filmmakers, she chose the former. Additionally, von Trotta was seen to be relatively privileged among women making films. She had gained considerable experience and access to the means of production through her husband Volker Schlöndorff's Bioskop studio, a fact that did not go without notice among her peers.

If her sole purpose was to get a feminist message across to a mainstream audience, one could argue that von Trotta made the correct decision. On the other hand, it would have been possible to articulate a diplomatic response to her interviewers' questions without alienating the feminist community or mainstream audiences by further contextualization or explanation of her position. At any rate, the effect of the interviews remained: although there were occasions of mutual support between other women filmmakers and von Trotta, her treatment by feminist reviewers in Germany has suffered.[9]

By far the most common approach to *Christa Klages* was to see the film as a message of utopian humanism and to interpret the character Christa Klages as a figure embodying characteristics belonging to a quasi-composite Iphigenie, whose humanity touches all those with whom she comes into contact, and Kattrin, the mute daughter of "Mother Courage," whose drumming saves her city from ruin. This approach not only enabled reviewers to lift the film out of a strictly feminist context, but also to maneuver away from the obvious parallels between the film and the contemporary political situation in Germany. "Universalizing" the content of the film de-historicized it, to be sure, and whatever the personal attitude of reviewers toward leftist sympathizers, they did not risk repercussions from readers, not to mention overt censorship from editors, by revealing their own positions ("Angleichung"; Beckert).

Women and Psychological Theory

Before looking more closely at the film text itself, one needs to examine a crucial area of discourse, one that has direct bearing on the appeal of *Christa Klages* for spectators in the late 1970s and early 1980s. One of the many changes enabled in part by the women's movement in Europe and the U.S. during those years was an unprecedented amount of attention devoted to the psychology of women. Many researchers believed that previous accounts of human moral development, because they had been based entirely on research using male subjects, needed to be rethought. Psychologists began to look at how the category of sexual difference complicated accepted notions of virtually every aspect of psychology. In particular, the work of Carol Gilligan in the U.S. and Margarete Mitscherlich in West Germany had a great effect on the degree to which these issues were discussed outside academic circles, since both women also published in non-academic magazines and discussed their research findings in newspapers, as well as on television and radio.

Both Gilligan and Mitscherlich were concerned primarily with the issue of the socialization of children and its effects on their moral development. While Gilligan was interested in how girls and boys differed in their moral decision-making processes, Mitscherlich looked at whether girls and boys were socialized uniquely into roles of peacefulness or aggression. It is important to note that both researchers were working from the assumption that the qualities historically attributed to women (nurturing, gentleness, etc.) were valuable. In other words, just as Gilligan and Mitscherlich were exploring how women were socialized to embody "feminine" qualities, they were clearly valorizing the qualities themselves. At this early stage of such research, neither the possibilities of differences *among* women—racial, class-based, experiential, to name a few—nor the reality that some women were aggressive and autonomous and some men gentle and relationship-oriented were of major importance. The problems surrounding what appears to be a quite essentialist assessment of women's psychology were yet to be articulated. Still, the recognition that work on moral development could be expanded to include the voices and experiences of women had a powerful resonance, and both Gilligan and Mitscherlich paved the way for numerous subsequent studies in this field.

Gilligan's *In a Different Voice* (1982) is particularly useful as we turn to *Christa Klages*. In this book she summarized some of the interviews she had been conducting on the subject of moral judgment, calling them collectively the "rights and responsibilities" study. Her research subjects were asked to discuss a hypothetical dilemma and propose a solution. The dilemma, devised by psychologist Lawrence Kohlberg, involved a man, Heinz, his deathly ill wife, Ruth, and a druggist. Heinz was financially unable to buy a life-saving drug for his wife and the druggist was unwilling to supply the drug without charge. The respondents were then asked whether, given the situation, Heinz should steal the drug to save his wife's life. Gilligan uses the responses of two children, Jake (who argues against stealing the drug) and Amy (who argues for stealing the drug), to exemplify gendered patterns of responses to the question. According to Gilligan, Jake's responses indicated that he perceived the solution to the problem to be absolute, impersonal and inevitable, given a consensus-based societal morality. Amy, on the other hand, saw a hierarchical order of rational principles as less urgent than a contextually contingent and communication-based solution to the problem that highlights relationship and connection rather than autonomy.[10]

Christa Klages and a Gendered Moral Code

The moral dilemma just outlined, as well as the gender-based solutions to that dilemma, are enacted in similar ways in *The Second Awakening of Christa Klages*. Again, the basic plot revolves around the chain of events precipitated by the fate of the day-care center. Christa's interest in saving the center stems not only from the fact that she founded it, she runs it, and her daughter attends it. Equally important is the fact that quality day care is needed by the community at large. The moral dilemma is set up as follows: the day-care center is unable to meet its lease payments and the city government is ready to evict it in favor of a new, paying tenant. Von Trotta intensifies the situation by polarizing the moral claims to tenancy of the two parties. The day-care center built by Christa attempts to provide an alternative, holistic pedagogy; accepts children regardless of parental ability to pay the full amount; admits the children of so-called "foreign guest workers"; and is run cooperatively. The new tenant, on the other hand, intends to open a pornography shop. For Christa, the absurdity of the fact that her operation would be halted by a city government unwilling to take into account the "righteousness" of her claim as opposed to the "sinfulness" of the counter-claim—money issues notwithstanding—leads her to bank robbery.

One could argue that von Trotta was indeed invoking clichés by making the new tenant a pornographer, especially since she presents pornography in an unquestioningly bad light. Not only does she ignore the contested nature of pornography itself, she allows the weight of the emotional public debates about the issue to make her argument for her. On the other hand, she could have been attempting to construct a dilemma perceived by her audience to be clear in its morality. If she thought her audiences were overwhelmingly opposed to pornography—and in the late 1970s they probably were, at least publicly—the decision to provide a "limit case" was calculated to force the audience to confront the act of breaking the law when the ends are justified, rather than highlighting *whether* the ends are justified.

Of course Christa broke the law. But for her, as for the subjects in Gilligan's study, the most important issues did not revolve around the letter of the law, but rather took into account the context of the particular situation. For her, blind acceptance of the law would have had terrible implications, ranging from her own unemployment and the failure of her project to the loss of child care for her daughter and, more importantly, the loss of the only safe haven for disenfranchised children in her city. Accepting the fate of the day-care center would also have had ethical and moral implications. Certainly the real results would have been tragic. What drives Christa, however, is the knowledge that her inaction would mean the squandering of an opportunity to confront society with its own skewed priorities. Presented with the chance to right a social injustice, she would have remained passive.

The character of Hans represents the other model of moral decision-making, what Gilligan would characterize as the "male" model. He is the pastor of a small village parish and has connections to one of Christa's accomplices. Christa's hope is that Hans will accept the stolen money into a parish bank account, and then transfer it into the account of the day-care facility as a charitable contribution. Once Hans learns the source of the money, however, he refuses to participate in the scheme, arguing: "I don't even want to see it. No, drastic times *do not* justify drastic measures" (von Trotta and Francia 30). Even when Christa pleads with him to consider the plight of the children and questions his Christian ethics, he stays with his initial decision. He tells Christa that the idealistic notion of "the Church" she invokes does not exist, and that he is really no more than an employee of a modern, bureaucratic institution. Thus, he makes his decision based on abstract law, emphasizing the need to work consistently within the parameters of the legal system. He refuses Christa's assertion that all other avenues had been fully exhausted, but insists that even if they were, he would still refuse to be implicated in the plan.

If Christa can be understood as an example of Gilligan's "female" model and Hans as her "male" model, then the character of Lena embodies the possibililty of transition between the two. In her, we witness the transformation from one who accepts and fully participates in the laws of the society in which she lives to one who questions those laws. As a bank employee taken hostage by Christa during the robbery for a short time, Lena is the only witness able to make a positive physical identification of Christa as the woman who had robbed the bank. At first, she not only cooperates with the authorities, she strikes out on an investigation of her own. She is so invested in her work that she views a transgression against her place of employment as a personal violation. More and more, though, she becomes fascinated with Christa and her life. Not only does Lena see in Christa the excitement her own life lacks, she also comes to realize the principles and motivation behind Christa's "lawlessness."

Through conversations with Christa's mother, daughter, and co-workers, and through newspaper accounts of the official investigation, Lena gradually gains sympathy for Christa and begins to see the promise Christa's way of being in the world holds for someone like herself. By the end of the film, then, when Lena is face to face with Christa and is finally able to make a positive identification for the police, she refuses to do so. The film ends with the following scene:

> Official: Miss Seidlhofer, try to remember. Look at the woman very carefully.
> Lena: Could she please take off the sunglasses and the stocking!
> (Christa slowly removes the stocking and the glasses.)
> Official: Was that the woman?
> (A few moments pass before Lena answers, but without ever removing her eyes from Christa.)
> Lena: No, she's definitely not the one.
> (Only then does she smile, almost imperceptibly, only recognizable for Christa, not for the official.) (von Trotta and Francia 87-88)

In this moment of solidarity with Christa, Lena achieves her own transformation and enables Christa's "second awakening." In this one act, Lena has changed from someone with allegiances to bourgeois society with its rigid laws to a literal "out-law," and from complicity with patriarchal institutions to solidarity with women. This shift is articulated visually through the smile she gives to Christa and *not* to the officials, and through von Trotta's composition of the shot. Lena is at the extreme left of the frame and Christa is at the extreme right, each facing the other. Occupying the space between them—separating them—is the police investigator, who is standing with his legs apart and arms crossed. All three figures are in focus. At the moment of Lena's denial, however, the camera moves in tightly to the faces of the two women, blurring the figure of the investigator and effectively wiping out his centrality in the situation. If institutions—from the Church to law enforcement agencies to city government—have been constructed in the film as oppressive, or at least rigid and unresponsive to human need, their power is effaced symbolically in this final scene. Indeed, it is through Lena's and Christa's recognition that their goals must be achieved through common work that this effacement takes place.

Like Lena, Christa's friend Ingrid is also a transitional character. Where I have attempted to explain how a continuum of moral decision-making in Gilligan's terms might look using the characters of Lena, Hans, and Christa, von Trotta and her co-scriptwriter Luisa Francia posit a more teleological model of (feminist) selfhood. According to them, Lena occupies the least developed position, Ingrid the next position, and Christa, because of her clearly developed sense of self, the most advanced position. They explain:

> Christa, Ingrid, and Lena each have a different level of experience and consciousness. But the paths taken by the three women could be the path of a single woman. It starts with Lena, the bourgeois bank clerk, with her traditional, interchangeable wishes for marriage and a small household. As Lena comes into contact with Christa and her other way of living, she recognizes how stalled and limited her own dreams are, and ultimately it becomes impossible for her to betray this woman.... Ingrid, the second woman, already has everything Lena still dreams of: a condominium, designer furniture, and a husband with long-term job security. But when she is reunited with her schoolmate Christa, she too recognizes the lack and emptiness of her surroundings.... Now Christa Klages already has these phases behind her. She has left her marriage and home, in order to seek a new way for herself and her child, but also for others (94–95).

Whereas Lena is transformed as much by her own relentless pursuit and observation of Christa as she is by any action on Christa's part, Ingrid is more directly influenced by Christa, who initially seeks her out in search of a place to hide from the authorities. Christa urges Ingrid to talk about her relationship with her husband, Heinz; she asks pointed questions about Ingrid's choice of lifestyle that bespeak her dubiousness about its rewards and she gets Ingrid to admit, finally, that her nightmares stem from her unfulfilling marriage. Their conversations sound more like therapy sessions than discussions, and the end result is that Ingrid leaves her husband, at least temporarily, to accompany Christa to a cooperative in Portugal. There Christa and Ingrid find anonymity. They are able to let their guard down under the blazing Mediterranean sun and do physical labor alongside the local residents in an agricultural cooperative. Together they adopt the local work attire and marvel over their chafed hands, sunburns, and scraped knees. They give haircuts to the cork farmers as the women look on in amusement in a scene that is warm, relaxed, and happy. Neither the local men nor women engage in any dialogue.

Such romanticization and "letting down one's guard" has its price, however. Christa's and Ingrid's close friendship raises eyebrows, and their German contact Erich warns them that they must move on, explaining: "Women think differently here, have a different sensibility. It's still a little like in the Middle Ages. One has to respect that, don't you think?" (77). Aside from the explicit designation of the local women as "different," the reference is to their "medieval" world view, which evidently precludes perceived lesbian relationships. Erich implies that the

Portuguese farmers would find such relationships offensive, whereas the (more modern, progressive) Germans would find little to criticize in them, which is hardly the case.

In this film, then, the archaic and nature-bound lifestyle of their Portuguese hosts allows Christa and Ingrid to get in touch with their physicality and revel in the prizes awarded for it (their scrapes and weathered skin). They can suspend rational thought—Ingrid cannot conjure up her reasons for leaving her husband—and they can ultimately validate their own progressive tendencies by identifying the regressive beliefs of the Portugese farmers (all of whom have remained conveniently silent and incidental) they have visited and left behind. Further, Ingrid's closeness to Christa is achievable only in this context, physically separate from Germany and her husband and surrounded by people who have been constructed as radically "different."

Although Lena and Ingrid respond differently to Christa, and with varying degrees of agency and initiative, both their lives have been fundamentally altered by their encounters with her. But regardless of von Trotta's own insistence that Christa represents some sort of "end station" compared to Lena's and Ingrid's tentative first steps toward liberation and that Christa, Lena, and Ingrid represent three equally weighted possibilities for female identity, the film must be seen principally as Christa's story. It must also be seen as the story of her process toward identity, not as any end result. The title of the film itself demands such a reading, as does the structure of the narrative.

The film text is divided into five "chapters," and the titles of the chapters correspond not to any particular action or plot twists, but quite specifically to Christa's psychic journey: "Approach," "Friendship," "Community," "Solitude," and "The Second Awakening" (9). The bank robbery itself comes before the five sections, as a flashback sequence accompanied by her voice-overs. As the title sequence is still rolling, we have our first glimpse of Christa. She is standing alone in an empty room and in a voice-over says: "First I had to create my own prison, in order to comprehend what was happening with me" (13). Upon first viewing, the opening scenes are quite confusing because they are not in chronological order. The empty room of the title segment is the room she occupies during the "Solitude" segment. It is followed by a shot of Christa and her accomplice, Werner, jumping onto a train with the stolen money. Only then do we see the actual robbery. This is followed by a cut to the train, a cut back to the site of the robbery, and finally a cut to the first segment, in which Christa and Werner approach the pastor Hans.

Immediately, then, we know that we are dealing with a personal account told in the first person, and that the plot will be motivated by a need to discover and comprehend the psychological or emotional aspects of the action. We should note that Christa does not say that she wants to comprehend "was mir passiert ist" ("what happened to me"), which would imply an external event, but rather "was mit mir geschehen war" ("what happened with me"), which, I would argue, connotes an internal process. Rather than articulating a series of events that happened *to her*—against her will—Christa indicates through the use of the construction "mit mir" ("with me") that she had agency in her own awakening.

The use of voice-over indicates that Christa also stands outside or above the narrative, just as she is in it. She speaks from the position of the newly "awakened" Christa, sharing with the viewer the process through which she came to occupy her new status. This use of the voice-over continues through the film as she interprets, relates, or summarizes the unfolding of the narrative. It also indicates the extent to which von Trotta wanted to allow her protagonist to control her own discourse, to recount her experience in her own voice, rather than have it shaped through the words of others. Von Trotta's use of Christa's voice-over to provide narrative perspective has another function as well. By foregrounding this formal element, she insists that form and content can never be neatly separated. The use of voice on the level of content—Christa's ongoing process of developing and "speaking" her own sense of self—finds formal articulation through the device of the voice-over. It is through language, through her own distinctive voice, as well as through Lena's cooperation and unspoken communication and connection with her, that Christa moves to her point of awakening.

In the segment "Solitude," Christa uses a piece of charcoal to cover the walls of her apartment with words. She isolates herself totally and carries on a dialogue with herself through verses of poetry, questions, and sayings. As she sinks deeper and deeper into herself, she becomes more and more still, until she finally lies flat on her back, not moving for days. When she does arise, she starts to drink a suicide potion, throws it away, leaves the apartment, and allows herself to be caught by the police. As we have already seen, the moment of truth comes in an unexpected way, as Lena does not betray Christa.

Christa as Messiah

In the final scene, we see how Margit Czenki is "redeemed" by Margarethe von Trotta. In reality, of course, Czenki was caught, tried, and jailed. Von Trotta has constructed in the character of Christa—whose very name is evocative, and whose "Second Awakening" is like a "Second Coming"—a quasi-feminist Christ figure whose intervention into the lives of those around her provides them with their particular salvations. While von Trotta uses parallels from the Bible positively in some instances, she subverts them in others. Consider, for example, the passages in which Christa is described as someone who works for the disenfranchised and the children of guest workers, and whose humane goals are held up by von Trotta as an attempt to justify to German society the robbing of the bank. This approximates conventional understandings of similar strategies employed in the Gospel According to Luke, where the good works of Jesus are used apologetically to justify Christianity to the larger Roman society. Similarly, Christa is constructed by von Trotta as someone whose unconditional advocacy for the most powerless in German society—her good works—should justify the transgression against that society's laws.

In another New Testament parallel, Christa withdraws before the "crucifixion" in the apartment building, just as Jesus withdraws to the garden of Gethsamene before he is crucified in the Gospel According to Mark.[11] Most strikingly, however, von Trotta replicates the moment of Peter's denial of Christ in the Gospel According to Mark, but with a radically different outcome. The scripture reads: "But he began to invoke a curse on himself and to swear, 'I do not know this man of whom you speak'" (Mark 14:71). Where this utterance is linked in the New Testament both to Christ's crucifixion and to Peter's recognition of his own fallibility, Lena's similar words—"No, she's definitely not the one"—lead to Christa's salvation. They also show the extent of Lena's empowerment: she now is able to act as Christa would have (von Trotta and Francia 88). Peter's denial of Christ, according to Christian belief, was part of the Passion drama that offered the promise of eternal life to the followers of the crucified Christ. In von Trotta's revision of this scene, a denial is no betrayal. Indeed, Lena's "No, she's definitely not the one" serves to lead *both* Lena and Christa out of the darkness; Lena's words represent her move away from a position as adoring apostle of German law and bureaucracy to a position of enlightened "outlaw." And this transformation, which could not have happened without Christa's influence, ultimately leads back again to Christa's own freedom and second awakening.

This kind of morality—the morality of the enlightened, humane "outlaw"—is what unites Christa's and Lena's actions with the actions of Amy in Carol Gilligan's studies. Certainly von Trotta saw in her female protagonists attributes that she felt would lead Germans to a better society. It is also clear that she was positing them as a counter to Hans, whose goodness was of little use in the context of a complicated moral dilemma. Recall the earlier assertion by Hans that the modern Church is no longer the idealized institution Christa imagines, but rather a bureaucratic structure. Thus, just as Christa and Hans embody polarities within the category of gendered morality, they perform the same function in questions of religion. Clearly, von Trotta is suggesting that Christa's unquestioning, instinctual act—in spite of its departure from worldly legality—is morally superior to Hans's refusal to operate outside the bounds of organized religion.

Almost two decades after the release of *Christa Klages*, Margarethe von Trotta seemed to have given up her hope of effecting change in German society. After directing five feature films there, all embedded to greater or lesser degrees in German political culture, she began working in Italy and has only recently returned to making films with specifically German themes.[12] Still, as critics begin now to write the history of feminist film in Germany and document the utopian impulses of the early days of second-wave feminism, *Christa Klages* must occupy a place in that endeavor. It displays what Thomas Elsaesser has referred to as von Trotta's ability to "locate a certain truth about Germany" in her films (237)—in this case, an evocation of the potential of a specifically German, specifically feminist response to the history of Germany in the late 1970s. Whether utopian-humanist, as reviewers have claimed, or messianic, as I have suggested, or morally righteous, as an interpretation based on Gilligan would reveal, the valorized attributes of Christa Klages were also embodied by Margit Czenki. But where Czenki ended up in jail for her actions, Christa Klages's "Second Awakening" brought a message of hope, if only on celluloid.

Notes

My thanks go to the editors and outside readers of the *Women in German Yearbook* for their generous and helpful comments on this article. All translations of quotes are my own, unless otherwise indicated.

[1] See, for example, Anton Kaes, Eric Santner, and Richard McCormick.

[2] See Julia Knight, Barbara Quart, and Renate Fischetti. More recently, the two-volume *Gender and German Cinema: Feminist Interventions* has appeared, offering extensive and sustained attention to women in cinema in general, but also including individual readings of films (Frieden, et al.).

[3] For a more detailed discussion of German film making during this era, see Elsaesser (36, 260). See also Frieden, et al., especially volume II.

[4] Although von Trotta's later film *Marianne and Juliane* (*Die bleierne Zeit*, 1981) deals more specifically with the events of 1977, *Christa Klages* deals with some of the same general thematic concerns.

[5] The verb "klagen" in German means to accuse or sue, as in a court of law, or to bemoan.

[6] The "Radicalism Decree" became law in 1972. It was known popularly as the *Berufsverbot* or "career prohibition" because it led to the denial of civil service jobs to persons suspected of leftist activity.

[7] For a more detailed treatment of the reception of *Christa Klages*, see Renate Möhrmann's essay in Frieden, et al., highlighting the degree to which von Trotta's first film was embraced by the public and critics alike. Also in Frieden, Barton Byg's treatment of *Marianne and Juliane* and Anna Kuhn's

study of *Rosa Luxemburg*—both later von Trotta films—offer additional insight into von Trotta's reception. See also Coates, as well as Linville, for recent assessments of von Trotta's films.

[8] See, for instance, Wolfgang Würker, F. J. Bröder, H. G. Pflaum, Frauke Hanck, and Heino Eggers.

[9] See the review of von Trotta's later film *Die bleierne Zeit*, for example, by Charlotte Delormé.

[10] Discussions about the division between rational versus communication-based decision-making are found not only in feminist psychological theory, but also form the basis of distinction between Enlightenment and Habermasian philosophies. I thank John McCarthy for this reminder.

[11] All Biblical references are taken from the *Greek-English New Testament*. See in particular Mark 14:31-42. I thank Elizabeth A. Castelli and Lyn Loveless for discussing with me the New Testament.

[12] Von Trotta's film entitled *Il lungo silenzio* (1993), was shown at the 1993 Toronto Film Festival. A film returning to the contemporary German scene is *The Promise* (*Das Versprechen,* 1994), which deals with post-unification issues and was Germany's entry in the Oscar competition for Best Foreign Film of 1994.

Works Cited

"Angleichung durch Masse und Macht: Deutsche Filme auf der 'Berlinale.'" *Frankfurter Allgemeine Zeitung* 27 February 1978.

Auffermann, Verena. "Idealismus und die Folgen: 'Das Zweite Erwachen der Christa Klages' im Heidelberger 'Gloria.'" *Rhein-Neckar-Zeitung* 18 April 1978.

Beckert, Michael. "Der Mut einer Frau: 'Das Zweite Erwachen der Christa Klages.'" *Saarbrücker Zeitung* 4 May 1978.

Blumenberg, Hans C. "Edle Räuberin: Margarethe von Trottas Erstling." *Die Zeit* 21 April 1978.

Bröder, F.J. "Mut zum Ausbruch: Margarethe von Trottas 'Das zweite Erwachen der Christa Klages.'" *Nürnberger Nachrichten* 14 April 1978.

Byg, Barton. "German History and Cinematic Convention Harmonized in Margarethe von Trotta's *Marianne und Juliane*." Frieden, et al. 259-71.

Coates, Paul. *The Gorgon's Gaze: German Cinema, Expressionism, and the Image of Horror*. Cambridge: Cambridge UP, 1991.

Delormé, Charlotte. "On the Film *Marianne and Juliane* by Margarethe von Trotta." Trans. Ellen Seiter, Susanne Böhmer, and Barbara Hoffmann. *Journal of Film and Video* 37 (Spring 1985): 47-51.

Eggers, Heino. "Leben jenseits der Einsamkeit: Margarethe von Trottas Film 'Das zweite Erwachen der Christa Klages' zielt auf die Gesellschaft." *Vorwärts* 15 June 1978.

Elsaesser, Thomas. *New German Cinema: A History*. New Brunswick, NJ: Rutgers UP, 1989.

Filmverlag der Autoren. *Deutschland im Herbst*. 1977.

Fischetti, Renate. *Das neue Kino*. Frankfurt a.M.: tende, 1992.

Frieden, Sandra, et al., eds. *Gender and German Cinema: Feminist Interventions*. 2 vols. Providence, RI: Berg, 1993.

Gilligan, Carol. *In a Different Voice: Psychological Theory and Women's Development*. Cambridge, MA: Harvard UP, 1982.

Greek-English New Testament, rev. ed. Stuttgart: Deutsche Bibelgesellschaft, 1971.

Hanck, Frauke. "Neu im Kino: 'Das zweite Erwachen.'" *tz* (München) 14 April 1978.

Kaes, Anton. *From Hitler to Heimat: The Return of History as Film*. Cambridge, MA: Harvard UP, 1989.

Knight, Julia. *Women and the New German Cinema*. London: Verso, 1992.

Kuhn, Anna. "A Heroine for Our Time: Margarethe von Trotta's *Rosa Luxemburg*." Frieden, et al. 163–84.

Linville, Susan E. "Retrieving History: Margarethe von Trotta's *Marianne and Juliane*." *PMLA* 106.3 (1991): 446–58.

McCormick, Richard W. *Politics of the Self: Feminism and the Postmodern in West German Literature and Film*. Princeton, NJ: Princeton UP, 1991.

Mitscherlich, Margarete. *Die friedfertige Frau: Eine psychoanalytische Untersuchung zur Aggression der Geschlechter*. Frankfurt a.M.: Fischer, 1985.

Möhrmann, Renate. "The Second Awakening of Christa Klages." Frieden, et al. 73–83.

Mudrich, Heinz. "Wenn eine Frau Regie führt: In der Saarbrücker 'Camera': Gespräch mit Margarethe von Trotta und François Duplat." *Saarbrücker Zeitung* 12 May 1978.

Naefe, Vivian. "Räuberin will Kindern helfen: Interview mit Margarethe von Trotta zu ihrem Film 'Das zweite Erwachen.'" *Abendzeitung* 14 April 1978.

Pflaum, Hans Günther. "Ausbruch aus dem eigenen Gefängnis: Margarethe von Trottas Regie-Debüt." *Süddeutsche Zeitung* 17 April 1978.

Quart, Barbara Koenig. *Women Directors: The Emergence of a New Cinema*. New York: Praeger, 1988.

Santner, Eric L. *Stranded Objects: Mourning, Memory, and Film in Postwar Germany*. Ithaca: Cornell UP, 1990.

Trotta, Margarethe von, dir. *Das zweite Erwachen der Christa Klages*. Bioskop Filmproduktion, 1977.

Trotta, Margarethe von, and Luisa Francia. *Das zweite Erwachen der Christa Klages*. Frankfurt a.M.: Fischer, 1980.

Würker, Wolfgang. "Film im Fernsehen: 'Das zweite Erwachen.'" *Frankfurter Allgemeine Zeitung* 17 October 1980.

"Germany, Pale Mother": On the Mother Figures in New German Women's Film

Renate Möhrmann

This investigation is part of a comprehensive book project on the representation of motherhood in literature, painting, fairy tales, film and television, theater, and advertising. Edited by Renate Möhrmann, it will be published in the spring of 1996 by Metzler Verlag under the title *Verklärt—Verkitscht—Vergessen: Die Mutter als ästhetische Figur*. Since this project will be the first examination in German of the aesthetic representation of motherhood throughout various disciplines—and from the perspective of the mother rather than that of the daughter—the focus is less on the critical interpretations of individual works than on the treatment of motherhood within specific genres. (RM)

Berlin, 2 February 1980. Scandal. Critics leave the auditorium in droves during the première of Helma Sanders-Brahms's film *Germany, Pale Mother* (*Deutschland, bleiche Mutter*) at the 30th International Film Festival. On their faces a mixture of exaggerated pain and arrogant distaste, indicating that they had been provoked beyond endurance. What happened?

A mother had caused bewilderment in the ranks of the male critics.[1] Filmmaker Helma Sanders-Brahms, in her eighth film, had had the audacity to narrate the National Socialist past as female memory-work, from the perspective of a mother-daughter relationship. Moreover, it was the perspective of her own mother, whose daughter—i.e., the filmmaker herself—was acted by Sanders-Brahms's daughter Anna. With this autobiographical approach to the Third Reich, she violated a taboo against the mingling of two conflicting discourses, the private and the political; that is, she transgressed against the then-prevailing forms of representing political history in general. If she had told her mother's life during the war and post-war years as a private story, there would have been no scandal. Or, a strictly political parable without any private tittle-tattle—as she had very capably done in her early didactic films *Violence* (*Gewalt*, 1971),

The Industrial Reserve Army (*Die industrielle Reservearmee,* 1971), or *The Machine* (*Die Maschine,* 1973), which some critics had patronizingly praised—would not have occasioned that February 1980 uproar.

One thing is certain: It was not the subject of National Socialism that produced the broad palette of defensive reactions and blocked analyses, as Olav Münzberg believed.[2] After all, Sanders-Brahms's film was not the first to treat it. Such films as Edgar Reitz's *Hour Zero* (*Stunde Null,* 1977), Hans Jürgen Syberberg's *Our Hitler* (*Hitler, Ein Film aus Deutschland,* 1977), Joachim C. Fest's *Hitler: A Career* (*Hitler—Eine Karriere,* 1977), or Rainer Werner Fassbinder's *The Marriage of Maria Braun* (*Die Ehe der Maria Braun,* 1979) had already been made. None had met with so much resistance, none had been the target of so much malice. The very titles of the reviews are revealing: "Recoiling from the Pale Mother" ("Schaudern vor der bleichen Mutter," *Frankfurter Neue Presse,* 22 February 1980), "Prodigal Rubble-Film" ("Verquaster Trümmerfilm," *Die Welt,* 25 February 1980), "Mothers, Daughters, War, and Terror" ("Mütter, Töchter, Krieg und Terror," *Frankfurter Rundschau,* 25 February 1980), "Giggles in the Auditorium for *Germany, Pale Mother*" ("Über *Deutschland, bleiche Mutter* wird im Saal gekichert," *Münchner Merkur,* 22 February 1980). The list could be continued.[3]

Here it should be noted that reviews by female critics were overwhelmingly more positive and contained no comparable defensive reactions. Gender-specific positionality clearly played a decisive role in *Pale Mother*'s reception. It is also striking that male critics unanimously confessed to a diffuse feeling of embarrassment toward the film—and indeed, Sanders-Brahms poses the question of embarrassment anew. By showing images of childbirth, such as labor pains, the birth canal, the blood-smeared newborn, the cutting of the umbilical cord—images that had been taboo in film until that time (1980)—she breaks through the prevailing barriers of shame and embarrassment. Radically. Thus, it is no coincidence that the critics' mass departure began during precisely that scene. The scene is of central significance for the film, as is its setting—during the worst air raids on the civilian population. Through a montage of childbirth and air raid, of life being created and life being destroyed, of the blood of parturition and the blood of killing, Sanders-Brahms connects events that are normally treated as separate discourses in cultural production. How closely these things are connected, what devastation the war causes to those at home, and how fundamentally it also changes mothers—Helma Sanders-Brahms and countless other children of the war experienced this first-hand.

But—and this never ceases to amaze me—the experiences of mothers from this period are almost never documented; they are virtually absent as the subject of serious cultural debate. History was always written from the perspective of men,[4] of rulers and generals, of commanders and officers, of heroic anniversaries and memorial services for those killed in action, of opportunistic war profiteers and uprooted war-returnees. Zuckmayer's *The Devil's General* (*Des Teufels General*, 1946), Borchert's *Outside the Door* (*Draußen vor der Tür*, 1946), Staudte's *The Murderers Are Among Us* (*Die Mörder sind unter uns*, 1946), and Böll's *Where Were You, Adam?* (*Wo warst du, Adam?*, 1951) are concrete examples. This point of view also defines the prevailing thresholds of embarrassment. Corpses are not a taboo for the audiovisual media, nor is the blood of crime victims and war casualties. They can be seen daily on television and in film; every news program presents them. But the blood of women is embarrassing and offends our sense of propriety. It belongs in the private sphere.

Sanders-Brahms does not recognize such distinctions. Thus she enters a debate that the women's liberation movement had launched in the early 1970s: the question of the relationship between the *political* and the *private*, and of the legitimacy of treating them as separate for the last two hundred years. The need for such a debate had been made obvious by the new patriarchal attitudes in the German Socialist Students' Organization (SDS).[5] There too the separation of the political and the private was the *conditio sine qua non* for maintaining traditional concepts of male and female roles and the hierarchical relationship between them. As women's interests were once again defined as merely "private," they inevitably lost importance and could be eliminated from the political agenda. This turned out to be practical. At least for the men. It absolved them from the laborious responsibilities of child-care and domesticity while leaving their status as emancipators intact. For at the time, emancipation primarily meant that of the workers and the Third World. Mothers and their double burden were not on the agenda.

That was the starting point of the new women's movement. It recognized the programmatic aspects underlying such strategies of exclusion and the far-reaching social and political consequences of reducing the entire sphere of motherhood and household to the private business of each individual woman, who had to cope with it on her own. This is true even today, especially for Germany and Italy, the only two European countries without full-day schools and full-time day-care. Thus it was absolutely logical for the new women's movement to define the private as political and initiate a public discussion.

That was not without consequences for artistic production in general or for the new German women's film in particular.[6] The women filmmakers of the 1970s were the first whose works treated the formerly excluded themes of contraception, the German abortion laws (Paragraph 218), pregnancy, and motherhood, as well as the question of the compatibility of career and family. Examples of such films are: *Children Are Not Cattle* (*Kinder sind keine Rinder*, 1971) and *Does the Pill Liberate Us?*

(*Macht die Pille frei?,* 1971) by Helke Sander, *The Weaker Sex Gets Stronger* (*Das schwache Geschlecht wird stark,* 1974) by Claudia Schilinski, or *Paragraph 218 and What We Have Against It* (*Paragraph 218 und was wir dagegen haben,* 1976) by Sabine Eckart. However, such films were barely acknowledged by male critics. According to prevailing conventions, they were ranked on the lowest level of the hierarchy of significance.

A difficulty for the women filmmakers was their self-imposed task of creating new, authentic female characters with whom they themselves could identify. Where was inspiration to come from? There was precious little to be found in the past, for official historiography had never been especially precise with respect to women. Female experiences generally slipped through the net of history, ending in public catastrophes or private happiness; they lacked historical continuity and were almost impossible to reconstruct. Again and again women had to start from scratch. The fact that there had been—in addition to the labor movement—an engaged and vigorous women's movement in nineteenth-century Europe was something very few girls learned in school.

Faced with this historical deficit, many women filmmakers resorted to exploring the pasts of their own mothers as source material for constructing a female "I." This gave rise, in the late 1970s, to a series of films in which mothers are the central figures. To this group—along with *Germany, Pale Mother*—belong Jutta Brückner's *Do Right and Fear Nobody* (*Tue recht und scheue niemand,* 1975) and *Years of Hunger* (*Hungerjahre,* 1980), *Something Hurts* (*Etwas tut weh,* 1979) by Recha Jungmann, and *Malou* (1980) by Jeanine Meerapfel.[7]

Here too women had to be pioneers, because there were virtually no models. Appeals to film history were not productive: Despite the broad palette of female characters, the mother paradigm was largely absent. As a rule, the great genres that constitute film history, such as the Western, the thriller, the gangster film, the road movie, the Italian historical film, or the German *Heimatfilm,* do not portray mothers. They are men's films in which he-men set the tone and horses set the pace—the horsepower and the gears, status symbols of the new equestrian class. The absence of the maternal is not even noticed. Even Italian Neorealism, celebrated after the end of World War II as a new beginning in film history, focuses hardly at all on Italian mothers. To be sure, Roberto Rosselini in *Rome: Open City* (*Roma Citta Aperta,* 1945) develops a very complex mother figure in a memorable performance by Anna Magnani. But that is an exception. Italian Neorealism introduces other groups to the silver screen—children appear as symbols of hope in its early phase, older people appear at its decline, when the principle of hope has turned out to be an illusion. Mothers are at best minor characters, as in mainstream cinema. The same is true for the New German Cinema. What this new generation of

German filmmakers understandably wanted first of all was to settle accounts with "Papa's Cinema," with the fossilized cinematic conventions of the 1950s. What ensued was a debate between fathers and sons in which, once again, there was no place for mothers.

Nevertheless there *is* a film genre that has developed as the classic site for the mother paradigm. Admittedly, this genre does not enjoy a favorable repute and—symptomatically—has only very recently received scholarly attention and revaluation, primarily from feminist theorists: the melodrama. Its directors have gone down in film history as women's directors, which is another signal of the genre's specificity; it was the only one in mainstream cinema that offered a site for women's concerns and became a medium for romance. Mothers play an important part here. The fact that the mother discourse is articulated in this very genre, long regarded as trivial, is no accident. It is related to the hierarchy of meanings mentioned earlier that negatively affected Sanders-Brahms's *Germany, Pale Mother* as late as 1980.

At best, the subject of mothers was considered significant in connection with the socialization of sons. Rousseau and Freud had seen to that. That mothers were admitted into film history at all was not least a consequence of economic necessity. To be successful, producers had to win the female audience too. The genre to which this task fell was the "maternal melodrama." It offered millions of mothers and housewives, who could participate only marginally in public life, something not available anywhere else: an avenue from their own sphere of influence for emotional identification and a "bigger-than-life-pathos" in an intimate alliance that was familiar to them.

To define the specificity of mother figures in the New German women's cinema more precisely, a look at the classic maternal melodrama is helpful. American film theorist E. Ann Kaplan, the first to analyze this genre from a feminist perspective, has derived the following basic narrative pattern: The central character is the beautiful, devoted young mother who sacrifices herself completely for her child—the personification of the "Cult of True Womanhood" (123 ff.). The strikingly close bond between mother and child has two defining factors: first, in the great majority of cases the child is male—here, the film has recourse to psychoanalytic models—and, second, the child is frequently illegitimate, so that the mother becomes the only emotional reference-point for her son and the sole architect of his fortune. But this architect of fortune has only one charge: to deliver the boy as soon as possible from his mother's protection to the order of the father. The basis for this is not only ideological, as in domestic tragedy (*bürgerliches Trauerspiel*), where only the father is the mediator of morality and education. Melodrama is more straightforward. The son's reintegration into the world of the father is motivated primarily by economics. The absent begetters are usually found in the upper reaches of society and have ample financial resources at their disposal. Thus, the search for the father determines the plot of these films, and the successful reunion is their happy end. But only for father and son. The martyred mother disappears from the story. She has served her purpose. Her elimination is the *conditio sine qua non* for integrating the son into society. In retrospect, it turns out that the touching mother-son sequences, which certainly provided a measure of happiness to the female spectators, nevertheless remain by and large illusory—even in the eyes of the mother. For ultimately she makes herself into an agent of male discourse and outlines the strategy for her son's new fortune, now guaranteed by the father, in which she has no part. The film, in its complicity with patriarchal society, demands this sacrifice of her.

The creator of this type of melodrama was David Wark Griffith. With works like *Mothering Heart* (1913), *True Heart Susie* (1919), or *Way Down East* (1920), he set the standards for the genre well into the 1930s. The basic pattern of such films corresponds to the device of dichotomous contrasts that is characteristic of silent film. In order to make the new medium understandable, good and evil had to be recognizable as separate realms: benefactors and malefactors, the Biedermen and the firebugs, good girls and bad girls all had to be characterized iconographically as clearly distinguishable types. With the refinement of filmic devices, this polarization was soon overcome in the case of male characters, and more complex male figures could emerge; however, female characters continued to be pigeonholed as comrades and pin-up girls, wives and mistresses, mothers and whores, saints and sinners—dichotomies that can be traced back to the medieval dualism of vice and virtue. The melodrama revives the medieval dualism and distinguishes sharply between "good" selfless mothers with few needs of their own and "bad" sexually active mothers.

The second type of mother, first seen in Frank Lloyd's *Madame X* (1920)—as Christian Viviani has shown (84 ff.)—constitutes the basis of another variant of the maternal melodrama, one that is diametrically opposed to the Cult of True Womanhood. It is the story of a decline, the fall from grace of a mother involved in forbidden passions. The consequence is her expulsion from the family unit—the equivalent of a social decline—and forced renunciation of motherhood. Only from afar can the outcast mother observe her son's rapid progress under the law of the father—and she can suffer. Maternal suffering is the basic sentiment of all these films, but it is also the means of reparation for past sins, in order to effect a return to the bourgeois family after all—i.e., repatriation, in the truest sense of the word. A happy end achieved through the mother's total self-sacrifice and self-denial. Films such as Dorothy Arzner's *Sarah and Son* (1930), Frank Lloyd's *East Lynne* (1931), Edgar Selwyn's *The Sin of*

Madelon Claudet (1931), Charles Brabin's *The Secret of Madame Blanche* (1933), Joe May's *Confession* (1937) and, with some variations, numerous melodramas of the 1950s and 60s such as Douglas Sirk's *All I Desire* (1953), *All That Heaven Allows* (1955)—here even the adult children deny their widowed mother's right to sexuality—and *Imitation of Life* (1958). All of these follow the basic pattern created by Frank Lloyd in *Madame X*. Both types of the mother-melodrama have one thing in common: the dissociation of motherhood and sexuality.

At this point psychoanalysis must be mentioned. For when all is said and done, it is Freud whose Oedipus theory provided the first systematic basis for dividing mothers into *good* and *evil*. It is the child's unconscious survival strategy, according to Freud, to create a negative mother-image to compensate for the fear of losing the idealized preoedipal mother, the fear that she will betray him with another man. The fact that Freud always saw the child as male is also reflected in the maternal melodrama. Here we find the psychological basis for the mother's desexualization. Only a mother who is imagined as lacking sexual drives of her own can satisfy her son's demands for love. Thus, the mother's obliteration as a woman is the price she has to pay to gain admittance into film history as a mother figure.

And so it becomes clear: In their quest for the authentic mother, the young women filmmakers of the 1970s find melodrama to be a richly revealing source, albeit not an inspiring one. It also yields explanations for male filmgoers' massive rejection of the mother figures in the new German women's film. For there is one thing that the new mother-films have in common despite all their differences: The story is no longer told from the perspective of a male child and the needs of a male audience. The father-discourse has had its day. Now the forgotten daughters make themselves heard to tell the experiences of their mothers in a new way: with more complexity and more contradictions, more radically and more precisely. Of course this can be irritating. Just how much so can be seen in the reception of *The All-round Reduced Personality—REDUPERS* (*Die allseitig reduzierte Persönlichkeit—REDUPERS*), Helke Sanders's film about an employed single mother who continually seeks new ways to fulfill the double demands of child and profession. *REDUPERS* was Sanders's first full-length feature film, completed after a series of documentary and semi-documentary projects. Together with Margarethe von Trotta's *The Second Awakening of Christa Klages* (*Das zweite Erwachen der Christa Klages*), REDUPERS premiered in 1978 at the 28th Berlin Film Festival, attracting immediate attention as the first example of the New German women's cinema.

In contrast to Sanders-Brahms' film, *REDUPERS* garnered positive reviews. It was hailed as "one of the most important West German films of the year" (1978) and chosen as "film of the year" by the editors of the

Film Yearbook (46). They recognized and lauded the filmmaker's particular intent: to make an authentic, unglamorous film anchored in the everyday life of divided Berlin from the perspective of a group of women photographers, most of them young mothers, and to reflect this genesis in the film itself. It was generally seen and accepted that *REDUPERS* was also a film about the new women's movement—its possibilities and limitations, its gains in liberty and its concomitant losses in intimacy and security.

So far—agreed. Opposition, particularly from male critics, was articulated only sporadically, with regard to the mother-child sequences. These were said to be intolerable and absolutely unbelievable—mothers would not treat their little children with such heartlessness and lack of self-control.[8] This was in reference to the scenes in which the stresses of motherhood are depicted: The protagonist, Edda Chiemnyjewski is seen exhausted and enervated at the end of a long working day, unable to respond to her daughter's emotional needs. Mother and daughter in dissociation. Such images dismantled one of the oldest Christian cultural codes: the metaphor of the unswerving alliance between mother and child, based on the emblem of Mary and the baby Jesus. No matter that empirical evidence contradicted it. In the sphere of the symbolic, of aesthetic positioning, such images must endure. That, at least, is implied by the remarkable aversion to the new film mothers.

What never fails to astonish is that no other artistic medium has so persistently perpetuated the stereotyping of women and mothers as film has done. Nowhere were transgressions against these clichés condemned as vehemently as here. In the cinema the archetypal images of man and woman, mother and child, love and sorrow could not be disturbed, the epic narratives of the patriarchy could not be reexamined. The interrogation of these clichés, which had its inception in theater, in painting, and in literature around the beginning of this century, did not take place in film—neither in Hollywood nor in the European art film—until well into the seventies. Claire Johnston is one of the first to have pointed this out (25). It was certainly no accident that the earliest outlines of feminist theory were developed in debates related to the audiovisual medium film.[9] Today, in the early 1990s, faced with a growing number of feminist conferences and congresses—in art history, architecture, theology, philosophy, literary criticism, dramaturgy, directing—we must not forget that the prelude to all these ventures was the Berlin Film Festival of 1973 which, as the first feminist conference in the Federal Republic, was brought into the world with the greatest of difficulties.

Film's voyeuristic basic mode, its threefold male gaze—the *director,* who decides on the subject matter, the *cameraman,* who organizes it for the screen, and the *male* protagonist, who makes the woman an object of his desire—consolidates the patriarchal myths into an authority that no other artistic medium possesses. Film critic Bice Curiger writes of her amazement that one can walk out of the cinema very much a man or a woman, though one went in as a human being. She stresses this as an aspect of film that must be taken seriously, one that distinguishes it from other arts. Such conclusions illustrate the difficulty of creating—and accepting—new images of women and mothers. We have learned that the existing images do not reveal the truth—a glance into the family photo album is proof of that. Radiantly smiling mothers and children are not evidence of a radiant life. Hardship is more difficult to record and does not conform to the conventions of preservation. Therefore, truth—the approximation of truth—must be reconstructed by taking a fresh look at the existing images, by re-vision, by examining memory in connection with the images remembered by others, by dialogue with the people involved, always mindful of the historical dimension. That is one of the first postulates of feminist film theory (Johnston 30 f.) and it was the background for the first feminist film about one's own mother, Jutta Brückner's *Do Right and Fear Nobody* (1975), made possible by the the institution of a special series on ZDF, the second public television channel, whose mission including the financing of minority subjects. Thus, the new mother made her way onto the German television screen through the loophole of minority status.

"We think back through our mothers, if we are women," said Virginia Woolf, emphasizing "that it is 'useless' to rely on great men for help" (79). It is in this sense that Brückner refers to her mother in order to form an image of herself (Möhrmann 220). For she had the feeling of being without an identity, her "I" buried under the conventionalized codes of mother and daughter. What she needed was documentation of her own and her mother's concrete existence, evidence of her presence as a female individual—or at least explanations for the shadowy existence of her pale mother, who had never in her life wanted anything for herself. What the mother did not fathom is what the daughter wants to show: that individual biography is part of a historical process, closely linked to prevailing social norms, and that individual dreams are often nourished by socially transmitted collective desires: Happiness is a custom-built oak kitchen. But how can genuine female desires make themselves known? How can one be a mother and an individual at the same time? That is what Brückner wanted to find out.

When she was planning this film, she was thirty-four years old, her mother sixty. She had studied political science, philosophy, and history, writing her dissertation on German statecraft in the eighteenth century. Except for a few contributions to Bavarian educational television and some scripts for the "Bavaria" series, she had until then not worked with film. The fact that she ventured into film so late was related to her general mistrust of the medium. The suggestive power of images had always seemed menacing and prejudicial to Jutta Brückner. She feared that critical viewing might be clouded and understanding impeded. Only after concrete experiences of working with the medium did she gain a better understanding of its potential. She recognized that film offers forms of pre-verbal communication that—much more directly than in literature—allowed her to portray people's sensual as well as intellectual desires. From that point on she identified film as her chosen medium.

This was the background for her first film, *Do Right and Fear Nobody*, a photo montage on the life of her mother Gerda Siepenbrink, for which she received as a production subsidy the grand sum of 80,000 German marks. She made do with this by imposing a radical restriction on herself. The film consists entirely of photos: photos from family albums, photographic collections, association archives, photos of the great realist August Sander, photos from magazines and catalogues. But she does not use them to create a photo-essay or a feature. Her work tells a story, but with different means. Brückner employs her self-imposed limitations to illuminate critically the relation between biography and history, between the individual and the collective destinies of mothers. She combines pictorial documents from each period of Gerda Siepenbrink's life with the few remaining family photos in such a way that they either confirm, supplement, or contradict her mother's subjective experiences. A family party appears in a series of party photos, a wedding in a series of other wedding photos, a child at its mother's breast with many similar pictures from the same epoch. In this way it becomes apparent how collective feelings define personal desires, that is, how little one's personal desires correspond to one's own experiences.

Gerda Siepenbrink, the petit bourgeois who had cleanliness and doing right drilled into her, along with diligence and bettering oneself—only a professional would be a suitable marriage partner, definitely not a blue collar worker—, a woman who had never attached much importance to sexuality, but rather had viewed her husband as a guarantor of public approval: At the end of her life, a life that she would live completely differently if she could start over—in any case, she would not marry—Gerda wishes for a big double bed. These are her last words in the film, musically underscored by the lyrics of a hit song "I'll dance into heaven with you, to the seventh heaven of love (looove)."

What the mother did not recognize, the daughter does—and so does the female spectator: The fragmented adult woman is a product of the petit bourgeois education of girls. Brückner does not just show the desexualized mother, as melodrama does. She demonstrates *how* the dissociation of motherhood and sexuality comes about and *how* its pattern is already determined in childhood. For it is then that the course is set for female self-renunciation, that "adieu-sexuality" is pre-programmed as an educational goal. "Social acceptance," the mother had taught her daughter, "in our situation (the father had died and the family was poor) is only attainable through respectability, reliability, cleanliness, and above all by restraint." And gaining social acceptance was the prime goal of all her motherly endeavors. In this life plan, with its aim of social prestige, sexuality was only a disrupting factor. It had to be avoided.

How these questions haunted Brückner is also evident in her next two films. The protagonist of *A Fully Demoralized Girl* (*Ein ganz und gar verwahrlostes Mädchen,* 1977) transgresses the rules of petit bourgeois respectability by not avoiding the disrupting factor of sexuality. In *Years of Hunger* (1980) Brückner continues on a fictional level what she had prepared the way for with documents in *Do Right and Fear Nobody*: her own mother's all-round reduced personality. Again, a mother-daughter relationship is central, again she is concerned with the fateful discontinuities and dissonances in the process of becoming a woman that had not been shown in such a radical way in cinema until then. Brückner makes skillful use of the specific possibilities of the film medium to illustrate these ambivalences.

It is a beautiful thing to become a woman and be able to have children—this is Frau Scheuner's emphatic response to Ursula's appalled reaction to getting her first period. A flood of prohibitions follows immediately: no more rough-housing with boys, no physical activity, no swimming, no playing ball, best not to play with boys at all. No short skirts, for that could be dangerous, could spoil everything, could lead straight to misfortune. Everyone knows this. And—don't talk about it. Thus, what is beautiful in a women's life manifests itself first and foremost as a jumble of prohibitions. The beautiful remains abstract. The prohibitions are concrete. Brückner deliberately translates the prohibitions into images, while the prophesied happiness is expressed only verbally. She follows the same procedure when depicting the mother's sex life. Frau Scheuner, who had just asserted that children are the most beautiful thing in a woman's life, is shown immediately after the sex act squatting in a bathtub where, with a tormented expression and vehement movements, she washes the sperm out of her body—as if she wanted to tear out her genitals. Again the visual message contradicts the verbally proclaimed happiness.

Interestingly, the classic maternal melodrama—if it thematizes ambivalences at all—works in the opposite way. Here it is the prohibitions that are communicated only verbally, while happiness is shown in the most gorgeous pictures. That makes it as seductive as it is unbelievable. And that means, in the end, that it is also harmless.

We know of no critic who walked out of a maternal melodrama with such indignation as in the case of *Germany, Pale Mother*, or who wrote comparably savage reviews. It wasn't necessary, because those films had never seriously called the untouched male world into question. That happened first in German women's film, and therein lies its subversive potential. It stages the swan song of patriarchal discourse and the entry of mothers into film history. The absence of the fathers, their departure for the Second World War, frees the mothers—as these films show us—from the limitations of their gender roles. Suddenly the helpmates turn into agents of history—with a hitherto unknown range of activity—who define the war and post-war history. For everyone to see. And even when the patriarchal principle returns in full force after the war and the mother is marginalized again, as in Sanders-Brahms's experience, the system is unmasked as deficient. The restoration of the patriarchal order is no longer the restoration of happiness and harmony as in the melodrama.

It is astonishing that it took thirty years for this paradigm shift to be translated into film. Keeping in mind that "the majority of German postwar films (67.5%) are set partly or completely in the postwar period" (Pleyer 150), this "overlooking" of the maternal presence is even more incomprehensible. The almost hysterical reaction of the German press in 1980 to *Germany, Pale Mother* shows how serious were Helma Sanders-Brahms's transgressions against the prevailing norms of historiography. She tells history as her-story. And criticism at the time had no evaluative categories for such a phenomenon.

Notes

[1] The heading "A Mother Bewildered the Germans" ("Eine Mutter verwirrte die Deutschen") introduced a review of *Germany, Pale Mother* in the *Corriere della Sera* on 25 February 1980; it signaled the prevailing attitude toward this film.

[2] Olav Münzberg wrote: "The film's subject, National Socialism, and thus the film itself, will probably meet initially with resistance on the part of many Germans—as compared to foreign—viewers" ("Einige Anmerkungen" 1).

[3] Münzberg provides a revealing reception study from the perspective of social psychology ("Schaudern").

[4] Historian Claudia Koonz has also remarked on the fact that theories about National Socialism developed since 1945 have ignored the role of women.

[5] On this point see Renate Möhrmann (22 f.).

[6] Today we distinguish between women's film and feminist film, but in the 1970s and early 1980s the term "women's film" (*Frauenfilm*) was used to signal the fact that, after years of female absence in the history of film directing, women were conquering this medium as well (cf. Möhrmann 24–32).

[7] See Angelika Bammer, Barton Byg, Barbara Hyams, Anton Kaes, Barbara Kosta, Richard McCormick, and Marcia Pally for recent Anglo-American critical discussions.

[8] Even some of the students in my film seminar "Der neue westdeutsche Frauenfilm," young men between the ages of 22 and 26, criticized the mother-child sequences in *REDUPERS* as inappropriate and unrealistic.

[9] An early example is the American journal *Women and Film* of 1972.

Works Cited

Bammer, Angelika. "Through a Daughter's Eyes: Helma Sanders-Brahms' *Germany, Pale Mother.*" *New German Critique* 36 (1985): 91–109.

Byg, Barton. "Extraterritorial Identity in the Films of Jeanine Meerapfel." *"Neue Welt" / "Dritte Welt": Interkulturelle Beziehungen Deutschlands zu Lateinamerika und der Karibik.* Ed. Sigrid Bauschinger and Susan Cocalis. Tübingen: Franck, 1994. 229–41.

Curiger, Bice. "Das 'buddy system.' Die Filme des neuen Hollywood." *Cinema* 3 (1977).

"Eine Mutter verwirrte die Deutschen." Rev. of *Deutschland, bleiche Mutter. Corriere della Sera* 25 February 1980.

Hyams, Barbara. "Is the Apolitical Woman at Peace? A Reading of the Fairytale in *Germany, Pale Mother.*" *Wide Angle* 10.3 (1988): 40–51.

Johnston, Claire. "Women's Cinema as Counter-Cinema." *Notes on Women's Cinema.* London: Society for Education in Film and Television, 1973.

Kaes, Anton. *From Hitler to Heimat: The Return of History as Film.* Cambridge: Harvard UP, 1989.

Kaplan, E. Ann. "Mothering, Feminism and Representation: The Maternal in Melodrama and the Women's Film 1910-40." *Home is Where the Heart Is: Studies in Melodrama in the Woman's Film.* Ed. Christine Gledhill. London: BFI, 1987. 113–37.

Koonz, Claudia. *Mothers in the Fatherland: Women, the Family, and Nazi Politics.* New York: St. Martin's Press, 1987.

Kosta, Barbara. *Recasting Autobiography: Women's Counterfictions in Contemporary German Literature and Film.* Ithaca, Cornell UP, 1994.

McCormick, Richard W. *Politics of the Self: Feminism and the Postmodern in West German Literature and Film.* Princeton: Princeton UP, 1991.

Möhrmann, Renate. *Die Frau mit der Kamera. Filmemacherinnen in der Bundesrepublik Deutschland: Situation, Perspektiven, zehn exemplarische Lebensläufe.* München: Hanser, 1980.

Münzberg, Olav. "Einige Anmerkungen zu *Deutschland, bleiche Mutter.*" *Pressemappe zu "Deutschland, bleiche Mutter": 30. Internationale Filmfestspiele Berlin* (18–29 February 1980).

———. "Schaudern vor der 'bleichen Mutter': eine sozialpsychologische Analyse der Kritiken zum Film von Helma Sanders-Brahms." *Medium* 10 (1980): 34–37.

Pally, Marcia. "World of Our Mothers." *Film Comment* 20.2 (April 1984): 11–17.

Pflaum, Hans Günther, ed. *Jahrbuch Film 78/79.* München: Hanser, 1979.

Pleyer, Peter. *Deutscher Nachkriegsfilm 1946–1948.* Münster: Fahle, 1965.

Schütte, Wolfram. Rev. of *REDUPERS. Frankfurter Rundschau* 21 April 1978.

Viviani, Christian. "Who is Without Sin? The Maternal Melodrama in American Film, 1930-39." *Home Is Where the Heart Is: Studies in Melodrama in the Woman's Film*. Ed. Christine Gledhill. London: BFI Publications, 1987.

Woolf, Virginia. *A Room of One's Own*. 1929. New York: Harcourt, 1957.

"Gender Censorship":
On Literary Production in German Romanticism

Barbara Becker-Cantarino

The discourse on writing and sexual difference in German Romanticism functions as a discourse of censorship. A philosophical justification for excluding women from the "author function" (Foucault) and for subjecting their writing to male control was elaborated by Fichte in *The Science of Rights*. Goethe and other men of letters developed aesthetic norms for women's writing that were based on a male perspective of appropriate gender roles for women. Women authors' self-representation and literary activity were shaped by gender censorship that they were able to subvert only superficially by such means as public disclaimers, accommodation to male-defined standards, and anonymous or pseudonymous publication. (JC)

The complex of "censorship" and "literary production" evokes an institution, a system, or an individual who censors, that is to say, controls, shapes, or even suppresses another person's words, text, and/or publications. Since the Enlightenment and the emergence of the modern public sphere, such official surveillance has been attacked, modified, and gradually abolished altogether as far as state and religious authorities are concerned; we believe in an individual's "freedom" to create and disseminate his or her literary work. But it can be argued that the institutions of church and state censorship were merely replaced with market censorship (Jansen 4). For the function of censorship as a social force is very complex; it is "the knot that binds power and knowledge" (Jansen) and is tied to literary politics. As arbiters of aesthetics and of what constitutes "good" or "publishable" literature, individuals or groups influence, if not control or censor, literary production. Authors, editors, publishers, critics, and readers may decide and/or influence what is to be included and what is acceptable in an individual work and in a certain canon of "literature." I want to turn to the canon of German Romanticism and look at the complexity of censorship and gender: I suggest that the discourse on sexual difference and writing functions here as a discourse of censorship.

I. Fichte's Discourse on Sexual Difference and Women's Authorship

In 1796 Fichte incorporated a section entitled "Concerning the Legal Relation of Both Sexes in General to Each Other in the State" into his *Fundamental Principals of the Rights of Family* (*Grundriß des Familienrechts*), concluding with some rather odd remarks about "women's desire" to take up writing. Here Fichte defined rather rigidly the terms by which women may write, prescribing how a woman is to position herself as an author and what kind of a text she may produce:

> A few words more concerning the passion of women to become authors (*die Begierde der Weiber, Schriftstellerei zu treiben*[1])—a passion which is constantly on the increase among them in these our days. Literary labor can have only two ends in view: to make known new discoveries in sciences for the examination of the learned, or to communicate that which has already been discovered to the people at large by means of popular representations. We have seen that women cannot make discoveries. Popular writings for women, writings on female education, moral books for the female sex, as such, etc., can certainly be most properly written by women.... Of course, the woman must write as a woman, and must not appear in her writings as a badly disguised man. I have presupposed...that a woman will write only for her sex, and only for the purpose of being useful and to alleviate a discovered need of her sex; but on no account for our sex, or from motives of vanity or ambition. Not only would her works (*ihre Produkte*) have little literary value in the latter case, but the moral character of the authoress would also be greatly injured (450-51).

Fichte sternly restricts women's writing to certain types of texts, to useful, moral, popular literature, excluding their "products," as he calls their texts, from the realm of art, from what was to become the new aesthetics of classicism and romanticism. He directs women to serve their own sex only and explicitly bars them from what he and men of letters of his age considered to be the male domain of scientific or philosophical works. Such restrictions are framed within the context of "natural law," which makes them appear as what Nature herself has ordained for women. It is very revealing that Fichte made these statements in the context of his "Fundamental Principals of the Right of Family," an appendix to his major philosophical text on natural law: *The Science of Rights* (*Grundlage des Naturrechts,* 1795-96),[2] his basic work on social theory. The statement on women writers then comes as an afterthought to what he describes as a "natural" cultural order, one prescribed by Nature to regulate the speech and interactions of all her (Nature's) subjects (Becker-Cantarino, *Der lange Weg* 55 ff.). Fichte consciously speaks of woman's literary activity in the context of marriage and the family, and he speaks as a matter of course from the male, indeed the husband's, perspective. The gender order (as it is ordained in this presumably "natural" and "objectively scientific" order of Fichte's *Science of [Natural] Rights*) is an unreflected continuation of "male tutelage" (*Geschlechtsvormundschaft*). Fichte also extends this tutelage, I submit, to male control over woman's intellectual and literary activity. Fichte emphasizes that man is "the administrator of all rights [of woman]," although he has no "right of *compulsion* " (*Zwangsrecht*), for

> woman [*das Weib*]... is subjected through her own continuous necessary wish—a wish which is the condition of her morality—to be so subjected. She has the power to withdraw her freedom, if she could have the *will* to do so; but that is the very point: she cannot rationally will to be free. Her relation to her husband being publicly known, she must, moreover, will to appear to all whom she knows as utterly subjected to, and utterly lost in, the man of her choice. Her husband is, therefore, the administrator of all her rights... and she wishes those rights asserted and exercised only in so far as *he* wishes it. He is her natural representative in the state and in the whole society. This is her *public* relation to society. She cannot even allow herself to think for a moment that she should exercise herself her rights in the state (441–42).

To be sure, Fichte refers here to married women who represent woman's "natural" state, the normal case, so to speak; he only briefly mentions the exceptional cases, the "widows and divorced women, and... maids who are no longer under paternal authority and yet have never been married" (445). But Fichte's natural-rights position cannot allow public office or a Latin School or university education even for this "exception," the "single woman."

Let us digress for a moment and follow Fichte's argument: A public office presupposes a free, autonomous person, and, according to Fichte, only the single woman fulfills this condition; but it cannot be expected that she will relinquish claim to her "natural" destiny for marriage and subordination to a husband. A public education, Fichte continues, is aimed toward practicing a profession or contributing to knowledge "so that culture does not stand still"; yet this is "precisely what they, women, cannot make use of, since they are to become neither teachers, preachers, doctors, or lawyers" (448). We see how Fichte has great difficulties in imagining a woman who is *not subordinate* to a man, a single, independent woman in the (male-defined and -occupied) public sphere of his day and his philosophical system. This inability, this reluctance to conceive of a woman who is socially, culturally, and intellectually independent of men is the very obstacle encountered by a woman who desires to write and (if she wishes to publish her texts) to function as an author, that is, to appear autonomously in public with an intellectual product under her own name.

Fichte grants women only the "results" of "intellectual culture" (*Geisteskultur*), and "these results women learn also in society" from men: "...by our conversations they are saved the trouble of working through this hull [the unessential, the formal], and can receive its contents directly." Fichte emphasizes that the intellects of men and women have "a very different character" (448). Man makes himself rational through knowledge; he attains clear conceptions through "*Räsonnement.*" Woman is "already rational by nature"; her "whole system of feeling is rational" and "she is especially practical, and not at all speculative in her womanly nature. She cannot and shall not go beyond the limit of her feeling" (449). It is to these systematically defined notions of gender roles (*Geschlechtscharakter*) that Fichte attaches his judgment on "the passion of women to become authors" cited above; and it is without compelling logic and in a mildly annoyed tone that he does this. Claudia Honegger in her recent *Die Ordnung der Geschlechter*, fed up with Fichtean logic, has fittingly labelled this Fichtean logic a "systematic production of nonsense" (187).

We might observe here that, on the one hand, the men of early Romanticism claimed that which is original and creative for their own literary production and that each strove to become an *Originalgenie*; on the other hand, they simultaneously insisted quite "naturally" upon exercising their traditional tutelary responsibility for women by supervising them in the literary and intellectual sphere (Cocalis). To be sure, they wanted to teach and encourage, but even more to watch over and control, that is, to act as mentors, guardians, and tutors, to "speak for them" (*bevormunden*). Then, when the author function, to use Foucault's formulation, "was placed in the system of property that characterizes our society" (108) between the end of the eighteenth and the beginning of the nineteenth centuries, the gender discourse defined the (male or female) author function as difference. Foucault goes on to describe the Romantic's game of "searching for the author":

> [L]iterary discourses came to be accepted only when endowed with the author function. We now ask of each poetic or fictional text: From where does it come, who wrote it, when, under what circumstances, or beginning with what design? The meaning ascribed to it and the status or value accorded it depend on the manner in which we answer these questions (109).

Fichte, I submit, excludes the "female author function" from the "author function."

II. The Discourse of Censorship and the "Female Pen"

Although individual aspects of Fichte's social philosophy and his ideas about marriage were criticized, intellectuals and men of letters of his time nevertheless shared the view that women, including women authors, were subject to men. And like Fichte they were very intent upon securing the narrow borders of female authorship and censuring any encroachment into their own sphere. Whether as fathers or husbands, as friends, competitors, publishers, or critics, they exercised a control function over female authorship that was in part very personal and private and in part openly articulated. This resembled the classic formula for the functioning of censorship: the control by a dominant group, that of men of letters and male intellectuals, over a comparatively weaker group, that of women writers. Having only recently entered the public sphere of literary culture—by publishing as a recognizable group by the 1790s—the women writers, also labelled "scribbling ladies" (*schriftstellernde Damen*) or "poetic females" (Schiller), were certainly considered to be a group, by virtue of their gender and growing number. This censorship, based on rigid gender roles in analogy to male tutelage, gave men authoritarian control over the women associated with them socially and through family ties. Traditional male tutelage also made possible the "surveillance of literary production and reception [the purchase and reading of books] by means of literary and/or cultural policy and censorship...by the powerful social groups" (Breuer 46). I call this control function "gender censorship."

In censorship research and in the history of censorship in Germany the criterion of gender has thus far, to my knowledge, not been taken into account.[3] There is, of course, the concept of self-censorship—a much-explored notion since Freud[4]—in Klaus Kanzog's very thorough article on literary censorship (1041 f.), but the major interest of German scholars has always been directed towards the censorship *institutions* of state or church, of a political or social group and its official representatives, with a particular focus on legal history and political writing. I wish to explore a framework of conditions for patriarchal "gender censorship," both private and public, similar to those of public, institutionalized censorship. Here, too, we are dealing with sometimes subtle and sometimes massive tutelage of the producers of literature (women authors), and with the impediment to, hindrance of, and intervention into the literary production of others. This was carried out by the self-appointed censors, men of letters and male intellectuals, in part motivated by self-interest, desire for power, vanity, or rivalry, but also (presumably) by feelings of responsibility toward women. Their actions were usually coupled with references to the aesthetic norms and literary practices (of their own group). Such surveillance of literary production sought to preserve prevailing moral and social standards from the censors' perspectives and to maintain the high quality of literary works (as defined by the censoring men). As long as men claim and are allowed to exercise intellectual dominance over women, and as long as men hold key positions, from author to publisher, in the production as well as distribution and reception of literature, we can observe a controlling behavior by men of letters and intellectuals, a kind of "gender censorship." Only since the male monopoly in literature began to falter under the influence of the second women's movement and the so-called women's literature of the last two decades has gender censorship given way to more subtle variations of repression. It may take the form of displacement from the market (of a lesbian author like Christa Reinig), or moral and artistic devaluation (such as the debate about Christa Wolf's *Was bleibt*), or clever appropriations of supposedly "feminist" or "feminine" forms for one's own text (for example, Günter Grass in *Die Rättin* or Robert Walser in *Verteidigung der Kindheit*). The control of literary standards and public opinion has given way to a more direct confrontation in literary criticism and reviews, in newspaper articles, and in indirect, critical debate. The tutelary relationship has been transformed into a multifaceted competitive game of give and take on the literary stage, in which claims to superiority, overtly, and gender difference(s), subliminally and covertly, play a role.

While Fichte's reliance on sexual difference according to "natural law" provided the philosophical justification for limiting women's engagement in literary activity, Goethe, in an 1806 review, exercised a more differentiated, aesthetic control of norms when he proposed the following limitations for novels by women:[5]

> We could not help but shake our head in noticing that the gracious and charming creatures who frolic in the novel by our friend Eleutherie [Holberg's *Wilhelm Dumont, ein einfacher Roman*, 1805] proclaim themselves to be anti-natural philosophers and in so doing become extraordinarily tiresome. "Ought one to discuss politics with a face like that?" said the Duke to his beloved as he led her to the mirror; and that is what one would like to say to Adelaide in this novel as well: Ought one to think about philosophy, let alone natural philosophy, with so much charm, emotion, and high spirits? The best thing about it is that she herself feels how unseemly such statements are for a female pen (382).

Goethe here expresses rigid and (later in the review) prescriptive ideas about the "female pen" or female authorship, much as contemporary reviews expressed them again and again, by the way. The "field of conceptual or theoretical coherence" (Foucault 111) from which "the female author" is here defined is her gender. By selectively choosing a series of signs that refer to a difference between his idea of womanhood and the heroine of the novel, Goethe also faults, in the same review, the heroine of Friederike Unger's novel *Bekenntnisse einer schönen Seele* (1806) for being "a virago, a woman as imagined by a man" (368). The novel's unmarried, comparatively autonomous female character, a lady companion and tutor (*Hofmeisterin*), is in Goethe's eyes an "Amazon" in whom the woman reader can see "neither daughter, nor sister, nor beloved, nor spouse, nor mother...neither the housewife, nor the mother-in-law, nor the grandmother" (376). A man's perspective on life and utility is advocated here as the aesthetic norm for a novel authored by a woman. Thus Goethe suggests that women who write have their manuscripts checked by men:

> Shouldn't sophisticated and talented women be able to win sophisticated and talented male friends to whom they would submit their manuscripts? Then all unfeminine aspects could be obliterated and nothing would remain in their work that could attach itself like an annoying counterweight to the natural feeling, the charming disposition, the romantic, heartfelt opinions, the graceful representation, and all the goodness that female writings possess in such abundance (383–84).

With this suggestion of copy-editing by "sophisticated and talented friends" (read: "male authors"), disguised as a well-meant piece of advice, Goethe concludes his review. The aim of such advice, which is part of a strategy for regulating perception and which in its asymmetry has the character of gender censorship, is the social control of women authors and their texts.

III. Literary Production and Gender

Reminded by the prevailing gender discourse of their difference from and dependence upon men in the production of literature, women felt obliged to adjust their writing to this norm themselves. They would have men revise it and, more often than not, have it published under a man's name; or they would even neglect to complete a work in progress. Consider what Caroline Schlegel-Schelling, who left only letters and published nothing under her own name, reports about her writing:

> On Thursday Schelling submitted an article that I...[had] composed; I would not have wanted it under my name in any case.... Schelling did away with the epistolary form I had initially given it and incidentally teased me a lot because of my great affection for the play and everything connected with it that had been so obvious; I had to laugh myself realizing what a feminine appearance it had. With much joking we removed the traces of gentle hands one by one (*Caroline* 2: 263–64).[6]

The article, published under Schelling's name, was a review of the Weimar performance (directed by Goethe) of August Wilhelm Schlegel's *Ion* in January 1802. Caroline let what she had written be "corrected" as a matter of course. Was her work so deficient? On the contrary: her numerous letters, published repeatedly since 1871 and used over and over again as a source for the literary culture of Romanticism, show that as a writer of private letters she was capable of accurate and graphic description as well as sensitive and analytic judgment. Thus, her lack of formal schooling and university education or an inferior or inadequate literary ability cannot have been the reason why (her husband-to-be) Schelling wanted to touch up her style and expressions of opinion. Rather, for Schelling, it went without saying that he as "sophisticated friend" was qualified to watch over and revise his (future) wife's literary product before it was published.

This control function, viewed as "natural" and exercised by the husband or friend over "his" wife's or friend's intellectual products, seems to have been reaffirmed during the period of social restoration around 1800 and with the rise of the young generation of Romantics to literary fame and acceptance in intellectual circles. Literary women were always dependent on their husbands' and to a large extent on male family members' approval for their publishing and literary production, unless they were willing and able to function as outsiders or even as exiles. But when the young men of letters associated with early Romanticism were just getting established, and Friedrich and August Wilhelm Schlegel were planning and editing the *Athenäum* (1797-99), their relations with their female friends were initially much more cooperative. Caroline and Dorothea—among others associated with early Romanticism in Berlin, such as Schleiermacher, Fichte, and Tieck—were important contributors, though they remained behind the scenes and unnamed. In December 1797 Friedrich Schlegel wrote to Caroline:

> Write me everything that you intend to do yourself [for the *Athenäum*], even *before* you are firmly decided. I will then advise you as best I can. You must advise me too, and consider most thoroughly and critically everything that I write for it [the *Athenäum*] from my projects. But especially, promote everything Wilhelm can and wants to do through your interest. When he implements my suggestion concerning the Master's [? Goethe's] latest lyric poems: you can surely help him a great deal in this. —Do not let [either] Wilhelm's doings or your own aversion to work affect your idea of making contributions yourself. Even if you cannot or do not wish to do this right away, there is still much you can do—to double and set right our zeal through your participation and advice. —I have always thought your natural form—for I believe each person by virtue of talent and intellect has one best suited to him—would be *rhapsody*.... So, exercise care in choosing a form and take into consideration that *letters* and *reviews* are forms that you have entirely within your control.... That which could be printed [from] your letters is so pure, beautiful, and delicate that I would not like to see it shattered into fragments, as it were, and *made* coquettish by mere compression. On the other hand, I think it would not be impossible for me to compose one great philosophical rhapsody from your letters.... Should you ever write a novel, perhaps someone else ought to draft the

plan for it and, if it were not to consist entirely of letters, also write everything that would not be [in] letter form (Schlegel 59–60).

In this long, detailed letter, from which I have cited only a short excerpt, Friedrich Schlegel proposes a fitting demarcation of the literary terrain. On the one hand, he courts his talented, unconventional sister-in-law and appeals to her female charms in order to have her collaborate in his literary enterprise; on the other hand, he would like to be master of her talents, to make them useful for his own ends, to mentor and control them. He would like to "edit and process" (*diaskeuasieren*) her literary production even before she has "finished" (*fixiert*) her literary text: She, for her part, is to help, take an interest in, advise, but not ultimately decide or define her text. Here Friedrich Schlegel precisely delineates the borders of their literary territory as well. He secures for himself the fragment, the preferred form in Romantic aesthetics, and he assigns to her the unsystematic, flowing, formless rhapsody ("One poetizes rhapsodies, pours them out," we read in one of Friedrich Schlegel's literary notes). Moreover Schlegel assigns to her the letter, the pre-literary, pre-aesthetic text.

Neither Caroline's autobiographical epistolary novel (to be written under male supervision and guidance) nor Friedrich's "great philosophical rhapsody" from Caroline's letters was ever realized. Caroline stuck to her intellectual support work, reading proofs, copying manuscripts, providing ideas, letters, and excerpts (for brother-in-law Friedrich and husband August Wilhelm, later for husband Schelling). Caroline let Schelling revise her theater critiques, book reviews, and translations from the French and the Italian for publication; only during her Munich period, 1806–09, were a few published, albeit anonymously. Ever since the period with Forster in Mainz (1792–93), Caroline had been politically compromised, as Friedrich Schlegel was morally compromised through his relationship with the older, married, Jewish Dorothea and through the publication of *Lucinde* (1799). Both were barred from returning to Caroline's native Göttingen, for example. Caroline's situation prevented her from risking, as Fichte warned women in general, "through her literary celebrity an independence which necessarily weakens and threatens to dissolve her relation to her husband." For, Fichte continues, "if criticism [of her work] is unfavorable, she will feel the reproof as an insult to her sex, and this will embitter her days and those of her husband" (451). Like most women between 1790 and 1820 who had a close personal relationship with a prominent man of letters or intellectual, Caroline was subject to private and public "tutelage" (*Geschlechtsvormundschaft*), and as a woman writer—and she was always thought of as a *woman*—to "gender censorship."

This "censorship" also forced women authors into the practice of anonymous or pseudonymous publication. Writers of the older generation, such as Sophie La Roche (1730-1807) or Anna Louisa Karsch (1722-1791), consciously presented themselves as professional authors after a first work received critical acclaim—though they remained well aware of their status as exceptions, if not anomalies, in literary culture. Karsch earned a living by writing, and in the case of the widowed La Roche, writing created an essential source of supplemental income. However, almost all women around 1800 published their works anonymously or disguised by a (male) editor or pseudonym. This was the practice with the younger women novelists, such as Caroline Auguste Fischer (*Gustavs Verirrungen,* 1801; *Vierzehn Tage in Paris,* 1801; *Die Honigmonate,* 1802; *Der Günstling,* 1808; *Margarethe,* 1812) or Benedikte Naubert, who published their works without revealing their real names. In her mostly historical novels that began appearing in 1785, Naubert even maintained her anonymity vis-à-vis her publisher.[7] This allowed them to attain greater freedom for their fictions—Naubert's historical novels were believed to be by a man and sold extremely well—without risking their good reputations as middle-class women.

Since work and person of the *female* author were equated, especially by *men* of letters, women writers were judged from the perspective of "natürliche Weiblichkeit" and thereby subordinated to social control by the patriarchy. Karoline von Günderrode used the pseudonyms "Tian" and "Ion" (decoded only by literary insiders) and Dorothea Schlegel published her only novel, *Florentin* (1801), under editor Friedrich Schlegel's name. When the middle-class public sphere was constituted toward the end of the century as a "league of men" held together by the "glue of brotherhood," as Reinhard Koselleck has observed, something like "a genuine political 'men's movement' with the goal of checking the influence of women and ladies on the state and in society" could be found in men's circles and clubs, as Honegger maintains (53). "Gender censorship" in literary discourse intensified and flourished with Romanticism, since, given the growth of literacy and the development of a large female reading public, these women also wanted to write, publish, and enter the literary market, which had only really expanded since 1750.

The female author's self-representation and justification of her literary activity was shaped by "gender censorship," which she subverted superficially through accommodation. In 1810, when she herself was already fifty-six years old, twice widowed and a successful professional author, Therese Forster-Huber constructed the following image of her literary career in a letter to her father:

> I wrote to make it easier for my husband to support a wife and children, and until Huber's death [1804] no one ever found out that I put pen to paper! —all they needed to assume me capable of was translating journal articles because these were brought to the printer written in my hand. So I earned about half our income with a child at my breast, next to the

cradle at night when all were asleep, clearing my head so I could compress all the passionate feelings of my heart and the flights of my fancy into clear images and line them up in the thread of a story.... Huber would then make a fair copy of my unwieldy drafts, polishing, expanding, and pruning them.[8]

With this construction of her authorship, Forster-Huber defends herself to her father, the Göttingen philologist Christian Gottlob Heyne, who continued to reproach her for her publications until her bestselling *Bemerkungen über Holland aus dem Reisejournal einer Frau* (1811) made her a literary persona. Therese Forster-Huber did not give up her anonymity until 1811, although since Huber's death she had depended heavily on her literary activities to support herself and her four children from two marriages. But to her father, later to her own children, and to all her friends, she emphasized over and over again that her "femininity" had not suffered under her literary activity, and that she had always written only under Huber's editorial guidance and only because she needed the income. "Gender censorship" shaped and demanded such self-representation.

IV. "Gender Censorship" as Textual Control Function and Repressive Moment for the Woman Author

"Gender censorship" led to repressions, omissions, concessions, and modifications in literary texts, especially in novels, which contemporaries read as representations of real life. In her first, very successful novel *Die Familie Seldorf* (1796–97), Therese Forster-Huber chose the narrative structure of the family novel, which supported the "natural" gender order, to foreground a representation of patriarchal society in order to thematize the daughter's (Sara's) refusal to marry (motivated, to be sure, by masquerading as an unfeminine, soldier-like female revolutionary). Forster-Huber could then let her protagonist Sara emerge from behind the portrayals of Father Seldorf, her brother, her family friend Berthier, her brotherly friend Roger, and her unscrupulous aristocratic lover. Or Forster-Huber displaced the political problematic of the Polish uprisings into mythological, historical narrative in her Poland novel *Klosterberuf* (1807) and in *Fragmenten über einen Theil von Polen: Aus Briefen einer Engländerin, im Jahr 1789 geschrieben* (1793), which was based on her own experiences in Vilna.[9] As journalist and author, she developed subversive communicative strategies within her works through encoding and masking. For the public she minimized her literary activity ("one of my worst sins," "my chit-chat"),[10] in order to weaken the impact of "gender censorship." Her approximately fifty novels and stories, her numerous magazine articles, her editorial work (from 1816 to 1823) for the *Morgenblatt für die gebildeten Stände* and other works published by Cotta, the most important belletristic press of the time, attest to her talents as an author. Yet her work was excluded from the canon of true art by the Romantics as well as by Schiller and Goethe; she was regarded as a "hack writer" (*Brotschreiberin*), meaning that she was an independent and politically different-minded female competitor.

In the incipient love affair between Sophie Mereau and Clemens Brentano, too, we are dealing with the control function (at first subconscious) of a male poet over a woman's literary production. After Sophie had not only declined his advances but also neglected to include the poems he had sent her in the *Göttinger Musenalmanach* of 1803 that she edited, Clemens complained in a long, ironic letter:

> *It is very dangerous for a female to write poetry and even more dangerous to edit a "Musenalmanach"*; among various dissertations I have ready to discuss, this one could especially interest you; others would deal with the extent to which a woman can run or frequent a coffeehouse without besmirching her honor, the extent to which female servants are necessary for the education of students in academies, the extent to which a proper woman may drive a coach or ride a horse, etc. (*Lebe der Liebe* 104).

Brentano's mocking, playful, but also irritated tone and his presumption of male superiority thwarted a dialogue or any objective discussion of literary questions. Since Brentano was financially well provided for and had no reason for professional jealousy, he was irritated more by the fact that it was a woman who had dared to reject his work: "The fact that you are not entirely dissatisfied with my feeble poetic efforts shall be a spur for me to make my future poems even more pleasant from the beginning to the end as well as in the rhymes..." (102), he wrote in a piqued tone, and then gave vent to his displeasure over female authorship. A woman was simply not authorized to criticize men's literary products.

To be sure, in 1803 Sophie Mereau could still reply with full self-assurance to Brentano's pages of subtly offensive criticism:

> What you tell me about female authors and, especially, about my humble efforts has touched me deeply, indeed, I am edified. Certainly it is not at all proper for our sex and only men's extraordinary magnanimity has been able to look on patiently this long. I would be shaking in my boots over a few pieces that are unfortunately in press already if I did not find some comfort in the thought of their insignificance and innocuousness. But for the future I will at least stop wasting my time writing verses and if I should find myself compelled to write, [I shall] seek to produce good, moral cookbooks. And who knows if your learned work, the publication of which you have most kindly called to my attention, will not persuade me once and for all to exchange my pen for a needle (*Lebe der Liebe* 116).

After marrying Brentano in November 1803, Sophie Mereau published no more independent works except translations. Similarly, Dorothea Schlegel completed a few longer translations after her novel *Florentin* (1801) and a few original pieces for Friedrich's journal *Europa*, but undertook no more independent writing from 1807 until her death in 1832. Bettina von Arnim only began her literary career in earnest after her husband Achim's death; brother Clemens criticized her publications too, finding them indiscreet and unwomanly. "Gender censorship" created artistic inhibitions among the married women Romantics that effectively silenced them.

At stake, however, was the control function of the new, belletristic literature, the creative and evaluative privilege, and monopoly of authors establishing themselves as artists. Thus, Friedrich Schlegel was appalled that Caroline had criticized his writing in a letter not sanctioned by her husband, and complained to brother August Wilhelm:

> Your wife has written me a very intense and insulting letter about the *Athenäum*, one you probably didn't see before it was sent. The two full days that this superfluous annoyance cost me can be replaced by extra effort and working through the night.... But my high spirits, my good mood are gone. Caroline thinks my fragments are often too long. That, of course, is one of those observations where the answer gets stuck in one's throat (1798; *Caroline* 2: 449).

Male authors did not easily tolerate criticism of their literary production by women, for they themselves set the standards and were the critics and judges of *their* literature. They functioned as a matter of course as guardians, judges, and censors of literature by women, emphasizing, ever since Wieland had supervised the editing of La Roche's *Geschichte des Fräuleins von Sternheim* and recommended it to a female reading public, that women should write edifying, moralistic "women's literature" for women in support of "natural" gender roles.

V. "Gender Censorship" and Patriarchy

The practice of "gender censorship," by which men of letters and male intellectuals directed and watched over the literary activities of women, especially those of their own wives, lovers, and girlfriends, was artistically inhibiting for most women Romantics. The literary tutelage that men of letters and intellectuals claimed with regard to all women turned help with literary production, even help that had been sought (as was often the case), into gender censorship. The emphasis on femininity and the narrow limits imposed on the "female pen" led into a ghetto of women's literature. The book market, controlled entirely by male publishers, editors, critics, and authors, was conducive to such "gender censorship," by which the authority, power, and economic positions of male authors, newly professionalized during the late eighteenth century as competitive, creative artists, could be reinforced.

"Gender censorship," I suggest, is part of the power discourse of patriarchy (Walby), of gender construction as difference and separate spheres that was reestablished around 1800. "Gender censorship" has its tradition in the patriarchal construction of gender, more concretely in the Christian "patriarchal" (*Hausvater*) model. Fichte also referred to and secularized this construction as a "natural right." In the reconfiguration of marriage and the household that became operative since Luther and the Reformation, the patriarch (*Hausvater*)—I am using Mary Ezell's concept of the patriarch—also functioned as "house-pastor." As the pastor's deputy, he would regularly read to family and servants from the gospels; he was also responsible for the religious education and thus the moral and intellectual horizon of his wife and children. The gesture of this mentoring and reading, educating, and moral responsibility, but also defining and regulating, was carried out, as we know from countless biographical reports, with strictness, a great sense of duty, and authority. This patriarchal religious and moral authority finds its "natural" variant in "gender censorship" when literary authorship and production was professionalized during Romanticism. At the same time, women in the act of writing and aspiring to become authors withdraw from the intellectually subordinate position of the patriarch's wife, who is to be subject to the patriarchal authority of husband as "Hausvater," and begin to struggle for creative autonomy vis-à-vis male intellectual tutelage.

Translated by Jeanette Clausen

Notes

I wish to thank the Alexander von Humboldt Foundation, which supported work on this essay. A German version appeared in *Zensur und Kultur: Zwischen Weimarer Klassik und Weimarer Republik.* Ed. John A. McCarthy and Werner von der Ohe (Tübingen: Niemeyer, 1995), pp. 87–98. My special thanks go to Jeanette Clausen for her translation of this version of the essay.

[1] In the late eighteenth century "Weiber" or "Weib" clearly refers to gender and was the preferred term during the sex role discussion of the 1790s (see Hoffmann). It is also used to designate the wife or a married woman of the lower middle class and is not yet as pejorative an expression as it is in today's German.

[2] The English translation, originally published in 1889, replaced the literal translation of the title "Foundations of Natural Right," with the now current one: *The Science of Rights*. This substitution obliterated Fichte's claim to "natural"

universality. His task in this work was the "determination of the essential principles which provide the necessary conditions for a social order in which individual freedom may be exercised" (xiii). Fichte's androcentric theory concerned itself with the individual freedom of men. And while his discussion of women's rights may appear to be "amusing" (xxi) to the modern editor of the work, Fichte's tenets were generally shared by his German contemporaries as the discussion of gender censorship will show.

[3] Censorship is the topic of the May 1995 issue of *Frauen in der Literaturwissenschaft* (Rundbrief 55, Hamburg). The (short) contributions deal with modern instances of censored women authors; of interest to my topic is Gaby Pailer's essay.

[4] See for instance Michael G. Levine.

[5] Goethe's detailed review of three women's novels—Friederike Helene Unger's *Bekenntnisse einer schönen Seele, von ihr selbst geschrieben* (1806) and *Melanie das Findelkind* (1804) as well as Holberg's *Wilhelm Dumont* (1805)—appeared in the *Jenaische Allgemeine Literaturzeitung* in 1806.

[6] Letter to her husband August Wilhelm Schlegel, 11 January 1802. Caroline was living in Jena with Schelling, separated from her husband with whom she corresponded regularly about literary (and other) matters. Her marriage was dissolved by Duke Carl August upon Goethe's mediation in early 1803 (see Sara Friedrichsmeyer). The review appeared in the *Zeitung für die elegante Welt,* but did not please August Wilhelm Schlegel, who then attacked this and other reviews in the same magazine and reproached Caroline because she did not know Greek, had never read even a bad translation of Euripides, and therefore could not judge his play.

[7] Her identity was revealed by a Prof. Schütz only in 1817 in *Zeitung für die elegante Welt* (Schindel 2: 32–47). See also Shawn C. Jarvis.

[8] Manuscript in the Göttingen University Library, Therese Huber Nachlaß, B 926. I would like to thank Magdalene Heuser, who is preparing the edition of Therese Forster-Huber's letters, for her kind assistance. See also my "Revolution im Patriarchat."

[9] Like *Die Familie Seldorf,* the *Fragmente* first appeared anonymously in her husband's journal *Flora: Teutschlands Töchtern gewidmet* (Tübingen 1793); for the treatment of political issues, see my "Therese Forster-Huber und Polen."

[10] In a letter to Karl August Böttiger on 7 December 1811. Father Heyne corresponded with his son-in-law, Therese's second husband Huber, about Therese's "ridiculous, unwomanly urge to write" and about her political attitudes (Heuser 146).

Works Cited

Becker-Cantarino, Barbara. *Der lange Weg zur Mündigkeit: Frauen und Literatur in Deutschland von 1500 bis 1800*. München: dtv, 1989.

———. "Revolution im Patriarchat: Therese Forster-Huber (1764–1829)." *Out of Line/Ausgefallen: The Paradox of Marginality in the Writings of Nineteenth-Century German Women*. Ed. Ruth-Ellen Boetcher Joeres and Marianne Burkhard. Amsterdamer Beiträge zur neueren Germanistik 29. Amsterdam: Rodopi, 1989. 235–53.

———. "Therese Forster-Huber und Polen." *Daß eine Nation die ander verstehen möge: Festschrift für Marian Szyrocki*. Ed. Hans-Gert Roloff. Amsterdam: Rodopi, 1988. 53–66.

Breuer, Dieter. "Stand und Aufgaben der Zensurforschung." *"Unmoralisch an sich...": Zensur im 18. und 19. Jahrhundert*. Wiesbaden: Harrassowitz, 1988. 37–60.

Caroline: Briefe aus der Frühromantik. Ed. Erich Schmidt. 2 vols. Leipzig: Insel, 1913.

Cocalis, Susan. "Der Vormund will Vormund sein: Zur Problematik der weiblichen Unmündigkeit." *Gestaltet und Gestaltend: Frauen in der deutschen Literatur*. Ed. Marianne Burkhard. Amsterdamer Beiträge zur neueren Germanistik 10. Amsterdam: Rodopi, 1980. 33–55.

Ezell, Margeret J.M. *The Patriarch's Wife: Literary Evidence and the Family*. Chapel Hill: U of North Carolina P, 1987.

Fichte, J[ohann] G[ottlieb]. *The Science of Rights: Grundlage des Naturrechts nach Principien der Wissenschaftslehre*. Trans. A.E. Kroeger. London: Routledge, 1970.

Foucault, Michel. "What is an Author?" *The Foucault Reader*. Ed. Paul Rabinow. New York: Pantheon, 1984.

Friedrichsmeyer, Sara. "Caroline Schlegel-Schelling: 'A Good Woman, and No Heroine.'" *In the Shadow of Olympus*. 115–36.

Goethe, Johann Wolfgang von. *Werke*. Pt. I, Vol. 40. Weimar: Böhlau, 1901.

Heuser, Magdalene. "Jakobinerin, Demokratin und Revolutionär: Therese Hubers 'kleiner, winziger Standpunkt als Weib' um 1800." *Sklavin oder Bürgerin? Französische Revolution und Weiblichkeit 1760–1830*. Ed. Viktoria Schmidt-Linsenhoff. Tübingen: Niemeyer, 1988. 52–65.

Hoffmann, Volker. "Elisa und Robert oder das Weib und der Mann, wie sie sein sollten: Anmerkungen zur Geschlechtercharakteristik der Goethezeit." *Klassik und Moderne: Die Weimarer Klassik als historisches Ereignis und Herausforderung im kulturgeschichtlichen Prozeß. W. Müller-Seidel zum 65. Geburtstag*. Ed. Karl Richter and Jörg Schönert. Stuttgart: Metzler, 1983. 80–97.

Honegger, Claudia. *Die Ordnung der Geschlechter: Die Wissenschaften vom Menschen und das Weib 1750–1850*. Frankfurt a.M.: Campus, 1991.

In the Shadow of Olympus: German Women Writers around 1800. Ed. Katherine R. Goodman and Edith Waldstein. Albany: State U of New York P, 1992.

Jansen, Sue Curry. *Censorship: The Knot That Binds Power and Knowledge*. New York: Oxford UP, 1988.

Jarvis, Shawn C. "The Vanished Woman of Great Influence: Benedikte Naubert's Legacy and German Fairy Tales." *In the Shadow of Olympus.* 189–210.

Kanzog, Klaus. "Literarische Zensur." *Reallexikon der deutschen Literaturgeschichte.* 2nd ed. Berlin: de Gruyter, 1984. Vol. 3. 998–1049.

Koselleck, Reinhart. *Kritik und Krise: Eine Studie zur Pathogenese der bürgerlichen Welt.* Frankfurt a.M.: Suhrkamp, 1976.

Lebe der Liebe und liebe das Leben: Der Briefwechsel von Clemens Brentano und Sophie Mereau. Ed. Dagmar von Gersdorff. Frankfurt a.M.: Insel, 1981.

Levine, Michael G. *Writing through Repression: Literature, Censorship, Psychoanalysis.* Baltimore: Johns Hopkins UP, 1995.

Pailer, Gaby. "'Lasst uns die Ketten soviel als möglich unter Rosen verbergen...': Zum Problem der Zensur in Dramen von Autorinnen des 18. Jahrhunderts." *Frauen in der Literaturwissenschaft. Rundbrief* 55 (May 1995): 39–44.

Schindel, Carl Wilh. Otto Aug. von. *Die deutschen Schriftstellerinnen des neunzehnten Jahrhunderts.* 1823. Hildesheim: Olms, 1978.

Schlegel, Friedrich. *Die Periode des Athenäums: 25. Juli 1797–Ende August 1799.* Ed. Raymond Immerwahr. Kritische Friedrich-Schlegel-Ausgabe, Dritte Abteilung: Die Briefe von und an Friedrich und Dorothea Schlegel. Vol. 24. Paderborn: Schöningh, 1985.

[Unger, Friederike Helene]. *Bekenntnisse einer schönen Seele von ihr selbst geschrieben.* 1806. Ed. Susanne Zantop. *Frühe Frauenliteratur in Deutschland.* Vol. 9. Hildesheim: Olms, 1991.

Walby, Sylvia. *Theorizing Patriarchy.* London: Blackwell, 1990.

Aspects of Censorship in the Work of Karoline von Günderrode

Dagmar von Hoff

This article examines aspects of "gendered censorship" in the work of Karoline von Günderrode (1780–1806), especially in her dramas. To understand the phenomenon, it is necessary to view censorship from both the outside and within. Eighteenth-century drama and theater were taboo fields for women. Consequently, Gunderrode reacted with a three-fold form of self-censorship: in her form of self-expression, in her determination to write under two pseudonyms (Tian and Ion), and in her decision to leave a number of the dramas unfinished. (DvH)

Expressive Interest

Before 26 February 1804, Karoline von Günderrode wrote to the law professor Friedrich Karl von Savigny that she had come to realize that Savigny had turned his attention to her friend Gunda von Brentano—the sister of Clemens and Bettina—and formed a liaison with her.

> My heart hasn't turned away from you, much less to another mortal; no, I'm so happy to think that in the future I will always belong to you and Gunda, but in the last four weeks things seem different than they did a couple of months ago. Gunda scolds me and says I am arrogant, that I don't love anyone and am remote, but she's wrong, or at least she is exaggerating a lot; I am not at all arrogant, because I don't have faith in my own excellence, I can only fleetingly believe in it and sometimes not at all, but do you know what the problem really is? I can only stammer foolishly: I'm writing a drama, my entire soul is taken up with it, I've gotten so involved, I'm so at home in it that my whole life has become strange to me; I am much inclined to such abstraction, to immersing myself in a stream of inner observations and fictions. Gunda says it's silly to let oneself be dominated by a talent as minor as mine, but I love this flaw in myself, if it is one, it often insulates me from the whole world! (Preitz II: 198 f.).[1]

This passage indicates an emphatic affirmation of the writing of drama, one that puts it into conflict with the real world. This declaration of allegiance to the imagination, to an "aesthetic subjectivity" (*ästhetische Subjektivität*)[2] displaces the private dimension. Günderrode distances herself from her feelings for Savigny, who has meanwhile married Gunda, by introducing an aesthetic dimension, transforming the autobiographic "I" into an imaginary one. She maintains that her "entire soul" has become identical with the desire to write a drama. This extract from her letter simultaneously appears to deny the aesthetic desire she describes in that it introduces the rhetorical figure of litotes. Moving into a mood of irony, Günderrode presents her literary production as a form of impermissible imagining and speaks of the "flaw" of writing a drama. This is a masquerade, to be understood as strategy, because the "immense stupidity" (*große Blödigkeit,* here translated by "stammer foolishly"—with an etymological spectrum including connotations like "diffidence" [*Zaghaftigkeit*], "fragility" [*Gebrechlichkeit*], and "sensibility" [*Empfindsamkeit*]) fails to hide her very clear enthusiasm for this form of literary expression and the access it provides to the public sphere and the world in general. This fluctuation between self-elevation and self-chastisement is the salient feature of this text. The posture of understatement that she adopts allows her to express her desire, while still submitting to the role society has ascribed to her and to her social context. Thus, as Max Holquist suggests, a form of censorship on a preconceptual level appears as litotes, a more radical variant of meiosis (15). For it is characteristic of censorship to have the structure of a paradox, so that the command "Don't think of a white bear" (14) makes it virtually impossible not to think of one. The very irony of her tone attempts to circumvent the censorship forced upon her from outside.

There are other texts, too, where Günderrode discerns with a kind of clairvoyance the instances of censorship that stand in the way of her desire for self-expression and threaten to force her into projections of the ego she does not want. For instance, on 20 October, she writes to Gunda Brentano at a time when their relationship already seems to be in some discord—or at least, she assumes it is—that Gunda will not understand her: "because I can almost certainly assume that you cannot really be interested in what I would like to tell you about myself" (Preitz II: 172). And she continues:

> You have almost grown too distant for me to take you into the innermost parts of my world; nonetheless you are not the kind of guest one likes to leave standing outside the door. A major dilemma? I thought you could be shown to a box seat not too far from the stage, and the actors (thoughts, fantasies, feelings) could be made to perform for you, but you wouldn't be allowed to go backstage nor to see the innermost workings.— But I can't do this, Gunda, at least it's too hard for me, I either

have to close down the whole theater or unveil its most secret aspects (172–73).[3]

What is interesting about this theater metaphor, which Günderrode first used in 1801, is that it demonstrates her ambivalence between the desire for uninhibited self-expression and the idea that a human being is an actor who disguises himself or herself—or plays a role. In this early letter she makes a plea for an affirmation of self-expression, identified with a theater open to the wings, even if this is bound up with the painful loss of self. In her diary of the following day, 21 October, she notes: "...but these blissful dreams dissipate; they seem like love potions; they numb, exalt me, then go up in smoke, that is the misery and impoverishment of all our feelings; and things are no better with our thoughts, it's easy to think about things to the point of shallowness..." (173).[4]

Günderrode's idea of space, in which she expressly formulates her theater metaphor, corresponds to Freud's topological definition of censorship. Although he does not actually use a theater metaphor, Freud employs metaphors of separate spaces to describe the notion of censorship, sometimes personified in the form of the censor: between the antechamber "in which human psychic activity resembles individual beings frolicking" and the "salon in which consciousness resides" (Freud 1989, 293) a more or less watchful and alert guardian officiates: the censor.

The Concept of Censorship

With Freud, as with Günderrode, this idea of separate spheres, of the unconscious and the conscious, of the tension between a will to express oneself and the action of censorship, is rooted in the concept of power that ensures that desire or the desire to express oneself meets some impediment, causing it to form compromises, as for instance in the rhetorical form of irony. In this sense, censorship is a social fact, inherent in language, which can never be circumvented.

Pierre Bourdieu understands Freud's concept of censorship as a general model and transfers it into the sphere of society. According to him, every expression is the result of a negotiation between "the expressive interest and the structural necessity of a field acting as a form of censorship" (269). The basic formula for this expression is always "a compromise between an expressive interest and a censorship" (137). According to Bourdieu, censorship works best when the actor only says what he is allowed to say, for "in this case he does not even have to be his own censor" (138). He points to effective methods of censorship in society, which keep particular actors apart from particular social groups or places or even block their participation in the sphere of communication entirely. If one considers these symbolic relations of power, then it is easy to detect mechanisms of repression or regulations that exclude women from the field of literature. The logic of conscious and unconscious marginalization leaves women bereft of language, excludes them as producers from the literary sphere, regulates their choice of reading material, or forbids them access to publication. Thus the concept of gendered censorship, which transcends the formal concept of censorship and draws on the legal concept of censorship (lat. *censura*: examination, judgment),[5] must be supplemented both by aspects of sociological and communication theory and by Freud's analysis of the syntax of the dream and the concept of censorship derived from it.

Freud first mentions the concept in a letter to Fliess of 12 December 1897, in which he describes hallucinations or gaps that appear in memory. He refers to Russian press censorship and describes how "entire sentences and parts of sentences are blacked out" (Freud 1986, 315). This idea that a continuous text may contain omissions of that which is considered unacceptable and which appears as gaps or deformations is also mentioned by Freud in the *Vorlesungen zur Einführung in die Psychoanalyse*. In his 1916 lecture on "Dream Censorship," Freud demonstrates that the content of the dream contains gaps and he describes three features that allow us to recognize the working of dream censorship. For instance, the content is erased by "murmuring" (*Gemurmel*). This erasure is compared to the working of newspaper censorship, in which whole passages of text, probably "the best parts," are omitted, i.e., censored (150). In the second case, the dream is distorted because censorship brings about a weakening of meaning or leaves only a veiled allusion to the real content. In the case of the press, this means that the author attempts to preempt the censor and tries to make his case without explicit references to his real topic. The third case has no parallel in press censorship. Here it is a matter of the regrouping of content elements, of a shift of accent, which gives the dream its characteristic "strangeness" (151).

Thus Freud's metaphor of censorship is ultimately derived from what in politics are called the blank spots, the omissions. In Freud, as Michael G. Levine notes, the externality of censorship is always bound up with a "textual metaphor" (22). The connection between writing and censorship also appears in Jacques Derrida's reception of Freud's "magic slate" (*Wunderblock*). Every written character points to a censoring gesture, which Freud expresses in the image of two hands: "Consider that while one hand is writing on the surface of the magic slate, from time to time another is lifting the top sheet from the waxed one" (Freud 1975, 369).

Discursive Barriers and Disciplines

Karoline von Günderrode,[6] born in 1780 in Karlsruhe, lived from the age of seventeen in a charitable foundation for women of the impoverished nobility run by the Protestant Church in Frankfurt. Apart from poems and short pieces of prose, she mainly wrote dramas, using the *nom de plume* of Tian (later Ion). Among her friends she counted Gunda and Friedrich Karl von Savigny, Bettina von Arnim, Clemens Brentano, Lisette and Christian Gottfried Nees von Esenbeck, and Susanne von Heyden. From 1804 on she had a relationship with a married man, Friedrich Creuzer from Heidelberg. Her suicide—she stabbed herself to death on 26 July 1806 in Winkel am Rhein, supposedly out of unrequited love for the older Creuzer—has given rise to numerous legends.

Many things in her era stood in the way of Günderrode's explicit embrace of the dramatic form. The normative rules within the poetics of drama and the conventions regarding access to the theater as a public institution marked drama as a taboo sphere for women. Drama was generally considered one of the higher genres, based on a unified and closed model. On a symbolic level it dealt with issues of political and historical power; it also ordered communication and introduced a temporal order. This structure was in clear contrast to what was understood as a feminine form of writing. Susanne Necker, wife of the French banker and politician Jacques Necker, who held an important salon in Paris, wrote of her fear of this literary genre: "If I were a dramatist, I wouldn't dare to think of it without trembling, because I would think that he [the dramatist] would be a fruitful source of vice or virtue for the human race, because he multiplies himself into infinity through his images" (Necker 107 f.).[7]

This contemporary definition from a female perspective assumed that drama possessed laws of its own that were opposed to the sphere of the feminine. Even to think of drama was an act of audacity, the trembling the result of a responsibility that seemed traceable to the very effect of drama itself. Drama was considered simply "unfeminine," which is why it was almost impossible for women to publish in this genre, unless they were actresses, which gave them access to the stage, or unless they hid their dramatic intentions behind a mask of virtue or a *nom de plume*.[8] Thus it was all the more important to find a mentor who had access to organs of publication and could take over the role of agent. In Günderrode's case, this was initially Christian Gottfried Nees, and later Friedrich Creuzer.

If one looks carefully at the interventions, good advice, recommendations, and comments of her friends, and the utterly destructive criticism and reviews to which Günderrode's writing was subjected, then it is clear how very difficult her task was made. Only when one listens to the voices of the censors does one become aware of the atmosphere of repression that characterized the literary public sphere in Frankfurt at that time and of Günderrode's social isolation in the charitable foundation for women.

Using the *nom de plume* Tian, Günderrode published her *Gedichte und Phantasien* in 1804. The review that appeared in Kotzebue's periodical *Der Freimüthige oder Ernst und Scherz* sounded dismissive:

> In the future the authoress ought to honor that which is good and beautiful, to stride majestically, free and unfettered, in her own beauty, to reject the corset as well as the fool's cap; she ought never to raise herself forcefully, never to sink into the depths of sinister mysticism, but rather to remain in her own realm of intimate feeling, beautiful and tender images... (Günderrode III: 62).[9]

The review reduces her to the contemporary stereotype of the feminine, prescribes which philosophical and literary directions she should avoid, and, moreover, reveals her identity, "Fräulein von Güntherode" (III: 61). Although, thanks to the efforts of the Esenbecks, this volume was given a second review in the *Jenaische Allgemeine Literaturzeitung* (9 July 1804), which did her book more justice, the first one had already publicly denounced her.[10] She could no longer hide behind a pseudonym as was usual for women dramatists writing around 1800 in a genre that was taboo.

Yet Günderrode, who only now began to publish drama,[11] refused to be led astray and based her dramatic writing on her philosophical studies, above all on the natural philosophy of Schelling. In June 1804, she wrote to Savigny: "I am diligently studying Schelling and working on a new drama" (Preitz II: 202).[12] In 1805 two dramas appeared in *Poetische Fragmente*: "Hildgund" and the most ambitious piece, "Mahomed." The same year saw the publication of the dramas "Udohla" and "Magie und Schicksal" in *Studien,* edited by Creuzer and Daub. Finally, in 1806, "Nikator" was published independently of Creuzer in *Taschenbuch für das Jahr 1806: Der Liebe und Freundschaft gewidmet.*[13]

If one follows the exchange of letters between the various partners and the changes made to her text, it becomes clear that Günderrode's emphatic embrace of the drama, her pathos, her dialectic of the moment and the eternal and of self and nature in the conception of her dramas always managed to give offense. Attempts were made to prevent her from speaking and to stem the flow of her literary production. She was accused of not having studied romantic poetry enough and of possessing a longing that, according to Lisette Nees, threatened to "dissipate in infinity" (Preitz I: 264). Again and again she was criticized for her extreme sensitivity, which seemed to be provoked by momentary impulses and the fantasies deriving from them. Savigny criticized her reading of Schiller and tried to force her to affirm the idea of totality and divine nature: "To love something with one's whole heart is divine, and every form in which this divinity is revealed is sacred. But to tinker with this, to use fantasy to raise this feeling beyond its natural limit is blasphemy" (Preitz II: 210).[14]

Günderrode, however, is no longer prepared to subordinate herself to a divine principle or to confine herself to Christian ideas and dogma. In a very long letter, Nees criticizes her drama "Mahomed." He cannot see any relation to a finite end (*endlichem Zweck*) (Preitz II: 234). He dislikes her ambivalence toward the tragic and the comic and considers the play not a real drama as much as a history of the Prophet of Mecca in the form of dialogue. Günderrode reacts to the criticism of Nees, who is preparing her drama for print, by agreeing to a concession: "A Dramatic Text [*Dichtung*] in Five Acts" becomes "A Dramatic Fragment by Tian."[15] Thus, the drama is related to the finite, as Nees demands, and cannot dissipate into the infinite. The drama sent to be copied was, however, not yet to be printed by him. After a disagreement with Nees, Günderrode turned to Creuzer as mentor. At the end of November, the drama was then sold to the publisher without Creuzer's knowledge. Nevertheless, Creuzer remained her mentor, taking care of contracts and printing until her death.

Creuzer, too, attempted to influence her work. His main criticism was aimed at historical references—"all drama that is rooted in *history*"—which he advised Günderrode to avoid (Günderrode III: 144). At the same time, however, it is clear that he used his position as her literary agent to establish a bond between them. When in 1804 Günderrode relinquishes any claim on Creuzer, as he seems tied to his wife—"Mahomed and all the poems that you know have been sold, so please stop all further negotiations" (136)—he tries to use the great name of Goethe as bait to persuade her: "I wanted to write to you how I am trying to have your Mahomed and other poems appear in the same publishing house as Goethe's" (136). It is also striking that Creuzer continually praises the dramas to her face, while adopting a more critical position towards them in the presence of others. In addition, he explains to her in detail the criticism of her drama by Clemens Brentano and his wife Sophie Mereau, as can be seen from various passages in their exchange of letters.

The *Poetische Fragmente,* and in them the dramas "Hildgund" and "Mahomed," were also subjected to harsh criticism in *Der Freimüthige oder Ernst und Scherz*. The main objection here is the fragmentary character of "Hildgund" (Günderrode III: 110 f.). Nees, who might have been responsible for publishing the *Poetische Fragmente,*[16] would later, after her suicide, render a harsh judgment on her literary production and establish a connection between her death and her transgression of "the bounds of the female imagination." She "wanted to write as a woman with a masculine spirit," but her "unnatural flight" was destined to crash (113).

The repressive mood that characterized the literary public sphere at the time, its specific form of external censorship, also left its mark on the literary production of Günderrode.

The Unheard of/Unspeakable Moment (*Unerhörter Moment*) and Drama Production

The correlation between literary production and self-censorship can be observed above all in the gaps in and deformations of the dramatic form that contribute to the fragmentary character of Günderrode's dramas. The play "Magie und Schicksal" has an open end, as does the drama "Nikator"; the mini-drama "Hildgund" breaks off without warning, and "Mahomed" is also a fragment. "Udhola: In zwei Acten" is the only piece that has an ending. This incompleteness can be regarded as a specific mark of Günderrode's dramatic production.[17] In the following I would like to examine two of these dramas, "Nikator: Eine dramatische Skizze in drei Akten von Tian" and "Hildgund," both of which deal with the assassination of a tyrant, in order to make the connection between censorship and the desire for self-expression more concrete and to define more precisely the formal elements of her work.

At the level of plot, the dramatic sketch "Nikator," set in ancient Greece, is trapped in the classic gender constellation. The dramatic conflict, which ends in the assassination of the tyrant, develops from the plot in which general Nikator falls in love with Adonia, the niece of the general he has defeated. Adonia, for her part, is pursued by the lust of the king whom Nikator serves. In the end, the tyrant wishes to drag Adonia, who refuses him, to the throne and Nikator to the scaffold (Günderrode I: 300). At this moment Nikator stabs the king and the soldiers surrounding Nikator challenge him to say something in his own defense: "Let him live, if he can justify himself" (302). The drama ends on this note, an open end in which the audience can guess that the soldiers will acquit Nikator, the victor.

The distribution of the action between the sexes is thus quite traditional, because Adonia makes no practical contribution to the assassination, whereas the male hero may publicly stand up to the tyrant and kill him. When a heroine thinks of killing a tyrant, as in another of Günderrode's dramas, the same kind of forcefulness can apparently not be shown in public.

The drama "Hildgund," which is based on the Attila legend, formulates women's claim to action without actually making the deed a part of the dramatic action. Hildgund has fled Attila's capture with her fiancé Walter of Aquitanien. Attila in this drama is presented less as a tyrant than as the incarnation of an ascetic ideal: "no slave to pleasure," he "wears a linen garment" and drinks "from a wooden cup the water of a pure spring" (Günderrode I: 89). He demands the return of Hildgund from her father. "I demand her return, she shall be pardoned. And she is my heart's desire as queen" (95). Walter is ready to fight for his fiancée with words such as "Demand as much as you like, tyrant, she will never be yours" (95). Yet Hildgund is ready to act. While pretending to Walter that she belongs to Attila, she has already decided on action, a decision that can be read in her dark look (*düstrer Blick*) (96).

The decision thus demands a disguise: if the social erosion of the female sphere and women's lack of power is a precondition for Adonia's being able to say in "Nikator" "I am always identical with the one I love" (289), then the heroism of Hildgund requires that she leave the sphere of love behind and define herself in a universal claim to freedom: "The God who liberates me abides in my own heart" (91).

Putting herself in Walter's position, adopting a man's position, demands building up an inner armory, which, in view of the unspeakable nature of her desire, can only be done via a monologue:

> Why do I hesitate, is it really so terrible,
> That a shy, pale lip cannot speak it?
> Murder! Ha, the only horror is in the name
> The deed is just, and bold and great,
> The fate of nations rests in my heart,
> I will free them, free myself.
> Let fear and childish scares be banned,
> A bold fighter alone attains a great goal (99).[18]

Hildgund portrays herself as a "virgin in arms," as a savior of humanity. She wants to stake the outrageous claim to "male" action but simultaneously appears alienated from herself because her words on the stage have no addressee. The monologue, however, represents the grandiose and excessive nature of her intentions:

> My dagger trembles, soon the great victim will bleed,
> Who, ruler of the world, is defeated by a mere woman.
> The strong chain is rent which has held millions in bondage,
> The powerful spring which has pressed upon the globe is released,
> Fear not, Italy! I will set you free,
> The scourge of nations falls by Hildgund's hand (101).[19]

The attributes of the ruler—his greatness, strength, and power—are related here antithetically to the weakness of the woman. Thus the universality of an almighty ruler is opposed to the utterly isolated weakness of the female protagonist imagining, in a delirium, her will to freedom. Hildgund remains trapped in this polarity, pinned down at the height of the scene's fantasy, no matter how much she intensifies her rage and desire to kill. For, unlike Nikator, Hildgund does not carry out the unspeakable deed. There is no final scene that might leave a sense of resolution; instead, the drama ends without warning with the last words of Hildgund:

> Ha! go on tyrant, celebrate
> the fleeing hours of thy final day (102).[20]

The drama inscribes Hildgund's outrageous claim to action and leaves a strange gap, an absence of sense. Where a male hero would be able to stab away, this drama breaks off, because the desire of the heroine, formulated in a monologue, appears immoderate. The censored spot functions like a blind spot, or a vacuum, in which words find no ears and no space. The claim to action that is formulated remains unheard and unspoken; the drama thus remains trapped in the excessive idea that it dramatizes, in the objection to a deed that displaces the constellation of the sexes and thus places itself on the borders of madness. The assassination of the tyrant, which is dealt with in both dramas, is not *per se* unspeakable, as long as it remains in line with the prescribed sexual constellation. It becomes a transgression from the moment the female protagonist does not content herself with functioning as an image of eternal love, but desires to act in the political sphere.

This unspeakable moment, which is subject to censorship, steals into the drama disguised as the "unheard of event" (*unerhörte Begebenheit*) and thus finds a way to express itself. "*Unerhört*" describes what is not yet known, what society does not hear, something unutterable. The drama is written around this unspoken demand. Günderrode allows it to be articulated only momentarily and then covers it with taboo and prohibition.

Suicide and Censorship

This background reveals to us that in Günderrode's literary production external and internal aspects of censorship correlate with each other. At the point where both factors intersect, the expressive interest is erased. The ever more depressing way in which her environment prescribes positions, her dependence on a forbidden love, Creuzer's termination of their affair, the consequent loss of her mentor and agent for her texts in the public sphere, the impossibility of a lasting affirmation of the dramatic form: all limited Günderrode's desire to write. Against this background, her suicide could be seen as a consequence of the tension between her desire to express herself and the censorship to which she was subjected, and, in the final instance, of the impossibility of finding a form for compromise. This uncompromising transposition of self into death, the break with reason, documents that Günderrode crossed herself out, just as one might do with a text to make it unreadable.

In the end what remained was suicide, the only way to imagine oneself immortal. She did this ultimately in a most theatrical way, by stabbing herself. It is striking that the kind of death she chose did not correspond to any kind of imaginary fusion; it was no dissolution of human limitation in the limitlessness of nature, but a heroically aggressive act. However, it must also be understood as the expression of a consciousness lacking in continuity. Her suicide is therefore not so much an Ophelia death as an act of censorship.

Günderrode's affirmative attitude, discerned in the opening quote, became trivialized and ultimately unmaintainable in the course of her struggle with her environment. The proofs of the volume *Melete,* which had already gone to press, were withdrawn by Creuzer immediately after her death. She was cut off from her public, yet simultaneously her name was on the public's lips on account of her forbidden affair and suicide. Not even her corpse was left untouched—she was given a post mortem in the attempt to establish an organic reason for her suicide.[21]

What Günderrode began as a diversion, delving into the stream of inner observation, finally consumed her entire ego. In a letter to Lisette Nees in July, 1806, she writes:

> You want to know about me? I am actually tired of living, I feel that my time is up and that it is only through an error of nature that I continue to live; this feeling is sometimes more, sometimes less vivid in me. That's the story of my life (Preitz I: 281).[22]

Notes

[1] "Mein Herz hat sich nicht von Ihnen abgewendet, viel wehniger einem andern Sterblichen zugewendet, nein, ich denke imer mit groser Freude daran daß ich Ihnen und Gunda in Zukunft angehören werde, aber es ist mir doch seit einigen Wochen anders als vor ein paar Monaten. Gunda tadelt mich, sagt ich sei hochmüthig, liebe niemand, und nähme keinen Antheil, aber sie irrt, wehnigstens übertreibt sie sehr; hochmüthig bin ich nun gar nicht denn es fehlt mir die Überzeugung, ich sei vortrefflich, ich kann es nur vorübergehend meinen, und dann wieder gar nicht, aber wissen sie was es eigentlich ist? ich kann es Ihnen nur mit großer Blödigkeit sagen, ich schreibe ein Drama, meine ganze Seele ist damit beschäftiget, ja ich denke mich so lebhaft hinein, werde so einheimisch darin, daß mir mein eignes Leben fremd wird; ich habe sehr viel Anlage zu einer solchen Abstraktion, zu einem solchen Eintauchen in einen Strom innerer Betrachtungen und Erzeugungen. Gunda sagt es sei dumm sich von einer so kleinen Kunst als meine sei, sich auf diesen Grad beherrschen zu lassen; aber ich liebe diesen Fehler, wenn es einer ist, er hält mich oft schadlos für die ganze Welt."

[2] The fact that Günderrode's letters, in comparison to those of her friends and others engaged in dialogue with her, are unusually thoughtful and well-constructed has been pointed out by Karl Heinz Bohrer, who has drawn parallels

between her letters and those of Heinrich von Kleist and Clemens Brentano. In her letters, as in theirs, Bohrer sees the signature of the modern in the specific discovery of aesthetic subjectivity, marked by the emphatic discovery of self, the discontinuity of consciousness, and the delimitation of the ego (80).

[3] "Beinahe wirst Du mir zu fremd um Dich in die eigentlichsten Theile meiner inneren Welt einzuführen; dennoch bist Du ein Gast den man nicht draußen vor der Thür möchte stehen lassen. Eine grose Verlegenheit. Ich dächte man führe Dich in eine nicht ganz ferne Loge und lasse so die Schauspieler (Gedanken, Phantasien, Gefühle) vor Dir spielen aber hinter den Coulissen lasse man Dich nicht kommen, überhaupt das innerste Getriebe nicht sehen.—Aber ich kann das nicht Gunda, wehnigstens hält es mir zu schwer, ich muß entweder das Schauspielhaus ganz verschließen, oder auch das innerste entschleiern."

[4] "...aber die seligen Träume zerfließen; sie kommen mir vor wie Liebestränke; sie betäuben exaltieren und verrauchen denn, das ist das Elend und die Erbärmlichkeit aller unserer Gefühle; mit den Gedanken ists nicht besser, man überdenkt auch leicht die Sache bis zur Schalheit...."

[5] See the concept of censorship in Killy.

[6] In her epistolary novel *Die Günderode,* Bettina von Arnim made sure that this author would not be forgotten. In more recent times, her life and her writings have become known through Christa Wolf's reception at the end of the seventies, and through the historical-critical edition of her writings edited by Walter Morgenthaler.

[7] "Wenn ich dramatischer Schriftsteller wäre, so würde ich keinen Gedanken daran wagen, ohne zu zittern, denn ich würde denken, daß, da er sich durch die Vorstellung ins Unendliche vervielfältigt, er für das menschliche Geschlecht ein fruchtbarer Keim von Tugenden oder von Lastern würde."

[8] For women's drama around 1800 see Dagmar von Hoff, Karin A. Wurst, and Susanne Kord.

[9] "Möchte die Verfasserin...in Zukunft nur dem Guten und Schönen huldigen, herrlich, frei und fessellos in eigener Schönheit wandeln, und die Schnürbrust wie die Hanswurstenjacke verschmähen; möge sie sich nie gewaltsam heben, nie in die Tiefen einer finstern Mystik versinken, und lieber in der ihr eigenen Sphäre des innigen Gefühls, der schönen und zarten Darstellung bleiben...."

[10] See Lazarowicz (139).

[11] In the volume *Gedichte und Phantasien* there are only two dramatic sketches, "Immortalita" and "Mora."

[12] Preitz assumes that this is a reference to the drama "Magie und Schicksal" (II: 202). Morgenthaler corrects this assumption and proposes a connection with "Nikator"; however, he does not exclude the possibility that it might be "Udohla" (156).

[13] Her posthumous papers also include "Der Kanonenschlag oder das Gastmahl des Tantalus" and the "Edda Fragment."

[14] "Etwas recht von Herzen lieben, ist göttlich, und jede Gestalt, in der sich uns dieses Göttliche offenbart, ist heilig. Aber daran künsteln, diese Empfindung durch Phantasie höher spannen, als ihre natürliche Kraft reicht, ist sehr unheilig."

[15] See Karoline von Günderrode (III: 101) and Günderrode's manuscript with the corrections of Christian Nees.

[16] This issue has not been satisfactorily resolved. See Günderrode (III: 108).

[17] On the open form of drama see Kastinger Riley (119), especially Chapter IV on Karoline von Günderrode.

[18] Was zag ich noch, ists denn zu ungeheuer,
Als daß die scheue, blasse Lipp' es nennen mag?
Mord! Ha der Name nur entsetzet,
Die That ist recht, und kühn und groß,
Der Völker Schicksal ruht in meinem Busen,
Ich werde sie, ich werde mich befrein.
Verbannt sey Furcht und kindisch Zagen,
Ein kühner Kämpfer nur ersiegt ein großes Ziel.

[19] Schon zuckt mein Dolch, bald wird das große Opfer bluten,
Das, Herrscher einer Welt, ein schwaches Weib besiegt.
Die starke Kette reißt, die Millionen bindet,
Die mächtige Feder springt, die einen Erdball drückt;
Italien zag nicht! ich werde dich befreien,
Der Völker Geisel fällt durch Hildegundens Hand.

[20] ...Ha! feire nur, Tirann,
Des letzten Tages schnell entflohne Stunden.

[21] See Achim von Arnim: "Schauderhaft ist mir die Sektion des Arztes gewesen, der ihren Tod aus dem Rückenmarke gelesen..." (Weißenborn 357).

[22] "Nach mir fragst Du? Ich bin eigentlich lebensmüde, ich fühle daß meine Zeit aus ist, und daß ich nur fortlebe durch einen Irrtum der Natur; dies Gefühl ist zuweilen lebhafter in mir, zuweilen blasser. Das ist mein Lebenslauf."

Works Cited

Arnim, Bettina von. *Die Günderode*. 1840. Frankfurt a.M.: Insel, 1982.
Bohrer, Karl Heinz. *Der romantische Brief: Die Entstehung ästhetischer Subjektivität*. Frankfurt a.M.: Suhrkamp, 1989.
Bourdieu, Pierre. *Language and Symbolic Power*. Cambridge: Polity, 1991.
Brentano, Clemens. *Briefwechsel zwischen Clemens Brentano und Sophie Mereau*. Ed. Heinz Amelung. Potsdam: Rütten & Loening, 1939.
Derrida, Jacques. *L'Écriture et la différence*. Paris: Editions du Seuil, 1967.
Freud, Sigmund. *Briefe an Wilhelm Fliess 1887-1904*. Ed. Jeffrey Moussaieff Masson. Frankfurt a.M.: Fischer, 1986.

———. *Psychologie des Unbewußten.* Studienausgabe. Vol. 3. Frankfurt a.M.: Fischer, 1975.

———. *Vorlesungen zur Einführung in die Psychoanalyse: Neue Folge.* Studienausgabe. Vol. 1. Frankfurt a.M.: Fischer, 1989.

Günderrode, Karoline von. *Sämtliche Werke und ausgewählte Studien: Historisch-Kritische Ausgabe.* Ed. Walter Morgenthaler. 3 vols. Basel: Stroemfeld/Roter Stern, 1991.

Hoff, Dagmar von. *Dramen des Weiblichen: Deutsche Dramatikerinnen um 1800.* Opladen: Westdeutscher Verlag, 1989.

Holquist, Max. "Introduction. Corrupt Originals: The Paradox of Censorship." *PMLA* 109.1 (January 1994): 14–26.

Kastinger Riley, Helene M. *Die weibliche Muse: Sechs Essays über künstlerisch schaffende Frauen der Goethezeit.* Columbia, SC: Camden, 1986.

Killy, Walther, ed. *Literaturlexikon.* Gütersloh: Bertelsmann, 1993. Vol. 14. 504–07.

Kord, Susanne. *Ein Blick hinter die Kulissen: Deutschsprachige Dramatikerinnen im 18. und 19. Jahrhundert.* Stuttgart: Metzler, 1992.

Lazarowicz, Margarete. *Karoline von Günderrode: Portrait einer Fremden.* Bern: Lang, 1986.

Levine, Michael G. *Writing through Repression: Literature, Censorship, Psychoanalysis.* Baltimore: Johns Hopkins UP, 1994.

[Necker, Susanne]. *Fragmente: Zwey Bändchen.* Giesen, 1804.

Preitz, Max, ed. "Karoline von Günderrode in ihrer Umwelt. I: Briefe von Lisette und Christian Gottfried Nees von Esenbeck, Karoline von Günderrode, Friedrich Creuzer, Clemens Brentano und Susanne von Heyden." *Jahrbuch des Freien Deutschen Hochstifts.* Ed. Detlev Lüders. Tübingen: Niemeyer, 1964. 208–307.

———. "Karoline von Günderrode in ihrer Umwelt. II: Karoline von Günderrodes Briefwechsel mit Friedrich Karl und Gunda von Savigny." *Jahrbuch des Freien Deutschen Hochstifts.* Ed. Detlev Lüders. Tübingen: Niemeyer, 1964. 158–236.

Weißenborn, Birgit, ed. *"Ich send Dir ein zärtliches Pfand": Die Briefe der Karoline von Günderrode.* Frankfurt a.M.: Insel, 1992.

Wolf, Christa, ed. *Karoline von Günderrode: Der Schatten eines Traumes. Gedichte, Prosa, Briefe und Zeugnisse von Zeitgenossen.* Darmstadt/Neuwied: Luchterhand, 1979.

Wurst, Karin A. *Frauen und Drama am Ausgang des achtzehnten Jahrhunderts.* Köln: Böhlau, 1991.

Woman as Will and Representation: Nietzsche's Contribution to Postmodern Feminism

Lewis Call

Friedrich Nietzsche is frequently dismissed as a misogynist. However, Nietzsche's texts contain many possibilities for postmodern feminism, since these texts strongly exemplify the two themes that characterize much of the postmodern feminist position: woman as multiple and woman as representation. Nietzsche redefines "truth" as a "mobile army of metaphors"; if he is right about the status of truth, then his attempt to construct a new representation or metaphor of woman can be viewed as the beginning of a radical new feminism. His texts simultaneously decry the failures of modernist feminism and illustrate the possibility of a feminist politics that is truly beyond the modern. (LC)

The successful introduction of a new idea of human subjectivity was one of the most impressive, and perhaps one of the most frightening, achievements of the Enlightenment. Its thinkers created a concept of subjectivity that has since been institutionalized throughout modernity, and this subjectivity has strict requirements. To meet Enlightenment standards, human subjects must be rational and autonomous; an implicit third condition is that they be male. Thus, although the *philosophes* claimed and perhaps even believed that they were pursuing a project of radical liberation, behind their bright utopia stood a dismal ghetto set aside for those who were not permitted to play the game of rationality. The creation of the rational, autonomous Enlightenment self thus simultaneously created the need for a new subject, a postmodern subject. And if the subject of the Enlightenment was invisibly male, the postmodern subject has at least the possibility of being female and feminist. This postmodern feminist subject is the focus of this paper.

What is the status and importance of this new female subject? It is a subject position that is constructed as multiple and without essence. What, then, is the meaning of the long-problematic category "woman," given the development of this new kind of subjectivity? My answer here is that woman must be thought of in terms of representation. The postmodern female subject must be understood as something radically different from "woman" as that term is conventionally used. Postmodern woman is, in short, no living organism with her own concerns and her own politics. To be sure, this definition is deeply troubling in its own way. It runs the risk of making a meaningful feminist politics impossible by denying women the chance to act as independent subjects. Yet the alternative is perhaps just as frightening, for it is to repeat the gesture of Enlightenment, to try to make women into autonomous subjects who are (at least implicitly) male.

As a case study of woman as representation I shall examine the works of Friedrich Nietzsche. Nietzsche's works contain a tense duality: he offers us on the one hand woman as a despised object, yet against this bitter misogyny he gives us the possibility of an affirmative concept of woman. My goal is, as David Krell puts it, "to disengage Nietzsche's identification of truth and woman from the banalities and analities of misogyny" (84). Nietzsche's texts contain many possibilities for postmodern feminism, because they strongly exemplify two related themes that characterize so much of the postmodern feminist position: woman as multiple and woman as representation. The latter theme is particularly crucial, given Nietzsche's views on representation and truth. "What, then, is truth?" he asks in a famous passage from *On Truth and Lie in an Extra-Moral Sense,* and provides his own answer: "A mobile army of metaphors, metonyms, and anthropomorphisms—in short, a sum of human relations, which have been enhanced, transposed, and embellished poetically and rhetorically, and which after long use seem firm, canonical, and obligatory to a people: truths are illusions about which one has forgotten that this is what they are; metaphors which are worn out and without sensuous power; coins which have lost their pictures and now matter only as metal, no longer as coins" (1).[1] If Nietzsche is right about the status of truth as metaphor, then his attempt to construct a new representation or metaphor of woman can be viewed as the beginning of a radical new feminism. The possibilities of this new feminism are reflected in a number of recent commentaries on Nietzsche. Thus as Keith Ansell-Pearson points out, "it might be no coincidence that the 'discovery' of Nietzsche—*the* philosopher of difference, according to Gilles Deleuze—by feminist writers is taking place at the same time that radical political theorists, including feminists, are seeking to articulate a philosophy of otherness and difference" (29). Nietzsche's representations of women have profound political implications. His texts simultaneously decry the failures of modernist feminism and illustrate the possibility of a feminist politics that is truly beyond the modern.

The postmodern female subject is, first and foremost, a multiplicity. Teresa de Lauretis defines this subject as "en-gendered in the experiences of race and class, as well as sexual, relations; a subject, therefore, not unified but rather multiple, and not so much divided as contradicted" (2). Nancy Fraser and Linda J. Nicholson offer a similarly radical idea that "would replace unitary notions of woman and feminine gender identity with plural and complexly constructed conceptions of social identity, treating gender as one relevant strand among others, attending also to class, race, ethnicity, age, and sexual orientation" (35). And Donna Haraway goes so far as to suggest that "there is not even such a state as 'being' female, itself a highly complex category constructed in contested sexual scientific discourses and other social practices" (197). In all three of these conceptions, postmodern gender is understood as being sensitive to a number of positions that are silenced in any modern or Enlightenment discourse. The postmodern female subject becomes everything that the (male) modern subject is not. She must be fractured, fictional, decentered. As Nancy Hartsock argues, "the philosophical and historical creation of a devalued 'Other' was the necessary precondition for the creation of the transcendental rational subject outside of time and space, the subject who is the speaker in Enlightenment philosophy" (160). But this "devalued 'Other'" now comes back to haunt Enlightened modernity, using its difference as a weapon against conventional ideas of subjectivity. Woman had to be marginalized before Man could be made a fully dominant category, but this very marginalization now gives postmodern feminism the opportunity to take apart the gender hierarchy, to remove the rational, autonomous subject from its privileged and exclusionary position and replace it with a kind of subjectivity that is less autocratic.

Jacques Derrida reads Nietzsche's concept of woman to suggest that the hallmark of female subjectivity is precisely its nonadherence to any conventional understanding of what it means to be a subject. Derrida speculates that for Nietzsche "perhaps woman—a non-identity, a non-figure, a simulacrum—is distance's very chasm, the out-distancing of distance, the interval's cadence, distance itself, if we could say such a thing" (49). In short, Derrida argues that by refusing to posit itself as "real" or "true," female subjectivity violates the qualifications of subjectivity imposed by an implicitly masculine post-Enlightenment modernity. Postmodern woman is also, according to Derrida's reading, without ground or origin. Derrida writes: "there is no such thing as the essence of woman because woman averts, she is averted of herself" (51). Derrida is right to suggest that the important thing about female subjectivity is the way in which it eludes traditional forms of identity and subjectivity. This elusiveness allows postmodern feminism to distance itself from any discourse about subjectivity that is dominated by the autonomous Enlightenment self. However, there is an important limitation to Derrida's position. Derrida does not pay enough attention to the importance of representation. He uses the idea of woman strategically, to undermine the validity of the conventional Enlightenment subject position. But once he has accomplished this, he has no further use for woman. She remains a "non-identity, a non-figure." Derrida thus falls into the trap mentioned above: he uses the concept of woman critically, but does not make the next move towards a possible feminist politics, the move of positing woman as representation. Derrida insists that "there is no such thing as a Being or an essence of *the* woman or the sexual difference" (121), and this may well be the case. But Derrida suggests that there can be no such thing as *any* woman. Worse, he attributes this position to Nietzsche. As I shall show, however, Nietzsche's description of truth as a "mobile army of metaphors" retains possibilities for female subjectivity that go well beyond Derrida's strategies. By associating truth and metaphor, Nietzsche enhances the value of metaphor and, in so doing, implicitly enhances the value of the metaphor that is woman.

One of the most interesting examples of woman as metaphor is Donna Haraway's cyborg. "The cyborg," writes Haraway, "is a creature in a postgender world; it has no truck with bisexuality, pre-Oedipal symbiosis, unalienated labor, or other seductions to organic wholeness through a final appropriation of all the powers of the parts into a higher unity" (192). It represents, in short, a new kind of subjectivity, one that does not rely upon any Enlightened notion of the subject. Haraway's cyborg thus demonstrates the infinite diversity of possible forms available to the female subject once this subject is seen as multiple. The space opened up by the postmodern redefinition of woman is open to anyone. As de Lauretis notes, "if Nietzsche and Derrida can occupy and speak from the position of woman, it is because that position is vacant and, what is more, cannot be claimed by women" (32). What has until now seemed a liberating move suddenly seems quite dangerous, because the multiple, decentered postmodern female subject, in its cyborg or other manifestations, is a tremendously difficult subject to be. This is the cry that Hartsock makes, insisting that "rather than getting rid of subjectivity or notions of the subject...we need to engage in the historical, political, and theoretical process of constituting ourselves as subjects" (170).

Haraway offers an interesting response to this position: "in a deep sense [woman] does not exist as a subject, or even potential subject, since she owes her existence as a woman to sexual appropriation" (201). Subjectivity as it has been traditionally understood is not even a possibility for women, since it is by its very nature defined against them. De Lauretis writes: "the discourse of the sciences of man constructs the object as female and the female as object. That, I suggest, is its rhetoric of violence, even when the discourse presents itself as humanistic, benevolent, or well-intentioned" (45). Women cannot win by trying to be conventional subjects; conventional subjects are male. And certainly succumbing to the rhetoric of violence that renders them objects is no solution. The alternative, it seems, is to be neither subject nor object. In the postmodern condition, the female "subject"—the word seems hardly appropriate—is fragmented and diverse. Woman can thus become representation: figure, symbol, image. Again, however, not all postmodernists take this turn; at the beginning of *Spurs,* Derrida writes: "the title of this lecture was to have been *the question of style.* However—it is woman who will be my subject. Still, one might wonder whether that doesn't really amount to the same thing..." (37). For Derrida, woman is not even an image but simply a *style,* and one must wonder if something as elusive as a style could form the basis for any meaningful kind of feminism. Ansell-Pearson is quite right to suggest that "it is Derrida who castrates woman by reducing the issue of woman's emancipation from a question of *politics* (of power) to one of style. Not once in *Spurs* does he engage with either the history or the theoretical and practical struggles of feminism" (36). Derrida's reading of woman as style has a very dangerous effect. To wit, it does not allow any meaningful kind of feminist politics. Derrida's interpretation thus unwittingly contributes to the marginalization of women begun by the Enlightenment.

De Lauretis notes that "gender...both as representation and as self-representation, is the product of various social technologies, such as cinema, as well as institutional discourses, epistemologies, and critical practices" (ix). For her, gender *is* representation; this is the only way it can reasonably be understood. "Although a child does have a sex from 'nature,' it isn't until it becomes (i.e., until it is signified as) a boy or a girl that it acquires a gender" (5). De Lauretis is arguing here against a kind of biological essentialism. What is important about women is not that they are physically female, but that they are constructed as women by a variety of discursive practices. The trick, it seems, is to avoid what Fraser and Nicholson call the "disabling vestiges of essentialism" (20) that lurk in so much feminist theory. In this way, possible modes of being other than the rational, Enlightenment subject become apparent. This kind of rational subject becomes increasingly unimportant in postmodern feminist discourse. Indeed, as de Lauretis notes, "in the phallic order of patriarchal culture and in its theory"—and this is the order we still inhabit—"woman is unrepresentable except as representation" (20). To be sure, as she goes on to note, "violence is engendered in representation" (33). Yet representation also contains the only possibilities for liberation. If the autonomous subject is and remains implicitly male, then subjectivity holds no hope for women. The only action left for women is to seize control of the apparatus of representation itself, to determine what the category of woman *means,* and in so doing to create a radical stance that, ironically, involves no actual, living "woman" at all.

Again, there are tremendous dangers involved in this move against essentialism. De Lauretis is certainly aware of these problems: "only by denying sexual difference (and gender) as components of subjectivity in real women, and hence by denying the history of women's political oppression and resistance, as well as the epistemological contribution of feminism to the redefinition of subjectivity and sociality, can the philosophers see in 'women' the privileged repository of 'the future of mankind'" (24). If "woman" is to be understood as a category of representation rather than as subjectivity, then what becomes of feminist political action? How can the oppression of actual, living women be combatted when it is forbidden to discuss women as subjects at all? As de Lauretis notes, the deconstruction of the subject "closes the door in the face of the emergent social subject which these discourses are purportedly seeking to address, a subject constituted across a multiplicity of differences in discursive and material heterogeneity" (24). The great irony here is that postmodern feminist discourse, which claims to have important and liberating things to say about women, in fact denies women the possibility of social and political agency. Hartsock voices this frustration with some vehemence: "Why is it that just at the moment when so many of us who have been silenced begin to demand the right to name ourselves, to act as subjects rather than objects of history, that just then the concept of subjecthood becomes problematic?" (163). Though this smacks of conspiracy theory, one can certainly appreciate Hartsock's point. The postmodern critique of human subjectivity denies women political and social agency at the exact historical moment that they begin to experience some of the possibilities of that agency.

This tension in feminism between woman as agent and woman as representation can, I think, be characterized in de Lauretis's apt phrase as "the twin and opposite pull exerted on any progressive or radical thinker by the positivity of political action, on one front, and the negativity of critical theory, on the other" (36). Critique demands that women not be subjects, for subjects are exclusionary. Yet politics demands that women *be* subjects, for if they are not, then political action becomes radically incoherent. It is difficult to imagine any way out of this dilemma. But de Lauretis thinks she has one. She writes: "to assert that the social representation of gender affects its subjective construction and that, vice versa, the subjective representation of gender—or self-representation—affects its social construction, leaves open a possibility of agency and self-determination at the subjective and even individual level of micropolitical and everyday practices which Althusser himself would clearly disclaim" (9). Representation, then, *is* political. By redefining the category of woman, the critic is in fact engaged in a profound kind of action, one that has far-reaching implications for actual, living women. The politics of representation make possible radical local actions. It thus becomes possible for women to determine what they will be and to actualize that impulse. These "micropolitical" possibilities are where the true radical impulses of feminist politics may be satisfied, for it is in this space that women are shaped and defined, and it is therefore in this space that the crucial politics of ordinary life are satisfied.

I now wish to turn to the texts of Friedrich Nietzsche. Negative images of woman appear in many places in Nietzsche's writing. For example, he describes woman as an object to be possessed:

> ...a man who has depth, in his spirit as well as in his desires, and also that depth of benevolence which is capable of hardness and severity and is easily confused with them, can think of woman only in an *oriental* way—he must conceive of woman as a possession, as property with lock and key, as something predestined for service and attaining her fulfillment in service—in this matter he must take his stand on the tremendous intelligence of Asia, on Asia's superiority of instinct, as the Greeks formerly did: they were Asia's best heirs and pupils and, as is well known, from Homer to the age of Pericles, with the *increase* of their culture and the amplitude of their powers, also became step by step *more strict* with women, in short more oriental (*Beyond Good and Evil* 238).

Nietzsche's attempt to link the cultures of ancient Greece and Asia here is very interesting, particularly given his well-known admiration for the former. Indeed, Nietzsche explicitly praises both Greek and Asian cultures in the *Genealogy*: "One cannot fail to see at the bottom of all these noble races the beast of prey, the splendid *blond beast* prowling about avidly in search of spoil and victory; this hidden core needs to erupt from time to time, the animal has to get out again and go back to the wilderness: the Roman, Arabian, Germanic, Japanese nobility, the Homeric heroes, the Scandinavian Vikings—they all shared this need" (I, 11). Nietzsche's inclusion of Arabs and Japanese in his list of noble races could be read as an attempt to break free from one aspect of white male European hegemony. This move is thus rendered extremely ironic by the fact that another type of hegemony, gender hegemony, remains very strongly inscribed within his racially cosmopolitan ethos.

The "oriental" possession of women must be absolute and unquestioning. Nietzsche writes:

> The more modest man counts the simple disposal of [woman's] body and sexual gratification as a sufficient and satisfactory sign of having, of possession; another, with a more jealous and demanding thirst for possession, sees the 'question mark,' the merely apparent quality of such a having and requires subtler tests, above all in order to know whether the woman not only gives herself to him but also gives up for his sake what she has or would like to have—; only *thus* does she count to him as 'possessed' (*Beyond Good and Evil* 194).

The possession of woman thus becomes one of the most urgent goals of man. "Sexual love betrays itself as a lust for possession: the lover desires unconditional and sole possession of the person for whom he longs; he desires equally unconditional power over the soul and over the body of the beloved; he alone wants to be loved and desires to live and rule in the other soul as supreme and supremely desirable" (*Gay Science* 14). Certainly woman is an interesting and exciting object: "a real man wants two things: danger and play. Therefore he wants woman as the most dangerous plaything" (*Zarathustra* I, 18). Yet she remains an object, incapable of action or agency. This is the origin of lust and jealousy in man. Love has a somewhat different meaning for woman, who "wants to be taken and accepted as a possession, wants to be absorbed into the concept of possession, possessed" (*Gay Science* 363). Man takes and woman permits herself to be taken, or more accurately, woman *is* taken—since woman has neither subjectivity nor agency here, an active verb is hardly appropriate. As Zarathustra succinctly summarizes it, "The happiness of man is: I will. The happiness of woman is: he wills" (*Zarathustra* I, 18). Thus the proper response when one encounters woman is, as Nietzsche sees it, to possesses and to control: "Seize forcibly the wench for whom you feel!" (*Gay Science* prelude, 22).

If woman is an object to be possessed by man, this possession must be motivated by a basic and irrational drive. For it is difficult to see why else one should desire the despicable object that Nietzsche describes. Woman is full of vanity and self-loathing: "behind all their personal vanity women themselves always have their impersonal contempt—for 'woman'" (*Beyond Good and Evil* 86). The passions of woman are severely limited. And for Nietzsche certain types of passion are among the most important parts of the human experience. Speaking of the scholar, Nietzsche says that "if love and hatred are demanded of him, I mean love and hatred as God, woman and animal understand them—: he will do what he can and give what he can. But one ought not to be surprised if it is not very much" (*Beyond Good and Evil* 207). Woman is hardly in good company with God and the scholar, two typical targets for Nietzschean invective. To be compared here to an animal almost seems the better choice. In any case, with her passions limited as Nietzsche seems to think they are, it is clear that woman will not easily become *Übermensch*.

Worse than limited, woman is weak, sick, decadent; in short, she is everything Nietzsche despises in modern Europe: "Finally: woman! One-half of mankind is weak, typically sick, changeable, inconstant—woman needs strength in order to cleave to it; she needs a religion of weakness that glorifies being weak, loving, and being humble as divine: or better, she makes the strong weak—she rules when she succeeds in overcoming the strong" (*Will to Power* 864). With her weakness, woman threatens to poison the strong. "Let men fear woman when she hates: for deep down in his soul man is merely evil, while woman is bad" (*Zarathustra* I, 18). To understand this accusation, it is important to consider the historical account of morality that Nietzsche constructs in the *Genealogy*. He begins with the Greek tradition, describing the distinction between good (understood as aristocratic) and bad (understood as common). He then argues that this noble morality was subverted by what he refers to as a "slave revolt" of morality, which propagated the Judeo-Christian distinction between good (humble, or in Nietzsche's terms common) and evil (proud, or aristocratic). Nietzsche hopes to transcend this newer formulation; he is therefore pleased to see the "evil" in man, for it hearkens back to an old tradition of nobility. But woman is "bad" or common. Woman, in short, "has so much reason for shame; in woman there is concealed so much pedanticism, superficiality, schoolmarmishness, petty presumption, petty unbridledness and petty immodesty" (*Beyond Good and Evil* 232). Perhaps worst of all, Nietzsche, who constantly subordinates abstract philosophical concerns to real physical considerations of life and health, finds that "woman does not understand what food *means*: and she wants to be the cook! If woman were a thinking creature she would, having been the cook for thousands of years, surely have had to discover the major facts of physiology, and likewise gained possession of the art of healing" (*Beyond Good and Evil* 234).

Many of the objections Nietzsche raises about women are in terms of aesthetics. He claims that women "'put on something' even when they take off everything. Woman is so artistic" (*Gay Science* 361). Nietzsche is probably not attempting here to mount a critique of art and artists as such, since he frequently shows a great deal of respect for true art. What he is criticizing here is woman as *bad art,* art that fails to accomplish what it should. "What has woman to do with the passionate indifference of the true artist, who assigns more importance to a sound, a breath, a heyday! than to himself? who strains with every finger to reach his innermost secrets?" (*Will to Power* 817). If woman fails as artist, she fares no better as work of art. "When we love a woman, we easily conceive a hatred for nature on account of all the repulsive natural functions to which every woman is subject" (*Gay Science* 59). Woman's body is, in this interpretation, artless.

Nietzsche's representations of woman would seem to be reactionary, even repulsive. But these are not representations of women in general. Rather, they refer specifically to the independent woman: "Woman wants to be independent: and to that end she is beginning to enlighten men about 'woman as such'—*this* is one of the worst developments in the general *uglification* of Europe" (*Beyond Good and Evil* 232). Here Nietzsche seems to be speaking against the *modern* woman specifically, against the woman who seeks to participate on equal terms with men and who refuses what Nietzsche has laid out as her natural role.

> Since the French Revolution the influence of woman in Europe has grown *less* in the same proportion as her rights and claims have grown greater; and the "emancipation of woman," in so far as it has been demanded and advanced by women themselves (and not only by male shallow-pates), is thus revealed as a noteworthy symptom of the growing enfeeblement and blunting of the most feminine instincts (*Beyond Good and Evil* 239).

Again, Nietzsche is speaking here against a particular representation of woman. He is suggesting that when women participate in modern liberal European society, *womanhood* suffers. The particular examples of this betrayal of womanhood that Nietzsche selects are illuminating: "It betrays corruption of the instincts—quite apart from the fact that it betrays bad taste—when a woman appeals precisely to Madame Roland or Madame de Staël or Monsieur George Sand as if something *in favour* of 'woman as such' were thereby demonstrated" (*Beyond Good and Evil* 233). It is precisely to this representation of woman—George Sand, woman as man—that Nietzsche objects.

Here, I think, is the key to understanding Nietzsche's apparent misogyny and his virulent anti-feminism. The negative representations of woman in Nietzsche's writing are part of a textual strategy. Nietzsche is attempting to counter a strong modernist impulse. His attacks on woman are arrows—Derrida would call them spurs—aimed at what Nietzsche sees as a tremendously dangerous concept of the female. This concept relies upon the Enlightenment ideal of freedom and emancipation and seeks to acquire these boons for women. In doing so it simultaneously reinforces the Enlightenment tradition from which it draws these ideas. Nietzsche thus inveighs against modern woman in the same voice he uses to attack modern man. Both are corrupt, sick, and weak; neither can produce the kind of world Nietzsche desires. But as Ansell-Pearson reminds us, these attacks on the modern can be most useful to postmodern feminism: "Nietzsche's critique of Christian and liberal notions of the self can certainly be of use to a noble and courageous feminist politics of difference" (31). Nietzsche's critique undermines the politics of modernist feminism by challenging the validity of the subject on which such politics must be based. However, his critique simultaneously makes possible a new kind of feminism, one that need not depend on the bankrupt idea of subjectivity created by the Enlightenment. Thus, as Peter Burgard writes, "beyond the context of Nietzsche's views on femininity, we must also consider his consistent condemnation of feminism in light of its embeddedness in his pervasive critique of democracy and the democratic ideal, both being for him examples of a striving for equality that disregards difference and that characterizes the herd mentality of the weak" (10).

It is precisely the inability of modernist feminism to account for difference that rouses Nietzsche's ire. Far from being reactionary, then, his "misogyny" emerges as part of a wide-ranging critical project. This project is an attempt to destabilize the institutions of modernity in preparation for a new construction. And one of the possibilities created by this new construction is a renewed, reinvigorated feminism. Thus as Lynne Tirrell argues, "the wider philosophical context of Nietzsche's thought provides grounds for taking seriously several passages of *The Gay Science* that reveal a more sympathetic understanding of women, since these passages take seriously Nietzsche's antidualism, his perspectivism and his early existentialist notion of the self" (158). Nietzsche's critical attacks on modern concepts such as dualism are motivated by a desire to overcome the modern and to create something new, and this project gives postmodern feminism some valuable opportunities.

In addition to his devastating critique of modern woman, then, Nietzsche offers a positive image of woman. Like the modern woman, this image refers to no actual woman. Rather, it is a representation of woman, a way of understanding woman. Yet for Nietzsche, there is nothing beyond representation, image, and metaphor. He writes in *On Truth and Lie in an Extra-Moral Sense*: "[Men] are deeply immersed in illusions and dream images; their eye glides only over the surface of things and sees 'forms'; their feeling nowhere leads into truth, but contents itself with the reception of stimuli, playing, as it were, a game of blindman's bluff on the backs of things" (1). This is the crucial importance of representation for Nietzsche. His extreme critique of truth suggests that representation, image, and metaphor are the only epistemological possibilities available to us. To be sure, Nietzsche is not always pleased with this conclusion. He laments: "Does not nature keep much the most from [man], even about his body, to spellbind and confine him in a proud, deceptive consciousness, far from the coils of the intestines, the quick current of the blood stream, and the involved tremors of the fibers?" (*On Truth and Lie* 1). But as much as he dislikes this conclusion, he can reach no other. Already in 1873 he flatly dismissed the possibility of true knowledge in the Kantian sense.

> The "thing in itself" (for that is what pure truth, without consequences, would be) is quite incomprehensible to the creators of language and not at all worth aiming for. One designates only the relations of things to man, and to express them one calls on the boldest metaphors. A nerve stimulus, first transposed into an image—first metaphor. The image, in turn, imitated by a sound—second metaphor (*On Truth and Lie* 1).

Creatures of language, Nietzsche believes, have no right to speak of abstract "things in themselves" as Kant does; these "things" exist beyond the realm of perceptions and are therefore incomprehensible. Instead there is image and metaphor. These express our relationship to the world and to each other, and as such they are the closest thing to truth that we have.

This, then, is the importance of metaphor for Nietzsche: it represents the only "truth" to which humans can legitimately claim access.

Thus in a famous passage at the beginning of *Beyond Good and Evil,* Nietzsche celebrates the power of woman as metaphor.

> Supposing truth to be a woman—what? is the suspicion not well founded that all philosophers, when they have been dogmatists, have had little understanding of women? That the gruesome earnestness, the clumsy importunity with which they have hitherto been in the habit of approaching truth have been inept and improper means for winning a wench? (preface).

Here Nietzsche combines a spirited attack on the methodology of conventional philosophy with an appreciation of the mysterious feminine nature of truth. Indeed, as Debra Bergoffen points out, he may well be doing much more than this. "Does this 'supposing truth is a woman...,' as the first line of a work dedicated to overcoming the truth of morality, tell the whole story?" Bergoffen wonders. "Does it, given the ways in which we find the masculine figure inscribed in the highest truths and grounding values of the Western tradition, sound as the echo of Nietzsche's announcement of the death of God?" (25). According to Bergoffen's interpretation, Nietzsche's critique of the Western philosophical tradition is simultaneously a subtle critique of the patriarchy that has defined that tradition: "God the father, the fraternal order, the paternal metaphor—all these strategies of undoing otherness are undone under the assumption of truth as woman" (28).

Clearly the metaphor of woman as truth holds some powerful possibilities for feminism. De Lauretis writes:

> Woman's skepticism, Nietzsche suggests, comes from her disregard for truth. Truth does not concern her. Therefore, paradoxically, woman becomes the symbol of Truth, of that which constantly eludes man and must be won, which lures and resists, mocks and seduces, and will not be captured. This skepticism, this truth of nontruth, is the 'affirmative woman' Nietzsche loved and was, Derrida suggests. It is the philosophical position Nietzsche himself occupies and speaks from (31).

Woman represents for Nietzsche the essence of truth, but truth not in the stagnant, disinterested sense of modern science. Rather, woman is a vibrant, living thing, a delightfully contradictory (non)truth. Derrida claims that Nietzsche "revives that barely allegorical figure (of woman) in his own interest. For him, truth is like a woman. It resembles the veiled movement of feminine modesty" (51). This resurrected woman, then, this woman who has no interest in truth and is therefore uniquely qualified to represent truth, serves Nietzsche strategically. But Derrida goes on to write: "Because, indeed, if woman *is* truth, *she* at least knows that there is no truth, that truth has no place here and that no one has a place for truth" (53). Again, one side effect of Derrida's use of woman as metaphor is the negation of woman. Woman is truth, but there is no truth. Therefore there is no woman. Nietzsche, on the other hand, uses the metaphor of woman to deny the existence of truth in the conventional sense, but he does so to open a broad space for new affirmations, new kinds of truth. To those who find Nietzsche's new metaphoric truth insufficient, who demand quick solutions and rational replies, he says: "Truth has so much to stifle her yawns here when answers are demanded of her. She is, after all, a woman: one ought not to violate her" (*Beyond Good and Evil* 220). Nietzsche is willing to defend his new (un)truth.

What are the characteristics of this new woman? She represents life, which is, after all, one of Nietzsche's central concerns. Nietzsche writes: "perhaps this is the most powerful magic of life: it is covered by a veil interwoven with gold, a veil of beautiful possibilities, sparkling with promise, resistance, bashfulness, mockery, pity, and seduction. Yes, life is a woman" (*Gay Science* 339). The key here is that woman exists as a positive possibility, beyond the modernist mockeries that too often are all that can be seen of her. She is more an ideal than a reality, of course: "All at once we believe that somewhere in the world there could be women with lofty, heroic, and royal souls, capable of and ready for grandiose responses, resolutions, and sacrifices, capable of and ready for rule over men because in them the best elements of man apart from his sex have become an incarnate ideal" (*Gay Science* 70). This description of woman as "the best elements of man" seems strange, for it hints at the masculinized woman that Nietzsche has already dismissed. Yet it is crucial to remember here that woman takes from man selectively, and that she can never take "his sex": she remains distinctly female. In any case, these "lofty, heroic and royal souls" certainly seem far removed from Nietzsche's misogyny. Stripped of her modernist dross, woman displays all the strength, the power that is so much a part of Nietzsche's superior individual. There are hints of "*Überfrau.*" As David Krell puts it, "The liberation of the woman in woman is to be something utterly new and unheard of: it is to be the very matrix of *Übermensch*" (30). Unconcerned with the trivial, meaningless pursuits of modern European man, woman exists in her own world. "When a man stands in the midst of his own noise, in the midst of his own surf of plans and projects, then he is apt also to see quiet, magical beings gliding past him and to long for their happiness and seclusion: *women*" (*Gay Science* 60). Yet despite her quiet power, woman also lies at the heart of the most profound kind of sound: "Does the concept grand style ultimately stand in contradiction to the soul of music—to the 'woman' in our music?—" (*Will to Power* 842). Truth, beauty, power, and soul: all are part of the infinite possibilities of Nietzsche's new woman.

It is precisely this woman who motivates Nietzsche's extreme hostility towards modern feminism. As Derrida notes,

> in truth, they too are men, those women feminists so derided by Nietzsche. Feminism is nothing but the operation of a woman who aspires to be like a man. And in order to resemble the masculine dogmatic philosopher this woman lays claim—just as much claim as he—to truth, science and objectivity in all their castrated delusions of virility. Feminism too seeks to castrate. It wants a castrated woman. Gone the style (65).

Again, Nietzsche makes an attack on one kind of woman for the sake of what he sees as a superior type:

> To blunder over the fundamental problem of "man and woman," to deny here the most abysmal antagonism and the necessity of eternally hostile tension, perhaps to dream here of equal rights, equal education, equal claims and duties: this is a *typical* sign of shallow-mindedness (*Beyond Good and Evil* 238).

Nietzsche is opposed to the modern woman, to the woman who wants to become man, who wants to give up the delightful (un)truth that she represents. "To be sure, there are sufficient idiotic friends and corrupters of woman among the learned asses of the male sex who advise woman to defeminize herself in this fashion and to imitate all the stupidities with which 'man' in Europe, European 'manliness,' is sick" (*Beyond Good and Evil* 239). But Nietzsche's critique of this impulse remains the same, essentially, as his critique of "manly" stupidity. What is modern is sick and must be overcome. What is beyond modern is *Übermensch,* and possibly "*Überfrau.*"

The woman whom Nietzsche loves is a Dionysian woman. Derrida writes: "beyond the double negation of the first two [negative types], woman is recognized and affirmed as an affirmative power, a dissimulatress, an artist, a dionysiac. And no longer is it man who affirms her. She affirms herself, in and of herself, in man" (97). Derrida is pointing here to the radical feminism that becomes possible through Nietzsche's affirmative representation of woman. This is one of the few places in his text where Derrida seems to acknowledge the possibility of a postmodern female agency. This move works against his earlier description of woman as non-figure. Here she is surprisingly not simply a figure or image but an image with power, a self-affirming image. Perhaps this is Derrida's reluctant nod to the radical possibilities created by Nietzsche's affirmative representation of woman. In this representation, woman becomes independent, joyful, and free. She admits and cherishes her nature:

> ...that in woman which inspires respect and fundamentally fear is her *nature,* which is more "natural" than that of the man, her genuine,

cunning, beast-of-prey suppleness, the tiger's claws beneath the glove, the naïvety of her egoism, her ineducability and inner savagery, and how incomprehensible, capacious and prowling her desires and virtues are (*Beyond Good and Evil* 239).

Let us make no mistake: when Nietzsche describes woman here in terms that conjure up images of wild beasts, he does so in an affirmative way. This cunning and savagery represents for him a positive strength that is all too rare in modern society. Nietzsche understands the power of the images he wields, and he uses these images to further particular goals. If he assaults woman as modern, as feminist, as sick and weak just as Europe is, it is so that he may return with a new affirmation. He attacks the woman who *is* under the banner of the woman who *might* be. It is possible, of course, to dismiss this as a utopian affirmation, but Nietzsche's attack on truth and the corresponding increase in the power of metaphor make this unnecessary. Nietzsche's positive image of woman may have no relation to the status of actual women in the world. But this image remains nonetheless a representation of sufficient power to affect dramatically the condition of those women.

Nietzsche gives us an excellent example of the various destinations available to the postmodern feminist. He understands the crucial importance of representational politics, and he also understands multiplicity. Woman means many things to Nietzsche. As Derrida writes, "He was, he dreaded this castrated woman. He was, he dreaded this castrating woman. He was, he loved this affirming woman" (101).[2] Here are two negative realities: woman bereft of any spirit, transformed into a pale caricature of sickly modern man, and woman who is perhaps partly responsible for the sorry state of that modern man. But against these two dismal realities stands a beautiful possibility: woman as Dionysian, as (un)truth, as free spirit. Nietzsche has thus provided some important tools for postmodern feminism: negative representation to critique the misguided varieties of feminism, and affirmative representation to celebrate new possibilities for women. There is in Nietzsche's writing a veritable arsenal of female subject positions. It remains to be seen how these positions will be transformed into a meaningful politics; perhaps they will be most significant on de Lauretis's "individual level of micropolitical and everyday practices." After all, it is here that representation achieves its most profound significance for actual, living women, as what it means to be a woman is defined by them and for them in an immediate way.

Notes

[1] Following Walter Kaufmann, I have given references by section number rather than by page number (e.g., *Beyond Good and Evil* 238) or, where appropriate, by book number and section number (e.g., *Genealogy* II, 15). The large number of editions and translations of Nietzsche's works makes such an approach attractive. Quotations in this article follow the excellent translations of Kaufmann and R.J. Hollingdale.

[2] The reference to castration suggests that Derrida is advocating a Freudian reading here; indeed he refers to Freud on the same page. While it is often difficult to present a compelling psychoanalytic reading of an historical figure, Nietzsche's problematic relationships with his sister and other women make it tempting to attempt such an analysis. I do think that David Krell goes too far, however, when he argues that "If we recall those recently discovered pages of *Ecce Homo* (6, 267–69) in which Nietzsche suggests that his mother and sister were the two irrefutable objections to the eternal recurrence of the same, then the case seems closed. Everything that Nietzsche or Nietzsche's Zarathustra celebrates in or about the female—as a symbol of life, truth, creativity, and eternity—we can accordingly reduce to overcompensation" (3). For more on Nietzsche's relationship with his sister, see, for example, H.F. Peters, *Zarathustra's Sister*.

Works Cited

Ansell-Pearson, Keith. "Nietzsche, Woman and Political Theory." *Nietzsche, Feminism and Political Theory*. Ed. Paul Patton. New York: Routledge, 1993. 27–48.

Bergoffen, Debra B. "Nietzsche Was No Feminist..." *International Studies in Philosophy* 26.3 (1994): 23–31.

Burgard, Peter J. "Introduction: Figures of Excess." *Nietzsche and the Feminine*. 1–32.

de Lauretis, Teresa. *Technologies of Gender*. Indianapolis: Indiana UP, 1987.

Derrida, Jacques. *Spurs: Nietzsche's Styles*. Chicago: U of Chicago P, 1978.

Feminism/Postmodernism. Ed. Linda J. Nicholson. New York: Routledge, 1990.

Fraser, Nancy, and Linda J. Nicholson. "Social Criticism without Philosophy: An Encounter between Feminism and Postmodernism." *Feminism/Postmodernism*. 19–38.

Haraway, Donna. "A Manifesto for Cyborgs: Science, Technology, and Socialist Feminism in the 1980s." *Feminism/Postmodernism*. 190–233.

Hartsock, Nancy. "Foucault on Power: A Theory for Women?" *Feminism/Postmodernism*. 157–75.

Krell, David Farrell. *Postponements: Woman, Sensuality, and Death in Nietzsche*. Bloomington: Indiana UP, 1986.

Nietzsche and the Feminine. Ed. Peter J. Burgard. Charlottesville: UP of Virginia, 1994.

Nietzsche, Friedrich. *Beyond Good and Evil.* Trans. R.J. Hollingdale. New York: Penguin, 1990.

———. *The Gay Science.* Trans. Walter Kaufmann. New York: Vintage, 1974.

———. "On Truth and Lie in an Extra-Moral Sense." Trans. Walter Kaufmann. *The Portable Nietzsche.* Ed. Walter Kaufmann. New York: Penguin, 1984.

———. *Thus Spoke Zarathustra: A Book for All and None.* Trans. Walter Kaufmann. New York: Penguin, 1988.

———. *Werke: Kritische Gesamtausgabe.* Ed. Giorgio Colli and Mazzino Montinari. Berlin: de Gruyter, 1967–78.

———. *The Will to Power.* Trans. Walter Kaufmann and R.J. Hollingdale. Ed. Walter Kaufmann. New York: Vintage, 1968.

Peters, H.F. *Zarathustra's Sister: The Case of Elisabeth and Friedrich Nietzsche.* New York: Crown, 1977.

Tirrell, Lynne. "Sexual Dualism and Women's Self-Creation: On the Advantages and Disadvantages of Reading Nietzsche for Feminists." *Nietzsche and the Feminine.* 158–82.

From "Halbtier" to "Übermensch": Helene Böhlau's Iconoclastic Reversal of Cultural Images

Alyth F. Grant

Böhlau's *Halbtier!* questions the images of femininity current in the arts and philosophy of the nineteenth century that idealized such notions as self-sacrifice and identifies their role in the continued oppression of women. It shows how women are seduced by such images, internalizing their messages, so that they help perpetuate their own subjection. Böhlau seeks to create a counter-image in her heroine, both drawing on and subverting the philosophy of Nietzsche; she critically examinines the sociological implications of the many variations of the animal motif to be found there, yet adopts his vision of the *Übermensch* as the model for her heroine. (AFG)

"But sometime, in a stronger time...he must surely come to us, the redeeming being...this being of the future who will redeem us from the hitherto existing ideal" (Nietzsche 6_2: 352).[1]

Helene Böhlau's *Halbtier!* rings with echoes of Nietzsche, from the direct use of Nietzschean vocabulary to the adoption of key ideas from his philosophy. Its heroine, for example, is modelled on Nietzsche's conception of "the redeeming being." Given the many well-known passages in Nietzsche's work that have contributed to his reputation as a misogynist, the question inevitably arises as to the nature of the reception of Nietzsche in Böhlau's work, a novel written by a woman, principally for women readers. My contention is that Böhlau, by using Nietzsche's vocabulary and creating characters who embody Nietzschean attitudes toward women, calls those attitudes into question. Where she draws on Nietzsche's key theories she remodels them to serve her own ends, envisaging, for instance, an *Übermensch* who is a woman, able both to avenge the injustice done to her sex by the very subjugation his philosophy propounds and to serve as a model or inspiration for others. Thus Böhlau seeks a way to empower women by using Nietzsche's language and images subversively, in an iconoclastic reversal of their original intent.

Gisela Brinker-Gabler has called *Halbtier!* "the most provocative woman's novel of the turn of the century" (2: 178). Certainly it provoked mixed reactions at the time of its appearance. *Das litterarische Echo* of 1901 reports it to have been "vigorously attacked" (*Echo* 1120). Among those rejecting it were representatives of both the bourgeois women's movement (Gertrud Bäumer)[2] and the socialist women's movement (Anna Schapire).[3] It is possible that some of the controversy surrounding the work arose through the obvious influence of Nietzsche in its language and thought. Bäumer's article clearly associates Nietzsche with what she perceived to be the individualism dominating the age and which she saw as a barrier to the social engagement necessary to improve the lot of ordinary people.

By the turn of the century Nietzsche's philosophy had been absorbed, at least superficially, into bourgeois culture. Perhaps surprisingly, his ideas had evidently found considerable favor with some women writers. Marie Hecht, writing in *Die Frau* in 1899, the same year that *Halbtier!* was published, attempts to analyze the reasons for Nietzsche's popularity, which she calls "a fashionable illness...which threatens to become a dangerous and infectious intellectual influenza" (486). Hecht finds it difficult to comprehend why a writer whose attitudes towards women were so blatantly anti-emancipatory—she points her readers to the appropriate passages in *Beyond Good and Evil*—should nevertheless hold such sway among them. Seeking possible explanations for Nietzsche's power over the female psyche, she speaks of the seductiveness of his language, with its musicality, its images, and its hypnotic qualities, of his "feminine sensuality" and "the wild, unbridled quality" of his superlatives. The women to whom he appeals, she claims, are those who respond not to the thinker but to the poet, those of undeveloped and undisciplined intellect, or those who are driven by radical feminism to take the other extreme position, which portrays "female nature in its pure form as lustful longing for the male, voluptuous desire for a child at any price" (489). Hecht feared for the future of the women's cause under this influence: "...such a strong influence on women at a time when they are striving to develop themselves independently into mature personalities true to their individuality...must be viewed as a phenomenon of grave consequence" (487 f.).

One might ask therefore whether the publication of *Halbtier!* supplied Hecht with further evidence of a woman writer succumbing to the seductively irrational philosophy of Nietzsche. But I shall argue that that is not the case. Böhlau is indeed in touch with the intellectual ideas of her time, showing not only a familiarity with Nietzsche and Schopenhauer,[4] but also an affinity with the early work of her contemporaries Freud and

Breuer.[5] However, she does not display the ill-disciplined intellect Hecht attributes to the female disciples of Nietzsche. Her use of Nietzschean vocabulary and concepts is conscious. Her work shows that she is aware and critical of the part played by the arts and philosophy in determining women's place in society through the images of femininity that they create. The anti-emancipatory ideas and images to be found in Nietzsche Böhlau recognized as part of a wider tradition of artistic imagery, still in currency in her time, that had become part of the social machinery keeping women in a state of subordination and preventing their becoming the subjects of their own destiny.

Halbtier!, which stylistically is a mixture of the exalted, the melodramatic, and the naturalistic, reveals a marked awareness of the repressive and limiting conditions under which women of the day suffered, made victims of a moral double standard, deprived of education and intellectual stimulation,[6] and condemned to living out roles and functions that gave them no outlet for their creativity and aspirations.[7] This state of affairs was noted by Breuer and Freud in their early studies on hysteria. But while they comment frequently that their patients are particularly intelligent women, they do not point to a direct causal connection between that and the illness of their patients. Nevertheless, Freud is aware of the often powerless situation women found themselves in, naming as a common cause for a later hysterical illness a "mortification" ("Kränkung," literally "making ill"), defined as "suffering that is endured in silence," to which the correct forms of social behavior for women prevented them from reacting and which consequently remained insufficiently "abreacted." Unlike men, they can demand no "satisfaction" in such a case (Freud and Breuer 8). Marlis Gerhardt, pursuing the causes of female illness, elaborates on this theory by interpreting the word "Kränkung" much more broadly, as an injury done to women as members of their sex by a society that demands adherence to an ideal equating them with nature and defines them through their role within the bourgeois family.[8] Where the conflict between the socially imposed ideal and the desire of the individual woman becomes too intense, the result is often an outbreak of hysteria, or some other nervous disorder. In the nineteenth century madness was considered to be a "female malady." In her book of that title, Elaine Showalter reaches similar conclusions to Gerhardt's, suggesting two explanations for the high incidence of madness among women: the confining nature of traditional female roles and life patterns on the one hand and the association of female images in European cultures with irrationality, silence, nature, and the body, on the other.

Böhlau's *Halbtier!* confirms these explanations and highlights the connections between the two. Its portrayal of the Frey's family life provides a detailed picture of the domestic oppression of women and of the double moral standard of the time that demanded innocence of its young women but condoned libertine behavior in their brothers. But Böhlau's criticism is directed not just at the social conditions of women's lives. Her novel also examines the part that cultural discourse plays in exacerbating women's unhappy situation. Art, literature, and philosophy are shown to be the vehicles of an ideology that exalts idealized notions of the feminine. There is an obvious disparity between such *images* of the feminine and the actual status accorded women in society; nevertheless they continue to exert ideological power, not only over men, but over women too, helping perpetuate women's willingness to participate in their own subjection.

Böhlau achieves her aims by means of a well-known plot, that of innocence betrayed. But here the seduction and betrayal is of the heroine's mind rather than her body and happens in the name of art. It has taken place long before the innocent heroine Isolde has met the man who later betrays her trust—through his etchings. The artist Henry Mengersen's work exalts a feminine ideal of self-sacrifice that links love inevitably with a sacrificial death. Isolde, fifteen when she first views an exhibition of his work, succumbs to the power of his images. Moved in particular by a picture portraying the grief of a young husband bending over the dead body of his wife while the figure of death looms over them bearing the body of the stillborn child, she believes she has found a new meaning to her destiny as a woman:

> She belonged to those—to those who must suffer so anonymously, so secretly, to those by whose love death stands, as she had just seen it, gigantic, serious, solemn death....
> Love and death! Oh to go to one's death loving like that! She felt proud, powerful—and was glad that she was a woman.... Yes, that is the greatest thing on earth: to be a woman! To sacrifice oneself! (87 f.)

Isolde has been raised in a family her own father labels "philistine" ("spießbürgerlich" 50). She has been denied the opportunity of an advanced education in favor of her younger, intellectually dull brother. Doktor Frey, her father, who shares Nietzsche's views on the place of woman when it comes to his own family, is adamant that to allow her to train as a teacher would be to admit her inadequacy as a woman: "She should marry, be a woman!... A woman is just a woman. If she is not woman enough to be just a woman, she should be put down!" (26). Her mother, a decent but unimaginative and cowed woman, is kept in the role of "domestic animal" by her patriarch husband, who limits her household budget to the extent that her entire energies are consumed by the effort to make ends meet. Her one claim to self-satisfaction is her success in shielding her two daughters from the ugly realities of her married life and thus protecting their innocence at all costs, as society deems appropriate for "daughters of the better classes" ("höhere Töchter"). Doktor Frey, meanwhile, leads a life in higher intellectual and social circles, celebrated as "poet" (66), "prophet" (46), "*Übermensch*" (67), and possible future "Member of Parliament" (21).

In this man and his relationship to the society lady Mrs. Wendland on the one hand and to the women of his family on the other, Böhlau exemplifies the disparity between the notion of ideal "womanliness" ("Weiblichkeit") central to the male propagators of the German tradition such as he and what women have become as a consequence of the patriarchal social order. At home a patriarchal despot who treats women as his personal valets, Frey complains bitterly that they are philistines who burden his purse, pry into his affairs, and inhibit his productivity, being an "obstacle to all greatness" (54). As examples of German womanhood he compares them unfavorably with the woman he has just met, Mrs. Wendland, a rich English widow whom he describes as "a woman in her perfection" (53). To the astonishment of his daughters, in her company he is transformed into an old-style cavalier:

> He guided her as carefully as if she were a Higher Being who he was afraid could be damaged merely by contact with the ground. One could see from his every step, his every movement that he could hardly contain himself in his earthy, rather naive delight and satisfaction (90 f.).

Yet this paragon to whom Frey shows such reverence airs in her salon outspoken views on the relationship between the sexes in Germany that might well be expected to cause offense to her guests—not just because of the grammatical infelicities of her speech. Mrs. Wendland is indeed "a Higher Being," but not in a sense Doktor Frey can appreciate. Although she is a woman, she aspires to a higher level of being, to Nietzsche's vision of the *Übermensch,* who transcends the conformity of the "herd animals" ("Herdentiere"). But the male bearers of culture in her circle misunderstand and fail to appreciate her aspiration. They give the title *Übermensch* instead to Doktor Frey, who has the least self-understanding or self-transcendence of them all.

Mrs. Wendland recognizes that the idea German men have of women is nothing more than a constructed image, as a consequence of which women enjoy a status little higher than that of animals:

> "There you go with the Middle Ages!—Naturally, all German men do that when they talk about women. A German man always sees women in the Middle Ages, dressed like that too. I believe, when a man speaks of 'the German woman' he thinks of one who has been carved in wood, never the living one, like the childlike ones you see on the title pages of all the German family magazines. There is nothing more naive in this respect than the German man" (77).

Böhlau's attribution of this view of male-female relationships in Germany to a foreigner functions like a Brechtian alienation technique, highlighting the unsatisfactory fact that the meanings and images associated with the abstract terms "woman" or "the German woman" in German literary discourse have little to do with the aspirations and lives of women in her society as she understands them. The limited image of women conveyed by bourgeois family journals[9] serves to perpetuate the idea that women's intellect is inferior to that of men. Mrs. Wendland blames the women themselves in part for tolerating this situation. "All German women are cows" (72), she sighs, while declaring her determination to enlighten those she can.

The omniscient narrator clearly sympathizes with Mrs. Wendland's views. Many variations of the animal motif—"herd animal" (2), "night animal" (57), "semi-animal" (95), "animal of prey" (96), "domestic animal" (163)—emphasize the degradation of woman to animal and evoke the two-class society of Nietzschean theory.[10] As the object of a man's love, or as housewife and mother, a woman is reduced to the physicality of her body and that determines her function in life. While in literature and the arts she is revered for her beauty and virtue, her "birdbrain" (Doktor Frey's term!) is never taken seriously. She is simultaneously "worshipped and despised" (290), as Isolde puts it. Decades before the advent of gynocritics, Mrs. Wendland recognizes the ideological power that abstract notions gain when given form in works of art and thought. The idealized images of womanhood acquire an autonomous life, even though their inner coherence bears little relation to social realities. She therefore lays the blame for the injustice done to women as a consequence of this power principally on the poets and philosophers, the manufacturers of images. Despite the dignity of her position as hostess, she gives vent to a revolutionary anger in her desire to throw a bomb amongst all those "who write and philosophize and speak about woman. I would throw it right into the middle of their arrogance" (76). Among the guests to whom she addresses these words are Doktor Frey and Henry Mengersen, as writer and artist, respectively, representatives of the very groups that help perpetuate idealized images of womanhood. Both, however, seem oblivious to the implications of her words.

The artist Henry Mengersen, Mrs. Wendland's former lover, is another intimate in her circle. Bored by the company of young German women who have been raised in accordance with the ideal of innocence, he appreciates her stimulating company: "One could talk and live with her without ever being bothered by naive comments" (94). His most recent work is a sculpture of Mrs. Wendland that is to be unveiled for the first time in the presence of her guests. Expecting a piece that will honor her, she is shocked and displeased when the figure is revealed to be that of a sphinx bearing her features. She realizes that the artist has seen in her not an individual, but an idea of womanhood that disregards her mind and reduces her to something animalistic, predatory; she sees herself portrayed as "an animal of prey" (95), an image reminiscent of Nietzsche's view of woman in *Beyond Good and Evil*.[11] The sculpture thus reveals the disparity between the male artist's portrayal of woman and a woman's perception of herself. Mrs. Wendland believes herself betrayed, recognizing that Mengersen has been unable to accept her intellectual openness towards him as he would from a man, and that his representation of her expresses his sense of being threatened by her. As she explains: "I know that I am a thorn in Mr. Mengersen's side, even though he is so charming to me, because I am a real human being, live just as he lives and am as clever as he is" (96). In empathetic identification with Mrs. Wendland, the narrating voice expands on these words:

> She had given herself to him openly. She had offered him the pleasure of getting to know woman fully in her most exalted form, as she thought, sophisticated woman.
> She had been without reservation toward him, completely honest, in trust, as one great free human being to another—and he had recognized the animal in her—only the animal—the brute beast (99).

Mengersen's artistic representation of Mrs. Wendland is a means of reasserting his power over her, returning her to her "proper" place in the scheme of things. The incident illustrates both the distortion the idea of woman undergoes in such art and the male will to power it serves.

Mrs. Wendland describes men's disregard for women's minds and their reduction to what are essentially animal functions as an insult and injury: "For us women it is always mortifying, whether they are passionate towards us or cold" (104). The concept of such psychological diminution as an insult is strikingly close to that of Breuer and Freud; but unlike many of their patients, Mrs. Wendland does not bear the insult silently. A more damaging example of such a "mortification," however, is to be found in the later marriage between Mengersen and Isolde's sister Marie, who repeats the pattern of her mother's marriage. She bears child after child despite the danger to her own life and provides for her husband's need for an ordered existence, protecting him from the unpleasant practicalities of childcare and domestic chores. To him these are "such unpoetic things" (255), as Marie wryly puts it, bitter at being denied the small reward she desires: being able to share in his intellectual and creative life.

The Frey sisters, as their names suggest, are ascribed different fates although they reflect aspects of the same nexus of problems, illustrating the consequences of a cultural tradition in which women are both worshipped and despised. Their divergent characters are indicated in the opening chapter through the description of their bedroom: "One senses two souls in the one room. Two completely different souls with completely different habits" (9). Marie's bed is immaculately made and snowy white, the wall above decorated with family photos and bunches of dried flowers, while Isolde's bed is draped like an altar with a piece of rich purple silk damask, and on the wall are reproductions of old masters. While Marie follows the prescribed path of feminine virtue and self-denying motherhood, ending up despised and rejected as her mother was before her, Isolde, like her namesake, seems at first destined for a more literary fate: passionate love unto death.

Such a destiny seems foreshadowed in the opening scene of the novel, when Isolde, under cover of a rainstorm, snatches up a skull that has been excavated in front of her window. In this skull, which she places on a pedestal above her altar-like bed, she sees a resemblance to the features of Henry Mengersen. The reverence she pays it, "like a nun over a holy relic" (19), demonstrates her inchoate sexual desire and incipient passion for the artist. She equates the man with the images he creates, assuming that the nobility of the ideas expressed in his paintings must be manifestations of the life and person of the painter. In this state of innocent awareness and awakening desire, which she understands only as a longing to be transported out of her mundane world into a higher sphere, she meets the artist himself and in his studio sees again the etchings that had first stirred her desire for the self-sacrifice she saw as her female destiny.

Mengersen, observing her from a distance, is fascinated—despite his contempt for young innocents—by the grace of her young body, and exploits her unconscious desire to give herself sexually by asking her to model for him in the nude. Believing he would only ask such a thing if he loved her, she identifies his request as her moment of sacrifice; she presents herself to him like the "Meierstöchterlein" to the doctor in *Der arme Heinrich*, so that through her sacrifice her master might live. But her willingness elicits no penitence in Mengersen. The artist in him observes and is moved by the parallel, but the cynical rake in him sees only the artfulness of a young woman scheming to get her man. "A clever woman after prey is incredibly cunning," he thinks (170). And so his marriage choice falls on Marie, who fits his needs: "My future wife must be well-to-do, young, modest" (214). This betrayal precipitates Isolde's transition from childhood to womanhood. In a night of tortured reflection she comes to understand that as a woman she is destined to be a lesser being, without the right to be the autonomous subject of her own life. The narrative voice of experience anticipates, even as it describes Isolde's state of innocence, the fall into knowledge that will drive her to despair: "The stupid, dull, vile sense of being a woman did not cling to her yet, that feeling of being a creature of a lower order—a being that is not a human but a woman, a being that cannot feel and act like a human being, that is limited to its sexuality" (231 f.).

As she reflects on the notion of "woman," Isolde begins to fear that the contempt of men for women is deserved, being forced to acknowledge the apparent absence of a female contribution to knowledge and to accept it as proof of women's inferiority: "Everything that had ever been thought, was thought by a man; everything that had ever been done, was done by a man.... Women and animals have done nothing and thought nothing that anyone knows about" (234). For the first time she thinks of herself not as a person like all others but as a being defined primarily by her gender, and realizes that Henry Mengersen's disdain is not personal but directed at the entire female sex.

Thus the traditional story of seduction and rejection ends with the heroine's self-loathing; she accepts on behalf of her female kind the blame for her own condition. No longer just innocence betrayed, she is woman as martyr, displaying the bleeding wound of her sex.

> Her frail body was martyred by a deathly agitation.
> There she lay, kicked, abused, sullied, lonely, and belonged to the despised, dull, thoughtless half of humanity that does not have the right to be a complete human being.
> Then tears welled from her eyes, burning, painful tears that flowed like drops of blood from a wound (236).

At this point there is a caesura in the narrative. It resumes five years later to portray an Isolde apparently transformed, a seemingly mature woman who has pursued the Nietzschean path to a higher form of existence, having spent the intervening years leading an ascetically disciplined life.[12] She has worked to transcend the semi-animal destiny prescribed for her kind by becoming an artist of note whom even Henry Mengersen must respect. The latter part of the novel reads as an answer to the first. Isolde, a German "daughter of the better classes," now succeeds Mrs. Wendland, the foreigner, as central figure and as the model for "sophisticated woman" (99). While Mrs. Wendland was merely a patron of the arts, Isolde is herself an artist, better able to fulfill through striving Nietzsche's vision of the purpose of human life.[13] Isolde the artist attempts to redress the imbalance of history by making a significant female contribution to the arts.

The climax of the novel counterbalances Isolde's earlier night of despair with a second, but the roles are reversed: the former victim resists a renewal of that role and becomes avenger. Her despair arises this time from the loneliness of her existence both as woman and as artist. Lacking the knowledge of a great tradition of female art from which she can draw strength and inspiration as do her male colleagues, she is assailed by doubts about her ability to achieve her artistic aims: "But she is a woman! The dead, lifeless past of woman lay over her then like a dead, dark mass and weighed her down, suffocated her, and made every movement difficult" (341). The burgeoning new life of the spring growth in the garden outside her door increases her sense of estrangement from the world around her and she yearns for the intimacy and haven of a great love and the joy of a child to cherish. As she kneels prostrate in her despair, Henry Mengersen enters the open door, misinterprets her distress, and tries to force himself upon her in the arrogant assumption that he is what she needs. Desperately resisting his unwelcome advances, she kills him with the weapon he himself has provided for her self-defense.

Böhlau's account of this attempted rape cleverly controls the potential melodrama of the scene by contrasting Isolde's silent and desperate struggle with Mengersen's importunate and arrogant words. Initially paralyzed by horror, unable to act or to scream, Isolde suddenly reasserts herself and puts up a wild and determined resistance, pitting her will against her assailant's. Mengersen's language reveals that the images he employs in his art determine not only the world of his fantasy but his most instinctual drives and that the sexually evocative power of these images is at the same time mixed with the fear and hatred of the "other" embodied in a woman. In his upsurge of lust he names Isolde in turn "thoroughbred animal," "demon," "bacchant," "martyr," speaks of her "divine body," and calls her "silly darling" (347-48). The irreconcilable images of his art and his daily life can no longer be kept apart; their fusion precipitates an explosion of violence towards their object. The Nietzschean motif of the "animal of prey" recurs, but this time used for Mengersen himself: the image he had imposed on his sculpture of Mrs. Wendland has been but the projection of the fear of the uncontrollable in himself[14] that now breaks forth. But the attempted rape is also the ultimate violent attempt at subjection of the "other," the woman who has resisted his will and his control of her, most recently in his attempt to put an end to her rovings through the woods and countryside at will.

Isolde's only words during this struggle puncture Mengersen's inflated metaphors as she breaks free, grasps the revolver, and shoots him—"like a dog!" The narrative voice, closing the incident with the words "Isolde had shot her brother-in-law Henry Mengersen, *the great artist*" (349, my italics), significantly marks the murder as an act directed against an artist. Isolde, in shooting a rapist, also shoots "the originator of the fatal image of woman," as Sigrid Weigel wrote of a similar figure in Louise Aston's *Lydia*.[15] The difference in this case is, however, significant. While in Aston's novel it is not Lydia who acts to free herself—she remains passive throughout—in Böhlau's work the victim of the "mortification," the psychological injury, casts off her status as object and becomes subject by this act, usurping male power and domination by turning the gun on its owner.

Isolde's act of self-assertion overcomes the passivity inherent in women like her mother and Marie. She feels no guilt—"What she did is not worth mentioning"—for it is an act of retributive justice: "She has passed judgment" (351). Instead she feels purified, and the injury that had so wounded her self-esteem and defiled her innocence five years before can no longer threaten her well-being. She will not become one of Freud's hysterics. On the contrary, the murder leaves her feeling "healthy,—strong,—calm" (350). She restores not just a personal sense of right, for "she stands here by the dead man as the very idea of woman" (350). She avenges the injury done not only to herself but to womankind.

The ending of the novel remains problematic, however. The conflict between ideology and social realities on which the plot of the novel is built becomes a problem for the writer herself, reflected in the two very diverse writing styles she uses—one a naturalistic mode and the other a poetic style infused with the abstract thought of Schopenhauer and Nietzsche. The conclusion is an example of the latter. Its highly evocative imagery suggests a new beginning and a becoming, and Isolde walks off into the night in a state of exaltation, awaiting the new dawn. Isolde is presented as Nietzsche's redeeming being. Yet the reader knows that when the sun comes up she will shoot herself. What message is Böhlau leaving her readers? Is Isolde to fulfill the destiny of her namesake after all? Can she not break out of the myth associated with her name? Is her act of vengeful self-assertion an inimitable, because unliveable, model, murder being in the real world punishable by death? Or must she die, as Monika Shafi has suggested, because a woman's erotic desire is too great a challenge to the power of the patriarchy to be tolerated.[16] Certainly, Böhlau has left the reader in no doubt that she is aware of the social realities of her time; as I have argued above, the novel seems designed to point to the distance between artistic images of women and their lives and the reality experienced by the women of her day. Particularly in the latter part of the novel Böhlau points most emphatically to the contrast between them. But at the end the novelist seems caught between the desire to convey a perspective that offers her readers some optimism for the future and the need to find a resolution to the story that convinces in the context of the realistic world she has created, drawn on the world of her own present. I shall examine the second half of the novel more closely, paying attention to the interrupted chronology of the narrative, in order both to clarify the development of the figure of Isolde and to examine how Böhlau has attempted to harmonize her ideology and her portrayal of social realities.

The second half of the novel contains a sub-plot that tells in naturalistic mode the story of another seduction, one of the more common variety that illustrates the moral double standard. It is perpetrated by the heroine's brother Karl Frey. The spoiled son of a bourgeois family whose first sortie into drunkenness while yet a schoolboy is treated indulgently by his father as a rite of passage, he seduces a respectable shopgirl, abandoning her when she becomes pregnant. Without means to secure the professional help of a midwife, she dies in childbirth and is delivered to the hospital dissecting room where, amidst the ribald comments of medical students, the body is cursorily dissected, then tossed with the dead child into the cheapest of coffins. This sordid procedure is observed by Isolde, whose help the young woman has sought too late and who only belatedly discovers that her brother is responsible for the tragedy. While this subplot seems at first a digression from the main storyline, it actually plays a crucial part in the development of Isolde's thought.

The figure of Isolde as a matured and successful young artist at the beginning of the latter part of the novel is actually contradictory. Although she no longer confuses the man Mengersen with the artist, she does not question the content of his art and she needs him to admire her work. He is still the measure of a great artist for her. Further, despite her pity for her sister as his wife, the idea of womanly sacrifice is still central to her thinking, even though she senses that the notion of it she held as a fifteen-year-old is in some way inadequate: "The sacrifice must be even greater. More humane, more beautiful, more conscious," she thinks (264). The sacrifice should not be that of a victim of the social order, but that of a self-determined subject.

But confronted with the dead body of her brother's young mistress, sacrificed to society's double standard, she at last sees through the artistic idealization of childbearing. The image of the young woman on the dissecting table is the counter-image to the one in the etching that had seduced her as a fifteen-year-old. Here the sacrifice made in giving birth is demythologized, divested of the glory with which the artist Mengersen had endowed it in his picture. Isolde now sees only the humiliation to which the young woman is exposed, both alive and dead. Yet as she looks into the face of the dead woman lying on the dissection table she sees also

> Something victorious.
> Yes, something in woman has grown great—invincible, great through humiliation. In the midst of her stupid, foolish, primitive nature a strength has grown, the strength that grows through suffering, contempt, rejection.... But the holy countenance of woman, the imperturbable quality in this countenance was the inspiring thing—the life, the great hope (282).

Although she is the victim of social oppression and male contempt, condemned to an existence as the lowest of the low amongst the "herd animals," the face of this suffering woman is nevertheless not an expression of resignation or renunciation, but rather of an unbroken will. Recognizing this, Isolde comes to see that such a woman's fate as an object of men's whims and desires has not been decreed by nature, and that in the strength and will still evident in the dead woman's face lies the potential for woman to be the subject of her destiny. The process of total empathy with the young woman's suffering, which Brinker-Gabler analyzes in terms of the Schopenhauerian "Tat twam asi!" (2: 180), results in an active expression of Isolde's own will, paradoxically in a renewal of her willingness for personal sacrifice, but now as an acting subject. (The sense of renewal implicit in her resolve is literally reinforced by the same imagery of spring and new beginnings that later accompany her walk to her last dawn.) Her sacrifice is no longer to be offered to art; it is imbued with a fighting spirit of solidarity on behalf of those who suffer: "She went, her whole soul full of the love of the world, prepared to sacrifice herself—ready to take on the whole world with her own life" (283).

The retrospective narration in the chapter that follows this episode explains how the five preceding years have prepared her for this altered point of view. Her study of the great philosophers and thinkers has left her disillusioned; she has discovered that all of them have contributed to the debasement of women: "Wherever she looked she found humiliating insults" (289). Even Buddha, "the wonderful one, the deepest of the deep, the redeemer of the world, the surmounter of suffering" (290), to whose sculptured image she has given the noble features of her friend, the philosopher Helwig Geber, has been a bitter disappointment, in that he too unaccountably excluded women from his "kingdom of suffering and understanding of suffering" (290). Implicitly, she has turned away from the guidance of the philosophers who deny the importance of the individual will and self, in search of another, her own, way.

Her goal initially was to transform the concept of "woman" in her own person by achieving success as an artist. Now, having studied the face of female suffering, her deeper understanding of its nature and causes has granted her a new vision and a new direction for her art. Her artistic aim now is to create "the countenance of woman" (291). To do that she has had to break free of the influences of the male artistic tradition. Its accumulation of images of the feminine can be of no help in the articulation of her vision and experience as a woman. Guided by her adviser and friend, the philosopher Geber, she has learned that she must find her vision within: "Create your own world; it is as you create it. It is only in you, in your imagination" (333). While these words clearly draw on Schopenhauer, they can also be seen to direct her to believe in the validity of her own vision. But in the absence of a female tradition that might confirm her in that belief, her situation is lonely, as is the destiny of a genius according to both Schopenhauer and Nietzsche. Her loneliness leaves her vulnerable to doubt in her own vision and capacities as an artist. She fears that she will produce only mediocre work. Here too one hears an echo of Nietzsche: "The most disgusting, most unpleasant thing on earth is the mediocre" (336). And she doubts the efficacy of her visionary world, when beside her others create a counter-world: "'And so I created it for myself!' thought Isolde, 'such a fine world! And my nearest and dearest created for themselves the counter-image to my world. Thus the dreams of people go into battle against each other and destroy each other'" (335).

In her search for a means to overcome her isolation she attends a meeting of the women's movement of the day. But their way is to imitate the forms of male society, running their meeting with the formality of a session of parliament. They are depicted as a self-satisfied group of worthy women without vision or the courage for radical change, who debate instead petty issues such as whether a woman should use her husband's title or not. The voices at this gathering seem to Isolde "unworldly" (295), and the stuffy atmosphere of the room smells autumnally of dying leaves; the words and actions are far removed from the radicalism of Isolde's desire: "I exhort you to do something kingly, something free!... Let the deeds of woman bubble forth with abandon like a spring that has been long buried and constricted—do something that shows that you have the powerful will that overcomes the world" (297).

Although her words remain unspoken, perhaps because she has no faith that women such as these can themselves achieve such heights, Isolde sees a role for them in fostering the young. In her silent exhortation she begs them to spread their motherly wings and to provide a space in which the creativity of the young female spirit can thrive, not just through its procreative function but also through work:

> The will of the individual creates the world! Why not make a nest for the young woman in which she can grow into what she wants to be and must become when she is able to breathe freely with both lungs like a creature of God, and has both things, a child and work. And from this little nest will come a new strong humanity—in defiance of all those who want a human race of slaves and domestic animals (299).

The language here once again echoes that of Nietzsche, but inverts his vision of the conditions that will lead to an improved model of human existence. Whereas Nietzsche argues in *Beyond Good and Evil* that "woman, like a more delicate, strangely wild and often pleasant domestic animal, must be cared for, protected, and carefully treated" and that the slavelike status of woman is the "requirement of every higher culture, every heightening of culture" (6_2: 183), Isolde envisages *woman* as the new being, Nietzsche's *Übermensch,* who by exertion of the "will to power" will find self-transcendence. In such a woman, who is also the bearer of children, lies the promise of empowerment for a new generation as well.

As she seeks a concept of herself and her way as artist, Isolde applies the abstract theories of the philosophers to the concrete shape of her life as woman and as artist. Each is found wanting, shown to lead to a further entrapment in the prescribed female roles. But the path of sacrificial self-denial, in several modes, remains a temptation. Upon the death of her father, Isolde appears at first to succumb to the seduction of Schopenhauer's "denial of the will to life" as the means to "redemption" (Schopenhauer 1: 533). She experiences in her mother's response to the death of her husband, even more intensely than in the case of her brother's young mistress, the nature of the sacrifice expected of women. Moved by the selflessness of her mother's tolerance and forgiveness of her husband's lifelong mistreatment of her to an ecstasy of identification with her mother, she embraces once again the ideal of self-denial attached to the wifely role, echoing her girlish response to Mengersen's images: "There is nothing greater on earth than to be a woman!" (318). But the closing lines of the chapter reveal in the subjunctive mood of the verb a scepticism towards the validity of this way, as the strength she perceives in her mother has been buried, inhibited in its potential to contribute to social renewal: "She felt the strength of her poor mother as if such a strength, if it were to pour itself freely and consciously out over old, tired humanity, could redeem and rejuvenate it; the strength that had been submerged and buried in her inconspicuous, oppressed mother" (318).

The rejection of this path is reinforced by the account in the following chapter of the ultimate subjection of Marie—her potential other self—who gives up all aspirations to sharing in her husband's creative life, accepting his ruling that it is her role "to fulfill the animal functions in life" (329). Ironically, her mother, now released from the tyranny of her own husband, becomes herself an agent of repression. She admonishes Marie's tendency to rebelliousness and her lack of patience, complaining that she "was not so selfless as a woman should be" (321). To encourage her daughter to rebel would be to invalidate the sacrifice of her own life. The ironic observation, clearly from Isolde's perspective—"No, Mama had a lot of worries with Marie too"—and repeated in modified form a page later—"Ah yes, Mama didn't have it easy with her daughters" (322)—makes it clear that Isolde has seen through the mechanism of oppression and has distanced herself once more from this path to Schopenhauerian salvation through "denial of the will." Even the rewards of motherhood that Marie enjoys are shown to be no real substitute for the intellectual life she is denied. Although in Isolde's hour of despair she doubts the fullness of her life and longs for the bliss of the symbiotic relationship of mother and child, she has already recognized that Marie's devotion to her children has been the only available compensation for all her thwarted desires: "At this moment Marie's despised soul clung to her love for her children, and this love grew into an ecstasy that overlaid every torment of the heart" (331).

The Buddhistic model of selflessness suggested to her by her friend Geber—"Give up the 'self' and you have the 'universe'" (343)—is the more persuasive because in Geber she has found a friend who respects her intellect and the relationship between the Gebers as a couple seems to represent an enviable ideal of a loving partnership. Yet even in her longing for a haven, "an island of the blessed" (241), such as they share, she recalls the shadow of anxiety that often mars Lu Geber's happiness.

Lu, who as Brinker-Gabler suggests (2: 182) may be seen as yet another aspect of Isolde, fits the description Nietzsche gives in *Human, All too Human* of the nature of intellect in a woman. To Nietzsche, intellectual life is foreign to the nature of woman; she best shows her intellectual strength by offering her own intellect as a sacrifice out of love for a man and his intellect. In compensation, directed by his intellectual interests, another intellect will grow in its place.[17] In other words, intellect in a woman can only be an offshoot of the male intellect, never an autonomous expression of her own being. Lu's happiness and fulfillment in the love for her husband and child, for which Isolde so envies her, was described earlier in the novel by Mrs. Wendland as a cross covered with a thousand roses. This image combines both the positive and the negative aspects of Lu's love: within her marriage she blooms with happiness, but it is also a cross to be borne, for the role she has adopted is that of support to her husband, protecting him from everyday worries and the wearying attentions of his many disciples. Consequently, Lu has allowed her concern that her husband might not complete his great work to consume her own creative energies. That too is a path Isolde cannot accept. In her last encounter with Lu, Isolde begs her to devote less of herself to her husband, who is self-sufficient, and to think of her own work: "Lu, work! Work yourself to death if you like, Lu. Use up your energies in your work, but not in love and anxiety. Be an intellectual creature" (355). Isolde's vision is of a loving relationship in which the productivity of one partner does not depend on the self-sacrificing ministrations of the other, but which instead, in respecting the autonomy of each, enables both to realize their talents.

In defiance of what Nietzsche deemed appropriate for a woman, or perhaps exploiting contradictions in his work,[18] Böhlau not only has her heroine affirm the importance of work as a means of self-realization and reject all notions of self-sacrifice, she also appropriates Nietzsche's most famous image, that of the *Übermensch,* turning it to her own ends by switching the gender and giving it Isolde's shape. Böhlau portrays Isolde after her act of revenge as transformed, no longer one of the "herd animals," and at peace, now at one with nature: it is "the sacred hour in which the wakeful lonely human being is for once not a herd animal, but something great, a now quiet piece of nature only just throbbing with the peace of life" (349). The death Isolde chooses and gladly embraces *is* a sacrificial death, one she believes symbolically necessary in order to break the pattern of willing self-subjugation. But in terms of Nietzsche's philosophy of "the eternal recurrence," she will return. And while Nietzsche does not assume that such a return will be to a better world, for Böhlau that hope exists. Isolde will return strong and powerful:

> Yes, she wanted to return—and she had to return. That was her firm, strong will, her sacred resolve.
> There existed here a world of dull, stupid, feeble souls, semi-animal souls! She wanted to sleep a deep sleep of death that would harden her powers; then she wanted to return, strong and pure and good—and powerful—capable of everything and with the power to redeem (360).

Whereas in her earlier despair Isolde had fallen on her knees, arms thrown out like the crucified Christ, she now stands as Nietzsche's redeeming being in female form, "unshakeable, mistress over life and death" (360).

To readers today, Isolde's sacrificial death in the name of suffering womankind may seem unsatisfactory and, as Gisela Brinker-Gabler has commented (2: 181), her elevation to the status of *Übermensch* perhaps implies a loss of solidarity with others of her sex who are condemned to remain "herd animals." Further, the novel leaves unresolved the tension between Isolde's desire for sexual fulfillment and the need to achieve selfhood through the lonely work of the creative artist. Perhaps limited by her own experience of marriage to a much older man, the one image of matrimonial bliss Böhlau creates is one of spiritual rather than physical union. Lu's love for Helwig is described as "naively maternal," full of "glowing warmth" (260), while his ideal is a "redeemed love" that is "itself cool, yet warming everything" (354). That is something other than what Isolde dreams of when, in the confidence born of her remaking of herself through her work, she feels "now she could love" (263). At this point, immediately prior to the shock of seeing the tragedy of her brother's abandoned mistress, it seems to her that work alone, without love, is insufficient: "A working woman without love! Oh, no! She smiled. No, she wanted to have all of life, all of it, full to the brim" (263). But events push her not to the harmonious integration of personal happiness and creative work but to her avenging act on behalf of womankind. Transcendence rather than fulfillment of desire is the solution Böhlau finds for the paradox of her situation. Yet the optimistic tone of the ending rests not just on the transcendental assumption of a rebirth: Isolde's alter ego Lu may, if she can follow Isolde's advice, achieve the autonomy that will allow her to fulfill all a woman's needs—physical, emotional, and intellectual—through self-fulfillment in a loving relationship, through motherhood, and through creative work.

Nietzsche, when writing of his vision of a redeeming being in *The Genealogy of Morals,* spoke in the words quoted at the opening of this essay of his function to release us from the hitherto existing ideal. Böhlau in *Halbtier!* deconstructs the prevailing ideal of woman in the arts, rejecting its inherent repressive implications for women. In its place she creates a new image, still an ideal, but one that makes apparent the inner conflicts of a woman who is striving for an autonomous existence.

Notes

[1] All translations of primary and secondary literature are my own, unless otherwise stated.

[2] Bäumer sees in Böhlau's heroine Isolde the "intellectually and sensually over-stimulated 'modern woman' [Frau] who ultimately sees only the semi-animal in woman [Weib]" (393).

[3] Shapire, for whom the answer to the oppression of women is to be found in their economic independence through a career, commends Böhlau's abilities as a writer but finds fault with her theoretical analysis.

[4] Brinker-Gabler's discussion of *Halbtier!* demonstrates in particular Böhlau's use of Schopenhauerian philosophy and how she integrates it with that of Nietzsche (2: 179–81).

[5] This suggestion is consciously tentative, since I have no direct knowledge of whether Böhlau actually knew their work *Studien über Hysterie,* which appeared four years earlier.

[6] Evidence for the paucity of girls' education can be found both in journalistic articles such as Amely Bölte's "Die höhere Töchterschule" and in literary works such as Hedwig Dohm's novel *Schicksale einer Seele,* which also appeared in 1899.

[7] Günter Häntzschel writes of the lives of upper middle class women whose domestic duties were declining as a consequence of new technological aids in the household: "Tied to the private sphere, and as a rule excluded from professional employment, they derive little stimulation or opportunity for self-development from the relatively great potential of their spare time. Their intellectual capacities must often wither and the awakening of interests in new areas of activity is impeded as a consequence of the monotony of their everyday lifestyle" (9).

[8] "The 'tale of suffering,' which follows from the silently borne 'mortification,' leads to what [Freud] calls the 'female wound.' This wound, the narcissistic injury of the woman is however, Freud assumes, incurable. It has to be borne as a biological imperative if the woman wants to measure up to the feminine ideal" (Gerhardt 13).

[9] Böhlau is clearly thinking of popular weekly papers such as *Die Gartenlaube*. For a discussion of the notions of femininity that magazine presented to its female readers see Kirsten Belgum's article in *Women in German Yearbook 9*.

[10] The Nietzschean vocabulary is present in the novel from the start: on the second page the passers-by on the streets of Munich are referred to as "herd animals," a motif elaborated on later by Isolde who with despairing insight accuses people in general of crawling on all fours, women, in particular her mother and sister, of creeping on their stomachs, and men as generally "philistine, hypocritical directors of institutes" on whose shiny top-hats she would like to spit (32).

[11] "What inspires respect for woman, and often enough even fear, is her *nature,* which is more 'natural' than man's, the genuine, cunning suppleness of a beast of prey, the tiger's claw under the glove, the naïveté of her egoism, her uneducability and inner wildness, the incomprehensibility, scope, and movement of her desires and virtues—" (Nietzsche 6_2: 184; Kaufmann 169).

[12] "Asceticism and puritanism are almost indispensable means for educating and ennobling a race that wishes to become master over its origins among the rabble and that works its way up toward future rule" (Nietzsche, *Beyond Good and Evil* 6_2: 78).

[13] "Our nature is to create a higher being than we are ourselves. To transcend ourselves in creation! That is the drive of procreation, that is the drive of deeds and works.—Just as all desiring postulates a purpose, so too a human being postulates a being that is not there, but which supplies the purpose of his existence" (Nietzsche 7_1: 213).

[14] Such a relationship between the artist and his work is described by Sigrid Weigel, writing of male authors: "As he fashions ideal, or alternatively dread-inspiring female figures in his text, the author can project on to them his wishes and anxieties with respect to the female" (*Topographien* 244).

[15] Weigel wrote these words about the perpetrator of a cruel experiment—the perverse prolonging of his wife's "innocence" by not consummating the marriage—who eventually repents and commits suicide, enabling the restoration of Lydia to health and sanity ("Der schielende Blick" 100).

[16] "An autonomous female sexuality is among the strongest challenges to patriarchal rule, so that even the erotic wish must be 'punished.' Isolde shoots Mengersen and will choose suicide" (Schafi 74).

[17] "The spiritual power [geistige Kraft] of a woman is best demonstrated by her sacrificing her own spirit to that of a man out of love of him and of his spirit but then, despite this sacrifice, immediately evolving *a new spirit* within the new domain, originally alien to her nature, to which the man's disposition impels her" (Nietzsche 4_3: 130).

[18] Brinker-Gabler points to a passage in which Nietzsche contemplates the possibility of the existence of "women with lofty, heroic, kingly souls" (Brinker-Gabler 2: 557).

Works Cited

Bäumer, Gertrud. "Die psychischen Probleme der Gegenwart und die Frauenbewegung." *Die Frau* 7.7 (April 1900): 385-95.

Belgum, Kirsten. "Domesticating the Reader: Women and the *Gartenlaube*." *Women in German Yearbook 9*. Ed. Jeanette Clausen and Sara Friedrichsmeyer. Lincoln: U of Nebraska P, 1994. 91-111.

Böhlau, Helene. *Halbtier!* Berlin: F. Fontane, 1899.

Bölte, Amely. "Die höhere Töchterschule." Häntzschel. 118-21.

Brinker-Gabler, Gisela. "Zwischen Tradition und Moderne: Literatur, Publizistik und Wertwandel im frühen 20. Jahrhundert." *Deutsche Literatur von Frauen*. Ed. Gisela Brinker-Gabler. 2 vols. München: Beck, 1988. 2: 169-205.

Dohm, Hedwig. *Schicksale einer Seele*. 1899. München: Frauenoffensive, 1988.

Freud, Sigmund, and Josef Breuer. *Studies on Hysteria*. 1895. Trans. James Strachey. London: Hogarth, 1955. Vol. 2 of *The Standard Edition of the Complete Psychological Works of Sigmund Freud*. 24 vols. 1949-74.

Gerhardt, Marlis. *Kein bürgerlicher Stern, nichts, nichts konnte mich je beschwichtigen: Essay zur Kränkung der Frau*. Neuwied: Luchterhand, 1982.

Häntzschel, Günter, ed. *Bildung und Kultur bürgerlicher Frauen 1850-1918: Eine Quellendokumentation aus Anstandsbüchern und Lebenshilfen für Mädchen und Frauen als Beitrag zur weiblichen literarischen Sozialisation*. Tübingen: Niemeyer, 1986.

Hecht, Marie. "Friedrich Nietzsches Einfluß auf die Frauen." *Die Frau* 6.8 (May 1899): 486-91.

Das litterarische Echo 4 (1901-02): 1120.

Nietzsche, Friedrich. *Beyond Good and Evil: Prelude to a Philosophy of the Future*. Trans. Walter Kaufmann. New York: Vintage, 1966.

———. *Human, All too Human: A Book for Free Spirits*. Trans. R.J. Hollingdale. Cambridge: Cambridge UP, 1986.

———. *Werke: Kritische Gesamtausgabe*. Ed. Giorgio Colli and Mazzino Montinari. Berlin: de Gruyter, 1967-1977.

Schapire, Anna. "Halbthier!" *Die neue Zeit* 18.1 (1900): 627-31.

Schopenhauer, Arthur. *Sämtliche Werke*. Ed. Wolfgang Frhr. von Löhneysen. 5 vols. Stuttgart: Cotta-Insel, 1960-76.

Shafi, Monika. "'Werde, der du bist': Eine vergleichende Darstellung des weiblichen Autonomiekonflikts in Theodor Fontanes *Frau Jenny Treibel* und Helene Böhlaus *Das Halbtier* [sic]." *German Quarterly* 61.1 (Winter 1988): 67-77.

Showalter, Elaine. *The Female Malady: Women, Madness and English Culture, 1830-1980*. 1985. London: Virago, 1987.

Weigel, Sigrid. "Der schielende Blick." *Die verborgene Frau*. Ed. Inge Stephan and Sigrid Weigel. Berlin: Argument, 1988. 83-137.

———. *Topographien der Geschlechter: Kulturgeschichtliche Studien zur Literatur*. Reinbek bei Hamburg: Rowohlt, 1990.

Vicki Baum and the "Making" of Popular Success: "Mass" Culture or "Popular" Culture?

Lynda J. King

This study examines the reasons for international literary star Vicki Baum's immense success. After first detailing the promotion of Baum and her works and briefly analyzing her 1928-29 novel *stud. chem. Helene Willfüer,* the study contends that advertising and writing for the marketplace were prerequisites to success, but did not ensure that she or her works would indeed become bestsellers. Based on theories of "popular" rather than "mass" culture, it goes on to explore the delicate and complicated balance of power between producers and consumers that leads to popular success. (LJK)

Vicki Baum: For many Germans born at the beginning of this century, hers is a name synonymous with the myth of the hectic, exciting life of Weimar-era Berlin. Her star status is reflected in a story about a prostitute who conned a man out of an evening's entertainment—and his wallet—by convincing him she was the famous Vicki Baum. As her contemporary Joe Lederer noted: "Well, it might have often happened before that a lady of the night passed herself off as an actress or an artiste—but as a writer? For that to happen you had to be as popular as Vicki Baum." Through the international success of her 1929 novel *Menschen im Hotel* (English: *Grand Hotel*), Baum's fame soon extended beyond Germany's borders as she became one of the few German-language writers to command world-wide acclaim. After having gone to Hollywood to write the screenplay for *Grand Hotel,* the film based on the novel, she decided to remain in California and became a well-known personality in the USA, too. While the star of this "prima donna of entertainment literature" (D.S.) rose outside Germany, her works were banned in the Third Reich, and it was not until after World War II that Germans could once more thrill to a Baum novel. She died in Southern California in 1960, but her books continue to appear in the USA, Germany, and other countries. *Grand Hotel* especially has retained its audience appeal; when reviewing the 1991 Berlin premiere of *Grand Hotel: Das Musical,* Klaus Geitel wrote in *Die Welt* that this story had become a cult object comparable to *Casablanca,* "a piece of big city mythology."

Baum's success has always been an important factor in German-language critical and scholarly response to her works. In the early 1920s, when she was not writing for the marketplace, critics were well disposed to her works, but after her bestseller *stud. chem. Helene Willfüer* (1928–29), opinions began to diverge, and the success of *Menschen im Hotel* prompted some critics to attack not her writing but the fact of her success (King, "Image"). Directly after World War II, when her works were reintroduced in Germany, most scholars ignored her, but after the serious study of "Trivialliteratur" began in the 1960s, they increasingly identified her with this type of writing.[1] Since the late 1970s, the prevailing attitude toward Baum has begun to shift. Some scholars have continued to analyze her works as examples of "Trivialliteratur" (Holzner), but most recent scholarship has focused on the topicality of her novels and her relationship to her synchronic literary community.[2] In addition, studies of German-speaking exiles in the USA have often incorporated articles on Baum (Bell, Ziegfeld).

This study examines the reasons for Vicki Baum's stellar rise and the success of her works, opening with arguments I first proposed in *Bestsellers by Design: Vicki Baum and the House of Ullstein,* then advancing an expanded explanation based on theories of popular culture. In the first section, I will summarize the partnership between Baum and her publisher, Ullstein, whose goal was to make Baum and her novels into bestsellers by interweaving its promotion of Baum herself with the promotion of *stud. chem. Helene Willfüer,* both of which revolved around the image of the 1920s New Woman. Next I will briefly analyze *stud. chem. Helene Willfüer* and its role in Baum's popularity. I will argue that, although the promotion and the text were expertly conceived and were prerequisites to success, advertising and writing for the marketplace did not guarantee that Baum or her book would indeed become bestsellers. Basing my arguments on recent theories that foreground "popular" as opposed to "mass" culture, I will assert that Baum and Ullstein could not completely control or manipulate consumers because popular success in an industrial society is based on a delicate and complicated balance of power between producers and consumers. In this power dynamic, producers use all the tools they have to attempt to control their products and the consumers who buy them, but consumers can assert their power by using the products for their own, rather than the producers' purposes. Doing so, however, undermines the efforts of producers at control and can ultimately subvert the underlying messages they might hope to communicate to consumers through their products.

Literature and the Marketplace in Weimar Germany

On 27 March 1929 Werner Mahrholz wrote in the *Vossische Zeitung*: "Let's not fool ourselves. The epoch of a purely literary culture mainly defined by books is over," and thus echoed the sentiments of those in the Weimar literary establishment who feared that traditional German culture was seriously, even terminally ill.[3] In the financially difficult times of the 1920s, they worried that the book would have to be transformed into a commodity produced, manufactured, and promoted for the marketplace if it were to compete with the products of the rapidly expanding entertainment industry. While some worried, others reevaluated their societal role and consciously chose to write for the literary marketplace. Writers like Robert and Alfred Neumann, Bruno Frank, Fallada, Roth, Feuchtwanger, Kesten, Kästner, Remarque, and Vicki Baum strove to combine high quality with a form accessible to the general reading public; the literature they created was intended as an exchange between the writer and the public (Hermand and Trommler 152-64).

To reach the public, these writers needed publishers willing and able to produce large numbers of their works, then market and distribute them to the potential audience. By the 1920s there were several publishing giants in Germany with the necessary know-how and capacity, among them Hugenberg, Mosse, Huck, and foremost Ullstein.[4] From its beginnings as a paper business in 1848 to its heyday in the late 1920s, the Ullstein company grew until it controlled the materials, technical and editorial production, sales, advertising, and distribution of a myriad of products. A linchpin of Ullstein's success was advertising and promotion, and Hermann Ullstein, the youngest of four brothers who owned the company, strove to make their business a modern, American-style enterprise firmly committed to advertising. Ullstein's genius for publicity and flair for success are nowhere more evident than in his company's partnership with Vicki Baum.

The Baum-Ullstein Partnership: The Promotional Campaign

The promotion of their new "property" testifies to Ullstein's instinctive understanding of a method that still is a given in the attempts of publishers to create bestsellers today: not only is the work promoted, but the image of the artist is also molded to suit the place chosen for her in the company's master plan *and* to suit the times.[5] The coordinated campaign that publicized Vicki Baum revolved around the New Woman, the 1920s version of the liberated woman, a topic of debate throughout the decade. As an intelligent, attractive woman with a career and a life out of the ordinary, Baum seemed the ideal candidate to be promoted as a New Woman, and efforts dedicated to establishing her image as such were orchestrated to dovetail with the publication of *stud. chem. Helene*

Willfüer, which Baum wrote at Hermann Ullstein's behest, spotlighting as its protagonist—a New Woman.

Ullstein's campaign to make Baum's name a household word had several facets, each fashioned to reinforce the other. First, Baum's physical appearance had to be adjusted to suit the image of the New Woman. On 24 April 1926, shortly after she joined the company, a small, dark photo of Baum printed in the *Berliner Illustrirte* (sic), Ullstein's mass circulation weekly, reveals her look before the campaign. This Vicki Baum is attractive, but soft and old-fashioned: her dark-brown hair is parted in the middle and coiffured with little attention to style, she smiles slightly, her soft, dark eyes predominate, and she wears a high-collared, lacy blouse. A year later she has been transformed. One Ullstein photo portrays a glamorous Baum in profile, her chin high in the air, with blond, stylish hair and perfect makeup, long jeweled earrings, pearl necklace, and an elegant, low-cut evening gown. Another feature of her new image is disclosed in the photograph that appeared with a short biography accompanying the last installment of *Helene* on 3 January 1929, when the release in book form was also announced. In the center sits Baum, with blond, bobbed hair, playing with her sons—but no husband in sight. This is Baum the New Woman as mother, taking time out from her busy career for her children. The photo thus meshed the "real" New Woman Baum with the fictional Helene, the single mother and successful career woman who finally has time to play with her son.

Another part of the Ullstein promotional campaign entailed assigning Baum to write articles that directly or indirectly fostered her image as an up-to-date and "serious" writer. One frequently printed photo of a trustworthy-looking Baum gazing at an abacus was captioned "Vicky Baum busies herself with the theory of relativity for her new Ullstein novel"; this photo was even caricatured on 4 January 1929 in the *Literarische Welt*. Another example was the article "Erfahrungen mit der Verjüngung" ("Experiences with Rejuvenation"), a popular explanation of scientific experiments on human rejuvenation through chemicals, complete with formulas. This piece confirmed that Baum researched her topics and thus was an authority on them, not just a writer of worthless kitsch who invented everything; it also performed as advance publicity for *Helene,* which also dealt with a rejuvenation drug. Because the promoters supposed that the novel's success depended at least in part on her audiences' belief that what Baum wrote was authentic and that her New Woman was "real," credibility was essential. In direct print advertising, the emphasis on authenticity continued. The key phrase in almost all the advertisements was "a young girl of our time," and personal testimony, which was supposedly sent to the publishers from those involved in the issues spotlighted in the novel, was often quoted. One example, which appeared in ads in several newspapers on 3 March 1929, was from a real "girl of the times," who, it was claimed, wrote to Baum: "You feel what we are grappling for, what we are struggling for...." (*Kölnische Zeitung, Berliner Tageblatt*).[6]

stud. chem. Helene Willfüer: The Successful Text

In all her writing, Baum did everything she could to produce a text that would appeal and thus sell to her target audience. In *stud. chem. Helene Willfüer*, she did that by mixing the tried and true elements of the romance novel with realistic and even gripping scenes of women's lives. In the opening pages, readers are introduced to Helene and Professor Ambrosius, her mentor despite his resistance to women's studying at university. During this chance meeting, Helene does not realize, but readers must, that she loves the professor. Through this story line, Baum keeps with the tradition of the romance novel, in which one of the sources of readers' delight—and comfort—is waiting for that moment they know must arrive when the heroine and her true love come together in the happy end.[7] Yet as appealing as the romance framework was to many readers, it alone would not have made the book the sensation it became among diverse readers. The sensation came from the challenges and hardships Helene experiences between this meeting and her romantic alliance with Ambrosius at the end.

Baum portrays Helene's difficult life with the mixture of sensationalism and sensitivity, fantasy and realism characteristic of all her works. Helene is a female chemistry student who must constantly prove herself in a male world, and her life becomes even more difficult when she becomes pregnant. Upon discovering her condition, she finds the idea of getting a Ph.D. and having a child "grotesque" (126), so she decides on an abortion. Her visit to the abortionist's "office" begins Helene's quest to regain power over her life, and the author's account of it maps the road unmarried pregnant women who sought an abortion were forced to take at the time. The novel now veers away from romance toward remarkable realism—or sensationalism, depending on one's perspective. For example, in a chilling scene, the abortionist "examines" Helene on a couch with a "greasy red" covering. In the face of his advances toward her, Helene flees in horror, "as if she had come directly from hell; but from now to the end of her life Herr Rauner would wander like a ghost through her nightmares, approaching her naked body with gnarled fingers and watery eyes" (128). Later Helene seeks sympathy from a female physician, Dr. Gropius, who only explains that she can go to one of the free homes for expectant mothers in Frankfurt and then continues: "Thank goodness, in the last few years we have managed to see to it that unmarried mothers have gained social rights" (135). When Helene confesses the actual reason for her visit, Dr. Gropius replies that it is wrong to deny responsibility for a child. If it were up to her, things would be different:

> Long ago a welfare institution would have been established to regulate child bearing. But we have a long way to go before that happens. And we have our ominous statutes.... Can you really ask me to put myself in danger of imprisonment, to put my whole existence on the line? (136-37)

A sympathetic midwife who also refuses to perform an abortion remarks that only quacks can help Helene, adding: "Idiotic law, idiotic state of affairs" (139). Finally, Helene turns to another unsavory abortionist, where she hears frightful groaning, as if someone were being tortured; when she hears this sound, she can only think of flowing blood (142). Only chance saves her from a similar fate.

Although the pregnancy and Helene's attempt to end it could be considered sensational or melodramatic, they are not out of place in a novel about women in Weimar Germany. With insufficient information on contraception and more open sexuality than in the past, at least in the urban environment, pregnancies among single women were not uncommon, and what to do about them was among the era's most vehemently debated issues.[8] Baum's own position was closest to Dr. Gropius's: she did not advocate abortion, but a regulated solution to illegitimacy.[9]

After the realistic depiction of Helene's pregnancy and her life as a single mother, the novel takes several melodramatic turns of plot. After reintroducing the smoldering romance with Ambrosius, Baum presents readers with a utopian vision of the possibilities that might be open to women in the future. Thanks to Ambrosius's intervention, Helene lands a new position with an aging chemist searching for a rejuvenation drug. All the members of the project live and work in an isolated house, and this secluded location enables her to raise her son in an extended family of unprejudiced scientists and their devoted servants, a utopian arrangement compared to the options available to most single mothers at the time. The utopian vision continues when Helene gains the rights to the wonder drug they invent and markets it herself, in effect selling her intellectual product in the same way Baum sold hers. A parallel to Baum's own negotiations with the important men of Ullstein is suggested by a scene in which Helene wheels and deals with the leaders of a large chemical concern (Baum, *Es war* 368-69). But whereas Baum admitted to being very nervous during her own negotiations, her heroine gives a cool performance, "as if she had never been accustomed to anything else" (268), demanding and getting everything she wants, including a percentage of the profits: "Success. Success. Made it. Made it. Made it.... And sitting all alone in the car she suddenly lets out a long suppressed cry, a single, high call of victory...(282)." Helene has been rewarded for her hard work in a way that was improbable for the 1920s—but not impossible. Indeed, Vicki Baum herself was evidence that such a triumph *was* possible.[10]

But Baum did not—and could not, given the romantic novel setting—close the novel on this note, for the romance was yet to flower. In a final chance meeting, Helene and Ambrosius recognize their affection for each other, and she acquiesces to his plea that they live and work together, with the implication that she will leave her position to dedicate herself to him and his work. Marriage is not mentioned. By now, however, an important change has taken place, for her beloved has been transformed from a man who was at the novel's outset both an all-powerful father figure and a sexually attractive potential lover—and thus disturbing for Helene. Now he is a still fatherly but considerably diminished, partially blind man who wants a partner in his work, someone to take care of him, and a lover who will not enrage him like his sexually threatening ex-wife. In the romance tradition, Helene can now accept him, for his combination of disturbing sexuality and fatherliness is gone.

The last installment of *Helene* ran in January 1929. People from all professions and classes had read the novel; during its run, the circulation of the *Berliner Illustrirte* exceeded two million. Reviewers wrote that it came "directly out of the present" (*Neue Freie Presse*), that its heroine was "a young girl of our time" (Kaus, Wolff) or a "a modern girl" who stood "squarely in the middle of life" (Arna), that it had caused "an uproar" (Walter). The reviewer for *Germania* even contended that "every stenotypist, the bank apprentice, the state functionary, the housewife, the maid, the female secondary-school teacher, young people" had read this novel (Becher). Most reviewers linked to the women's rights movement praised its positive portrayal of women's issues as well as its capacity to stimulate discussion about the New Woman and to supply a much-needed positive model for women; they largely ignored or downplayed the romance elements. Even when reproaching what they felt was a disappointing ending, as Gabriele Reuter did, critics nonetheless concluded that the merits of the novel outweighed its negative aspects.[11]

Baum, Ullstein, and *Helene*: Success as "Mass" Culture or "Popular" Culture?

Helene was a success. But do Baum's and Ullstein's efforts alone explain why so many bought and read the novel? A clever, manipulative campaign, a woman willing to change herself to suit the campaign and able to supply a text with up-to-the-latest-minute topics portrayed in a way that was alternately realistic, sensational, or utopian? Were Ullstein and Baum simply very good at mixing up the "formula" for making best-sellers? And another, perhaps even more important question, do those who try to produce commercial success like Ullstein and Baum have a covert ideological goal? Is this goal the supplying of soothing entertainment to divert consumers from thinking about the ills of society and thus keep them from working to change the status quo? For many twentieth-century intellectuals, the only possible answer to these questions was yes. These intellectuals, strongly identified with men like Theodor W. Adorno and Max Horkheimer, have mostly explained commercial success with references to "mass culture." They have charged that the culture industry manufactures uniform and predictable products in a rigidly controlled production process and manipulates consumers into buying "worthless" products. The goals are profit and maintaining the exploitative capitalist society; as Herbert Marcuse explained: "The products indoctrinate and manipulate; they promote a false consciousness which is immune against its falsehood..." (26–27). Indoctrinated in this way, consumers suffer from stunted political imagination (Storey 102). Thus mass culture, to use the words of popular culture advocate John Fiske, is said to be "imposed upon a powerless and passive people by a culture industry" to produce "a quiescent, passive mass of people, an agglomeration of atomized individuals" (*Understanding* 20). Central is the concept of a monolithic, mechanistic dominant culture of capitalism working single-mindedly to sell its products. In "The Culture Industry: Enlightenment as Mass Deception" Adorno and Horkheimer asserted that the products of the industry "make up a system which is uniform as a whole and in every part." They believed in an "agreement—or at least the determination—of all executive authorities not to produce or sanction anything that in any way differs from their own rules, their own ideas about consumers, or above all, themselves" (122).

For intellectuals who see themselves as representatives, even preservers, of high, autonomous culture against the onslaught of this other culture, such an explanation is seductive. But it can and has been challenged in several ways. For one thing, the reality of the entertainment business does not substantiate these critics' estimation of its power. Recent research has proved that infallible formulas for extreme success do not exist: estimates place the failure rate of new entertainment products as high as 80–90% (Fiske, *Understanding* 31; Frith 147). The entertainment industry is actually characterized by extreme tension between the desire for control, which aims at maximizing predictability of sales, and the uncertainty resulting from the need for novelty and innovation. Novelty and innovation are needed, the industry believes, because of the notorious fickleness of consumers (Jarvie 40; Lewis 32; Cosner et al. 23).

The notion of the single-minded, uniform, and highly controlled production of the culture industry so central to the arguments of mass culture critics has also been contested, and the Baum/Ullstein story provides another example of a striking lack of uniformity. In fact, even within the Ullstein organization itself, the word "uniform" hardly applies. For instance, the family's business interests often clashed with their democratic, egalitarian position on political and social issues and their support of a republican form of government, both in the days of the Empire and during the Weimar Republic. The Ullstein brothers backed the left-liberal German Democratic Party, throwing their support behind progressive causes through their influential newspaper *Die Vossische Zeitung*. Hermann Ullstein went further, buying his own newspaper in Leipzig to voice his more liberal views. While they undeniably believed in capitalism, they also felt responsible to their employees, offering them benefits not available to many of their contemporaries. One observer, Arthur Koestler, wrote that "their motto was political liberalism and modern culture. They were anti-militaristic and anti-chauvinistic and in the best sense European" (Schwab-Felisch 214–15). On the other hand, despite the clear political viewpoint expressed in the *Vossische Zeitung*, in Ullstein's mass-circulated products like the *Berliner Illustrirte Zeitung*, entertainment was emphasized and overt political messages downplayed for commercial reasons. Overall the *BIZ* tended toward "an honest belief in progress" (Luft 10), but the company still published works by more or less reactionary authors. After it had been taken over by Nazis, Hermann Ullstein recognized that his family's company, like other democratic publishers of the Weimar Republic, had underestimated the danger and not fought hard enough to resist the far right (Ullstein 197–217).

But despite their naivete in dealing with the right-wing danger, neither the Ullstein company nor the family can be justly accused of having worked with the other publishing giants of the Weimar era in a "cabal of executive authorities," to use Collins's version of Adorno's and Horkheimer's phrase (10). Such a cabal would have necessitated collusion between companies with diametrically opposed political philosophies, like Alfred Hugenberg's concern, which openly championed right-wing and even anti-democratic causes.[12] Moreover, Ullstein's publication of *Helene* and its hiring of Baum did not fit into a capitalist master plan. Printing this positive portrayal of a New Woman with its sympathetic stance on premarital sex and progressive views on abortion, single motherhood, and women's higher education was one way to sell magazines and books, but it was also risky. As Richard Dyer notes, "...to draw attention to the gap between what is and what could be, is, ideologically speaking, playing with fire" (25–26). Hiring Baum at a high salary for a relatively influential position was also risky. Certainly it would help business in the short term, but making her into a well-known personality and giving her the resources and power to become financially and socially liberated—a real New Woman—could also have paved the way for greater social change by creating a female role model for other women of the era.

Baum as producer does not fit easily into the mass culture critics' idea of uniformity, either. Perceiving herself as a "first class writer of the second rank" (Baum, *Es war* 405), she freely admitted that she wrote to earn money (404), but she also contended that she did good research and did not cut corners or try to trick her readers, whom she respected and never spoke down to (387). She believed she understood and felt the pulse of Germany in the late 1920s and could capture it on paper in a way that readers recognized as authentic. Her role was that of mediator, an "impartial observer," who because of her talent could put into words what others felt, the real life of real people (57). In this quest to combine earning money within the capitalist system, portraying the pulse of the times realistically, *and* entertaining a broad audience, Baum set herself a difficult task. As John Storey points out, using the example of rock musicians in 1960s West Coast counterculture, those who try to use commercial forms within the dominant culture system for system-contrary messages face a difficult predicament.[13]

Because of this quandary, the product created by such artists—or commercial craftspersons—is often contradictory, and Baum's *Helene* is no exception. Her covert criticism of existing laws, clear support of regulations to ensure the rights of unmarried mothers, and suggestion that such institutions as homes for expectant mothers should be available to all women were progressive ideas, probably similar to those held by many liberal-minded Weimar citizens. Probably motivated by Baum's own trust in the existing social system which had offered *her* the opportunity for success, Helene's victory over hardship and discrimination is offered as a positive model for individual women, a utopian hope for an emancipation gained not by political movements but by each woman's hard work.[14] Baum also makes the New Woman more acceptable and less threatening by placing Helene between the two extremes of "liberated" female behavior represented by her intellectual roommate and the *femme fatale* wife of Ambrosius. Thus her portrayal of Helene is progressive but hardly revolutionary. Baum stopped short of any precise demands for systemic changes that would force the "idiotic laws" to be altered.[15] Still, the potential influence of even her mild form of criticism on her readers in the 1920s should not be underestimated. Progressive thinking may have dominated the urbane Berlin world of "liberal intellectualism" (Baum, *Es war* 370), and her attitude may seem tame today, but in other urban circles and in the conservative provinces where the *BIZ* was widely circulated, it may well have appeared radical. Because of the magazine's huge readership, more people likely read *Helene* than most of the "serious" works addressing abortion or other "women's issues"; thus this novel's message could have had an impact on public opinion.[16] Then again, the romance framework seems to contradict even her mild version of liberation. This framework was necessary exactly because she had to remain part of the existing social system—represented by the place in which her novel was published, the mass-circulation magazine—within which her personal prosperity was evolving. From the mass culture perspective, we can speculate that the romantic framework could have negated the novel's positive message; in the light of recent theories that move away from the mass culture viewpoint to stress the consumers' role in the creation of success, however, we can equally well speculate that it did not.

Such research has focused on the type of contradictions evident in the messages that Ullstein and Baum conveyed—consciously or not—to consumers. Stressing the profit motive, Terry Lovell, for example, argues that individual capitalists will produce cultural commodities that challenge or even subvert the dominant ideology if doing so means additional profits for these individuals (61). Another view is posited by Dyer, who maintains that entertainment firms run the risk of revealing the gap between what is and what could be; the popular product has to "work through these contradictions at all levels in such a way as to 'manage' them, to make them seem to disappear. They don't always succeed" (26). He believes that entertainment does sometimes point to gaps or inadequacies in capitalism, "but only those...that capitalism proposes itself to deal with" and that "entertainment provides alternatives *to* capitalism which will be provided *by* capitalism" (25). Also recognizing the contradictions in popular texts, Fiske stresses the power of the consumer by contending that the successful text is "producerly" or a "popular writerly text," an explanation based on the distinction made by Roland Barthes in *S/Z* between readerly and writerly texts. According to Fiske, the meaning of Barthes' writerly text is open; it challenges readers to make sense of it, "foregrounds its own textual constructedness, and invites the reader to participate in the construction of meaning." The meaning of Barthes' readerly text is relatively closed; it is preferred by "an essentially passive, receptive, disciplined reader who tends to accept its meaning as already made" (*Understanding* 103). Fiske's producerly text stands between the two, accessible like the readerly text, but open in meaning like the writerly one. The producerly text

> exposes, however reluctantly, the vulnerabilities, limitations, and weaknesses of its preferred meanings; it contains, while attempting to repress them, voices that contradict the ones it prefers; it has loose ends that escape its control, its meanings exceed its own power to discipline them, its gaps are wide enough for whole new texts to be produced in them—it is, in a very real sense, beyond its own control (*Understanding* 104).

This recognition of consumers' power to make their meanings from a text openly defies the mass culture interpretation of commercial literature, a position already called into doubt by Walter Benjamin. In "The Work of Art in the Age of Mechanical Reproduction" (1936), Benjamin moved away from insisting that the importance of a text lay in its production and that the way it was produced necessarily determined how it was received or used by its consumers. He instead proposed that "meaning is produced at the moment of consumption; significance is determined by the process of consumption, regardless of the mode of production" (Storey 190).

The shift from an exclusive concern with the production of "popular culture" to a focus on consumption is typical of a cultural studies approach, in which the "themes are pleasure, empowerment, resistance and popular discrimination" (Storey 185). This "cultural populism" (During 17) asserts that consumers, far from being helpless dupes, are engaged in a war with the occupying army of the power bloc in which they exploit the gaps and weaknesses of capitalism and its products (Fiske, *Television* 316). Seen in this light, popular culture is not imposed from without or above but is made from within and below, and if the products of the culture industry do not offer consumers resources out of which they can make their own meanings, the products will be rejected and fail to sell (Fiske, *Reading* 2). Working from a feminist perspective within cultural populism, Ien Ang avows that the "paternalism of the ideology of mass culture" must end. This paternalism locates women as "passive victims" of "deceptive messages" and disregards their pleasures (*Watching Dallas* 118-19). She argues that a woman's pleasure in a popular text does not mean that she fails to understand its underlying ideology, nor does it make her incapable of political action. This does not mean, according to Ang,

> ...that feminists must not persevere in trying to produce new fantasies and fight for a place for them.... It does, however, mean that, where cultural consumption is concerned, no fixed standard exists for gauging the "progressiveness" of a fantasy. The personal may be political, but the personal and the political do not always go hand in hand (*Watching Dallas* 135-36).

Adherents of this "ideology of populism" (Ang, "*Dallas* and the Ideology" 416) have been criticized, for example by Jim McGuigan, for presenting an uncritical view of popular culture by stressing unduly the ways consumers interpret texts while ignoring the historical and economic context of consumption. Storey counters this argument:

> Even Fiske...does not celebrate an achieved utopia, but the active struggle of men and women to make sense and space in a world based on exploitation and oppression.... It simply isn't the case that claims that audiences produce meaning are in some profound sense a denial of the need for political change (184).

These theories of cultural populism shed new light on Ullstein, Baum, and *Helene* and its readers in Weimar Germany. For example, in suggesting that entertainment furnishes those alternatives to capitalism that capitalism itself will provide, Dyer proffers one explanation of why Ullstein was willing to validate Helene's problems and existence through the production and distribution of her story: everything Helene does can be seen as a part of existing paternalistic capitalist structures. Even if Helene had not decided to live with Ambrosius, her salvation from poverty was initiated by him, she worked within the structure of an enlightened capitalist company, and she became rich and famous by marketing herself and her product. Through Helene's two male professors, symbols of authority, the novel proposes that men in positions of power are willing to accept a woman if she works hard enough. The message could be that male leaders of society are not inherently against women; they are willing to accept *individual* women, as long as they fulfill certain expectations: they must be hardworking, nurturing, and motherly. Seen this way, Helene's success does not represent a victory for women, but rather an example of their "taming" or neutralization within the capitalist, paternalistic social structure. And to be sure, Helene and Baum were both co-opted to work for the system by men who believed they were doing them a favor by admitting them to their exclusive club.

Yet the implications of cultural populism in evaluating *Helene* go still further, for even if this were the text's "preferred meaning" (Fiske), the one the producers intended, cultural populism also reminds us not to overlook the power of the consumer in making meaning of a text. *Helene* is full of the "loose ends" that Fiske attributes to the successful, "producerly" text that consumers can potentially use in creating their preferred meanings. For example, although Helene chooses Ambrosius at the end, Helene's full life, with her highly successful job, money, and a marvelous son, leave much room for doubt about the ending; thus *Helene,* too, has "vulnerabilities, limitations, and weaknesses of its preferred meanings; it contains...voices that contradict the ones it prefers" (Fiske, *Understanding* 103). Assuming that readers do make of a text what they will, then *Helene*'s readers in the 1920s could have recognized these contradictions as well as any scholar can today. There are no data on how Weimar-era general readers interpreted *Helene*. But reviewers, the readers we can trace, *both* accepted the image Ullstein and Baum promoted *and* made their own meanings from the text by choosing what part of the novel they would accentuate, the realistic depiction of women's issues.

Finally, Ang and another feminist popular culture researcher, Janice Radway, offer new ways of thinking about the romance novel that suggest yet another perspective on *Helene*. Although the romance has often been vilified as a main contributor in the indoctrination claimed by the mass culture ideologues, Radway and Ang have called that apparent certainty into question. Radway's *Reading the Romance* presents and interprets the results of her study of a group of avid female romance readers. Radway hopes through the study to sort out or articulate "the difference between the repressive imposition of ideology and oppositional practices that, though limited in their scope and effect, at least dispute or contest the control of ideological forms" (221-22). Women, she concludes, "at least partially reclaim the patriarchal form of the romance for their own use," in part by choosing to consume "only those stories that will reinforce their feelings of self-worth and supply the replenishment they need" (184). Thus women do not read out of contentment with or acceptance of the patriarchal status quo; instead, their reading is a form of unarticulated protest—and thus resistance—against it. Radway's findings also reveal that romance readers, usually considered "category readers" (53), in fact discriminate among various kinds of romances, selecting to read only those they consider acceptable and enjoyable. This seldom-recognized ability to select empowers readers, allowing them to determine which romance novels are commercially most successful. Criteria for accepting or rejecting a text include the amount of sexually explicit description, the level of violence and cruelty, and relationship of the hero and heroine (53). The good novel satisfies readers' "needs for fatherly protection, motherly care, and passionate love" (149).

Even a brief look at *Helene* in the light of Radway's findings and conclusions helps to explain its popularity as a romance novel. In several scenes depicting Ambrosius's life before divorcing his wife Yvonne, the professor is overcome by his emotional and sexual desires; in fact, he nearly rapes his wife. Mixing these scenes with others showing his fatherly affection for Helene, Baum made Ambrosius into a character who should interest her audience. But Ambrosius, as a man capable of rape, is not a suitable mate in the romance preferred by Radway's readers; a man capable of rape might be "interesting," but the heroine cannot commit her life to him unless his lack of emotional control can be neutralized. Realizing this, Baum does change her character into an acceptable mate by the end of the novel. When he asks Helene to live with him, Ambrosius has retained some of his fatherly qualities, but is a chastened man who no longer wants the seductive Yvonne but the nurturing Helene. Helene feels needed by him, but she can also admit to her passion for this type of man. Thus their relationship and the ending are the very type Radway's romance readers favored.

Ang goes further than Radway in validating women's pleasure in consuming the products of popular culture. She chides Radway for retaining a dichotomy between the feminist scholar and the female romance reader, who, according to these scholars, should stop reading the novels and use their time to become actively involved in political change. Ang, who does not believe pleasure in the fantasy of popular culture excludes a feminist approach to politics, postulates that pleasure, far from always working "against their own 'real' interests," can "empower" women ("Feminist desire" 188). So, even if the romance framework seems regressive in comparison with the progressive elements of Baum's novel, this does not mean that contemporary readers necessarily received a regressive message from the romance; these feminist theories suggest that her readers could have used the romance for their own purposes just as readers do today.

Like colleagues in other disciplines, scholars exploring German-language literature and culture must face challenges to the apparent certainties of the past. When we address popular culture, we can no longer cling to a simplistic explanation that pits exploiters against exploited, relying on the assumption that producers follow recipes for success and that consumers are helpless to resist their traps. The study of popular culture has become more complicated as we include the experiences of producers in creating *and* consumers in recreating texts, but it has also been opened to fascinating, new ideas. In a global society increasingly influenced by popular culture, we must strive to understand this culture by working *with* its consumers, and abandon the tendency only to criticize the culture and pontificate *at* consumers. After all, the warnings and criticisms of "mass culture" advocates in the past have not led consumers to so-called "high" culture. A fresh approach is necessary, and it is time we took it.

Notes

Unless otherwise noted, all translations are my own.

[1] The first in-depth study of a Baum work was Bayer's analysis of *stud. chem. Helene Willfüer* in 1963. Using the value system of traditional literary studies, Bayer condemned it as substandard.

[2] See, for example, Hermand and Trommler; Berg et al; King, "The Woman Question" and *Bestsellers*; Harrigan; Soltau; Thunecke.

[3] For more on the literary establishment and Baum's relationship with her synchronic literary community, see King (*Bestsellers* 145–54).

[4] For details on Ullstein, see King (*Bestsellers* 45–71).

[5] For details on the campaign, see King (*Bestsellers* 81–98).

[6] Baum herself later wrote an article about letters she had received from young women saying that her portrayal of the circumstances of abortion in Germany were *not* authentic. These women, Baum claimed, insisted that abortions were much easier to get than she had shown ("Frauen").

[7] In a stylistically different story of another intellectual New Woman of the 1920s, Marieluise Fleißer's "Die Ziege," the ending is almost exactly the same,

reflecting, according to Wittmann, the same social reality for these women, and not only in Germany (269).

[8] Literature of all kinds was part of this debate, and one notable example among many was Friedrich Wolf's 1929 play *Cyankali*, which demonstrated the injustice of the statute criminalizing abortion, Paragraph 218.

[9] See Baum ("Frauen").

[10] See King for some statistics on women working during this time ("The Woman Question"). There was one woman working in an Austrian private chemical firm in a position similar to Helene's, so Baum's portrayal is not so farfetched.

[11] See King (*Bestsellers* 99–106). In her review, Hilde Walter made this very point, remarking that most of the debate on the novel revolved around what problems were presented rather than how they were depicted. In her analysis of how the novel was written, Walter showed she understood that it was the *combination* of the realistic portrayal of genuine problems with romance-novel sentiment and melodrama that constituted the true appeal of Baum's writing.

[12] This view is supported by Peter de Mendelssohn in his history of Berlin's newspapers and their publishers. He distinguishes two groups of publishers, those who supported the Republic and those who worked to undermine it. Hugenberg worked against it, Ullstein supported it. That they would work *together* at the end of the Weimar Republic was unthinkable (371–72).

[13] The music of these groups was an expression of opposition to the military-industrial complex and particularly to the Vietnam War, yet while it promoted and inspired resistance to the capitalist system, it also made profits, which the musicians did not control, that helped to finance the system and continue the war (Storey 122).

[14] Baum's memoirs also indicate her belief that the only way people could get ahead was by relying on themselves, as she had done (*Es war* 500, 508).

[15] In her memoirs, Baum in fact expressed her disdain for politics, for she believed that direct political action was useless (*Es war* 480).

[16] Walter's review cited above supports this argument. She notes that although there were other books with the same themes, none of them had caused the uproar *Helene* had.

Works Cited

Adorno, Theodor W., and Max Horkheimer. "The Culture Industry: Enlightenment as Mass Deception." *Dialectic of Enlightenment*. New York: Seabury, 1972. 120–67.

Ang, Ien. "*Dallas* and the Ideology of Mass Culture." *The Cultural Studies Reader*. Ed. Simon During. London: Routledge, 1993. 403–20.

_____. "Feminist Desire and Female Pleasure: On Janice Radway's *Reading the Romance: Women, Patriarchy and Popular Literature.*" *Camera Obscura* 16 (1988): 179-90.

_____. *Watching Dallas: Soap Opera and the Melodramatic Imagination*. London: Methuen, 1985.

Arna, Alfred. "Modernes Mädchen." Rev. of *stud. chem. Helene Willfüer*. *Vorwärts* 1 February 1929. n.p.

Barthes, Roland. *S/Z*. Trans. Richard Miller. New York: Hill and Wang, 1975.

Baum, Vicki. "Erfahrungen mit der Verjüngung: Ein Rundgang durch die Laboratorien einer neuen Wissenschaft." *Uhu* (December 1927): 32-40.

_____. *Es war alles ganz anders: Erinnerungen*. Berlin: Ullstein, 1962. In this study I have cited the Zürich edition (Buchclub Ex Libris, 1964).

_____. "Frauen unter Frauen." *Vossische Zeitung* 5 April 1931. n.p.

_____. *Menschen im Hotel: Ein Kolportageroman mit Hintergründen*. Berlin: Ullstein, 1929.

_____. *stud. chem. Helene Willfüer*. Berlin: Ullstein, 1929.

Bayer, Dorothee. *Der triviale Familien- und Liebesroman im zwanzigsten Jahrhundert*. Tübingen: Tübinger Vereinigung für Volkskunde, 1963.

Becher, Lucie. Rev. of *stud. chem. Helene Willfüer*. *Germania* 3 (February 1929). n.p.

Bell, Robert. "Depicting the Host Country: Vicki Baum's 'The Mustard Seed.'" *Kulturelle Wechselbeziehungen im Exil—Exile Across Cultures*. Ed. Helmut F. Pfanner. Bonn: Bouvier, 1986. 139-50.

Benjamin, Walter. "The Work of Art in the Age of Mechanical Reproduction." *Illuminations*. Ed. Hannah Arendt. New York: Schocken, 1969. 217-52.

Berg, Jan, et al. *Sozialgeschichte der deutschen Literatur von 1918 bis zur Gegenwart*. Frankfurt a.M.: Fischer, 1981.

Collins, Jim. *Uncommon Cultures: Popular Culture and Post-Modernism*. New York: Routledge, 1989.

Cosner, Lewis A., Charles Kadushin, and Walter W. Powell. *Books: The Culture and Commerce of Publishing*. Chicago: U of Chicago P, 1985.

D.S. "Eine Primadonna des Unterhaltungsromans: Der schlichte Handel mit Buchstaben: Erinnerungen an Vicki Baum." *Einheit* 16 (1963): 7.

During, Simon, ed. *The Cultural Studies Reader*. London: Routledge, 1993.

Dyer, Richard. *Only Entertainment*. London: Routledge, 1992.

Fiske, John. *Reading the Popular*. Boston: Unwin Hyman, 1989.

_____. *Television Culture*. London: Routledge, 1987.

_____. *Understanding Popular Culture*. Boston: Unwin Hyman, 1989.

Frith, Simon. *Sound Effects: Youth, Leisure and the Politics of Rock*. London: Constable, 1983.

Geitel, Klaus. "Berlin: Bühnenwirbel im 'Grand Hotel.'" Rev. of *Grand Hotel: Das Musical*. *Die Welt* 28 January 1991: 18.

Harrigan, Renny. "Die emanzipierte Frau im Roman der Weimarer Republik." *Stereotyp und Vorurteil in der Literatur*. Ed. J. Elliott, J. Pelzer, and C. Poore. Göttingen: Vandenhoeck and Ruprecht, 1978. 65-83.

Hermand, Jost, and Frank Trommler. *Die Kultur der Weimarer Republik*. München: Nymphenburger Verlagshandlung, 1978.

Holzner, Johann. "Literarische Verfahrensweisen und Botschaften der Vicki Baum." *Erzählgattungen der Trivialliteratur*. Ed. Z. Skreb and U. Baur. Innsbruck: Germanistisches Institut, 1984. 233-50.

Jarvie, Ian. *Movies and Society*. New York: Basic Books, 1970.

Kaus, Gina. Rev. of *stud. chem. Helene Willfüer*. *Wiener Allgemeine Zeitung* 19 February 1929: 5.

King, Lynda J. *Bestsellers by Design: Vicki Baum and the House of Ullstein*. Detroit: Wayne State UP, 1988.

———. "The Image of Fame: Vicki Baum in Weimar Germany." *German Quarterly* 58 (1985): 375-93.

———. "The Woman Question and Politics in Austrian Interwar Literature." *German Studies Review* 6 (1983): 75-100.

Lederer, Joe. "So sehe ich Vicki Baum." *Die Welt am Sonntag* 19 January 1958.

Lewis, George H. "Uncertain Truths: The Promotion of Popular Culture." *Journal of Popular Culture* 20.3 (1986): 31-44.

Lovell, Terry. *Pictures of Reality, Aesthetics, Politics and Pleasure*. London: British Film Institute, 1983.

Luft, Friedrich. *Facsimilie Querschnitt durch die Berliner Illustrirte*. München: Scherz, 1965.

Mahrholz, Werner. "Die Verwandlung des Lesers." *Die Vossische Zeitung* 27 March 1929: 1.

Marcuse, Herbert. *One Dimensional Man*. London: Sphere, 1968.

McGuigan, Jim. *Cultural Populism*. London: Routledge, 1992.

Mendelssohn, Peter de. *Zeitungsstadt Berlin: Menschen und Mächte in der Geschichte der deutschen Presse*. Berlin: Ullstein, 1982.

Neue Freie Presse. Rev. of *stud. chem. Helene Willfüer*. 17 February 1929: 30.

Radway, Janice A. *Reading the Romance: Women, Patriarchy, and Popular Literature*. Chapel Hill: U of North Carolina P, 1984.

Reuter, Gabriele. Rev. of *stud. chem. Helene Willfüer*. *Vossische Zeitung* 17 March 1929.

Schwab-Felisch, Hans. "Bücher bei Ullstein." *Hundert Jahre Ullstein 1877-1977*. Ed. W. Joachim Freyburg and Hans Wallenberg. Berlin: Ullstein, 1977.

Soltau, Heide. "Die Anstrengungen des Aufbruchs: Romanautorinnen und ihre Heldinnen in der Weimarer Zeit." *Deutsche Literatur von Frauen*. Ed. Gisela Brinker-Gabler. München: Beck, 1988. Vol. 2. 220-35.

Storey, John. *An Introductory Guide to Cultural Theory and Popular Culture*. Athens: U of Georgia P, 1993.

Thunecke, Jörg. "Kolportage ohne Hintergründe: Der Film 'Grand Hotel' (1932)." *Die Resonanz des Exils.* Ed. Dieter Sevin. Amsterdam: Rodopi, 1992. 134–52.

Ullstein, Hermann. *The Rise and Fall of the House of Ullstein.* New York: Simon and Schuster, 1943.

Walter, Hilde. "Aufruhr um Helene Willfüer." *Frau und Gegenwart vereinigt mit Neue Frauenkleidung und Frauenkultur* 25 (1928–29): 656.

Wittmann, Livia Z. "Liebe oder Selbstverlust: Die fiktionale Neue Frau im ersten Drittel unseres Jahrhunderts." *Der Widerspenstigen Zähmung: Studien zur bezwungenen Weiblichkeit in der Literatur vom Mittelalter bis zur Gegenwart.* Ed. S. Wallinger and M. Jonas. Innsbruck: Germanistisches Institut, 1986. 259–80.

Wolff, Emmy. "Studentinnen im Tagesroman von heute." *Die Frau* 36 (1928/29): 481.

Ziegfeld, Richard E. "The Exile Writer and His Publisher: Vicki Baum and Doubleday." *Deutsche Exilliteratur: Literatur der Nachkriegszeit. Akten des dritten Exilliteratur-Symposiums der University of South Carolina.* Ed. W. Elfe, J. Hardin, and G. Holst. Las Vegas: Lang, 1981. 144–53.

Motherhood and the "New Woman": Vicki Baum's *stud. chem. Helene Willfüer* and Irmgard Keun's *Gilgi—eine von uns*

Katharina von Ankum

The article situates Vicki Baum's *stud. chem. Helene Willfüer* (1926) and Irmgard Keun's *Gilgi—eine von uns* (1931) in the gendered political and cultural discourses of the inter-war years. The protagonists of both texts embody a new idealized female type: the rationalized, desexualized, yet compassionate worker of the modern age. By advocating this reconfiguration of the "New Woman" into the "New Mother," both texts participate in the adaption of an essentialist femininity to a cult of rationalization that supported patriarchal and capitalist structures, preparing the ground for the backlash against women in 1933. (KvA)

In her assessment of the status of women "Zurück zur guten alten Zeit?" (1933) published three days before the Nazi takeover, sociologist and cultural critic Alice Rühle-Gerstel deplores the fact that the vision of the "New Woman" had been abandoned before it could take hold in the lives of most women. Only a few pioneering individuals, she observes, were able to incorporate the emancipatory content of this cultural construct into their personal lives. Discouraged by tough competition in the job market during the post–World War I economic crisis and disillusioned by the limitations placed on their professional advancement by patriarchal prejudice, many women by the mid-1920s had begun to fantasize about returning to traditional models of femininity. In this context, Rühle-Gerstel criticizes the revisionist orientation of women's literature, which she feels is at least partially to blame for this development:

> Literature should present us with the woman who is not frustrated by occasional failures or temporary defeats. It should show a woman who will not stray from the path that she has found to be correct and necessary. What we need is the female protagonist who proceeds courageously to win new allies for her cause, ventures into unknown territories, not for the benefit of a few isolated individuals, but for the benefit of her entire sex (6).

Rühle-Gerstel's critique reflects a characteristically left-liberal belief in the didactic function of literature and utopian nature, a belief that overlooks the inevitable interdependence between culture and discourses of power. In my analysis of two of the most successful Weimar "women's novels"—Vicki Baum's *stud. chem. Helene Willfüer* (1926) and Irmgard Keun's *Gilgi—eine von uns* (1931)—I will demonstrate just how these texts reflect the dominant cultural discourses of their time and suggest that this accounts for their powerful impact on contemporary readers.[1]

In their attempt to construct progressive role models for the modern woman, both texts work with the problematic emancipatory concept of "spiritual motherhood" developed by bourgeois feminists in the 1890s. By emphasizing "spiritual motherhood," "feminist" activists had hoped to justify women's participation in the public sphere and achieve political representation in exchange for their essential, gender-specific contributions to society.[2] In many ways, the Weimar Republic turned this concept into political reality. Women received the right to vote and Weimar sociopolitical debates were strongly affected by efforts to integrate into society what was perceived to be a specifically female principle of humanitarianism, derived from women's ability to be mothers. The emphasis on a "politics of motherliness," which would soften the rough edges of modern society, reflected a societal consensus, reached after Germany's disastrous defeat in World War I, that men had forfeited their dominant position in society, and that a rebalancing of male and female principles was essential for restoring peace and prosperity to the German nation. The emphasis on this "female essence," however, also aimed to halt the development of what many regarded as the dangerously androgynous "New Woman"—the sexually liberated, economically independent, and self-reliant female—who threatened to erase accepted markers of gender difference.

Alongside social changes preempting a return to traditional roles after the war, modern society needed women to meet their reproductive responsibilities as well as the demands of paid labor. Thus Weimar political activists—among them doctors and lawyers—proposed and supported initiatives that were geared towards integrating (middle-class) women's traditional reproductive roles with their new responsibilities in the workplace. Pragmatic measures such as revised abortion legislation, easy access to contraception—championed by the Sex-Reform Movement—or legal equality for children born out of wedlock—advocated by the *Mutterschutzbund*—undoubtedly acknowledged the new social reality for women. Yet, underlying these progressive measures to facilitate women's new dual roles as producers and reproducers was a clearly antiemancipatory political agenda (Grossmann, "Girlkultur"). Public interest in reproductive issues was far less an expression of a new morality or solidarity with women than the result of a perceived need to channel female sexuality into forms where it could best be functionalized.

Women as workers and mothers were assigned a crucial role in the creation of a morally, economically, and eugenically superior German nation. The essay collection *Die Frau von morgen wie wir sie wünschen* (1929) documents the integration of "spiritual motherhood" into the Weimar discourse on the "New Woman." In this volume, prominent intellectuals of all political hues expressed their hopes that women, after having conquered traditionally male domains, would not become mere imitators of male ways, but rather develop viable alternative lifestyles. Rather than indulging in promiscuity and careerism, the authors agree, women should strive to maintain their internal balance and use their maternal instinct in the interest of the future of humankind.

Through mothering, women would draw the necessary energy for the redemption of modern society: "The continuous stream of energy that exists between mother and child is, more clearly than ever before, the source from which she draws the strength to respond to the demands involved in the construction of a new societal order" (Jahnn 145–46). The emphasis on the mother-child bond—yet unaffected by the alienation and functionalization of modern society—reconstructed the modern family as the mother-child unit, effectively eliminating the role of the male as father. With Weimar welfare policies facilitating the existence of "incomplete" families, men were free to advance their careers and celebrate their individualism. For women, in turn, the "New Mother," as I will call the single working woman with child, emerged as a model of identification that replaced that of the "New Woman."

Single motherhood appeared as emancipatory image in countless texts by women writers of the 1920s and 1930s (Roberts 216). The single mother represented a singularly convincing new sexual identity for women of the time. Its attraction lay in the combination of old and new: the familiarity of the traditional mother role as mode of identification, its at least apparent emancipation, and its promise as antidote to frustrations experienced in the working world. In my readings of Vicki Baum's *stud. chem. Helene Willfüer* (1926) and Irmgard Keun's *Gilgi—eine von uns* (1931), I analyze the ways in which these texts reinforce this popular, yet problematic model of emancipation offered to women in Weimar Germany. Both texts portray their protagonists as representations of a new female type: the ideal, rationalized, desexualized, yet compassionate worker of the modern age. By advocating the reconfiguration of the "New Woman" into the "New Mother," however, both texts participate in adapting an essentialist femininity to a cult of rationalization that supported patriarchal and capitalist structures, thus preparing the ground for the backlash against women in 1933.

I

Fictional texts addressing the difficulties facing the "New Woman" who strove to combine a satisfactory personal life with a successful career were typically situated in the office. Making her protagonist Helene Willfüer a student of the sciences rather than a representative of the new female profession, the typist, Vicki Baum places her novel in the tradition of an earlier *Frauenliteratur* whose portrayal of pioneering women professionals—be they teachers, artists, or politicians—focused primarily on the demonstration of female competence and less on the difficulties of juggling the double burden (Soltau 221). However, given the increasing numbers of women entering the universities after World War I—by 1932-33 18.8% of the student population were women, compared to only 10.8% in 1923-24 (Weyrather 25, 27)—Baum's novel does reflect a female life experience more common to the 1920s than it would have been at the turn of the century. The discussions on the status of women at the universities that run through women's journals of the time focus primarily on the compatibility of academic endeavors with the preservation of a womanly disposition. To diffuse potential criticism, female students were urged to contribute the "spirit of femininity" to the institution, carefully balancing their academic efforts with the harmonious image of "true womanhood." Their special womanly contributions would justify their presence at the university, just like the quality of "spiritual motherhood" made women's work desirable in fields like social work, teaching, or medicine. A woman neglecting to maintain her feminine appeal in favor of her commitment to her work would be perceived as unwanted competition by her male colleagues, and would endanger the hard-won place of her sex in her profession. A woman's aspiration to excel in any professional area bore traces of a dangerous individualism that threatened to come in conflict with her other, natural profession: motherhood (Weyrather 29).

Elisabeth Knoblauch's study *Zur Psychologie der studierenden Frau* (1930) identifies the question of the compatibility of a lengthy academic training with the wish to found a family as the central conflict experienced by female students: "Characteristic for the female student is the desire for the maternal profession [*Mutterberuf*], frequently combined with the wish to continue in her career" (445). The noted desire among women to combine motherhood and work perhaps also reflected the interviewees' desire not to deviate too far from the social norm. To place their profession at the center of their existence was considered an unhealthy imitation of male ways, which not only damaged the individual woman's emotional and physical health, but had detrimental consequences for society as a whole.

The many competing theories on female student typologies propagated in the numerous women's journals of the time attempted to explain and categorize the ways in which women responded to the challenges presented by their new career options (Tönniessen, Dieckmann, Caspar-Köslin). In recreating the student milieu at the University of Heidelberg, Vicki Baum draws on several such typologies. The archeologist Gudula Rapp embodies the type of the pathological student whose excessive devotion to her subject of study affects her physical and nervous constitution. In her article "Innere Probleme des Studentinnenlebens," Elfriede Dieckmann describes the physical degeneration of the overcommitted female student:

> I've had numerous opportunities to observe the development of those poor creatures. Based on the study of their physiognomy, I have been able to determine the following: either their facial features became firmer, giving the whole face a certain sternness.... The well-known line betraying excessive willpower appeared between both eyes. Their entire personality became harder, more rigid.... Or—their eyes became restless, their note-taking during the lectures more and more nervous and driven, until their facial expression became increasingly tortured and desperate (33).

Baum's portrayal of Gudula Rapp goes even further, suggesting that her exclusive attention to her scholarly work is motivated by her desire to repress her "deviant" sexual orientation:

> Poor Gulrapp. Fighting against herself day after day, night after night in a vain attempt to cover up the bitter truth, to repress her sick and deviant desire. Her small frame becomes more and more disembodied, the gaze behind her glasses increasingly hysterical, her thin ebony hands more and more unsteady. As she loses her inner balance, the successful completion of her project moves ever more out of her reach (168).

Following contemporary theories on hysteria, Baum links increased intellectual activity in women to the spread of nervous disorder, und ultimately sexual "disorientation." The intellectual woman as lesbian is deprived not only of any gender identity and relegated to a "third" neuter sex—her friends call her "das Gulrapp"—but of her professional fulfillment as well. Denying herself the experience of woman/motherhood, she is unable to tap into the specifically female energy center that would allow her to find personal wholeness and professional satisfaction. The character of May Kolding represents the other extreme of the female student typology: the *Modestudentin*. Financially independent, she spends time at the university primarily to enjoy the academic lifestyle, thus compromising the respectability of her fellow women students. "In many of us, feelings of shame and embarrassment about women like her have reinforced our sense of responsibility to our sex and awakened our sensibility about women's place," observes Dieckmann in her study on female university students (33).

By contrast, Helene Willfüer succeeds in balancing all aspects of female student life. She is the ideal woman student "who not only wishes to be a scholar, but a human being" (Dieckmann 34). Not only does her commitment to chemistry not threaten her womanly qualities, she is able to enhance the work environment with her housewifely and motherly talents: "Helene Willfüer possess the talent to create an ambiance of comfort in the middle of a messy, pungent laboratory" (32-33). In the novel's first chapter, Helene's positive encounter with a pregnant mother in the train compartment on her return to Heidelberg immediately signals to the reader that Helene does not pursue her studies at the expense of her femininity. Her natural disposition for motherhood, however, threatens to be repressed by outward necessity and the adverse circumstances of her pregnancy later in the text. Yet, the hardship she faces, struggling to complete her degree and raise her child, are presented as proof of Helene's "true womanhood," i.e., her ability to integrate intellect and motherliness. As her mentor and future husband Professor Ambrosius observes, attaining one's professional goal via the most direct route and without complications is not at all ladylike: "A zig-zag course is more attractive, more humane" (15), that is, more womanly.

Helene's vain attempt to find a doctor who will abort her illegitimate child can be read as a final act of resistance towards fully assuming her female role.[3] She discovers true professional inspiration only after she has accepted her fate of single motherhood. While sitting in her prison cell, awaiting exoneration from the false accusation that she had assisted in the suicide of her lover (and father of her child), she finds the answer to her scientific problem at the same time that she feels the first movements of her baby (198-99). Her sober approach to science bears fruit only in conjunction with a specifically female intuition: "Something new is happening to her. Far removed from the laboratory, without access to practical experiments, she encounters a creative, an intuitive force within her" (198). Through the experience of motherhood, Helene discovers a genuinely female approach to chemistry that enables her to become a self-sufficient individual who is resourceful enough to attain professional excellence as a woman in a male-dominated field.

With this plot development, Baum draws on theories of female creativity developed at the turn of the century. Against the argument that women's reproductive capacities preempted their need or ability for creative expression (Scheffler 29-30), bourgeois feminists proposed that motherliness held a central place for women of high artistic and intellectual ability, raising the experience of physical motherhood to a "spiritual motherhood" that permeated their lives and work (Stöcker 85, 88).[4] Insisting on a biologically determined female essence, Helene Stöcker, one of the movement's main proponents, compromises her own argument in favor of the compatibility of motherhood and professional commitment by identifying "spiritual motherhood" as the crucial factor responsible for the inferiority of women's achievements.

> Spiritual motherhood, motherliness in its highest sense is at the root of women's intellectual inferiority to men. But at the same time that she becomes aware of this dilemma, she realizes this painful conflict is in fact her most valuable asset (Stöcker 88).

Incapable of truly outstanding performance, the intellectually and artistically creative woman is constructed as a masochist, thriving on the suffering caused by the two contending forces within her: the creative spirit requiring extreme self-centeredness and the motherly spirit propelling her to retract her own ego.

In pursuit of her goal to complete her education and support her child, Helene aptly demonstrates that she is able "to deny her own self" (243): Living without sufficient food or sleep, in dark, unheated rooms, she nonetheless completes her doctorate with distinction.[5] The working conditions under which she ultimately gains professional recognition and influence are equally stressful. Completely isolated from public life, she is able to subordinate any personal interest to the advancement of science and the well-being of her son. While Helene already possessed all the qualities that made her the perfect female student, her life as a single working mother suggests even more strongly that she is the ideal woman of the modern age, able to integrate a feminine sense of caring with superior professional discipline. With her research, she contributes to the discovery and mass production of the rejuvenating drug Vitalin, which will supply her fellow human beings with an inexhaustible source of energy similar to that which she as a mother possesses naturally.[6]

The text represents Helene's successful response to the dual role of nurturer and breadwinner as a function of her ability to control her body and redirect sexual desire into mothering. Already early in the text, Helene's regular morning routine serves to illustrate the central role of order and discipline in her life:

> 6.a.m....In the valley below you can hear the first whistles from the factories, and right away the windows light up in the little houses on the hill. There are people who have no trouble getting up in the morning. Like Helene Willfüer who, at the first sound of her alarm, sits up in bed wide awake. She always gets up on the right foot, puts her kettle on the burner and pours a few buckets of cold water over her tall body (20).

Helene willingly integrates herself into the mechanism of the university town of Heidelberg, "a twitching, feverish, restless workshop of the mind," and derives pleasure from her status as functional element in the machinery of a modern city (20). Her brief relationship with the artist Rainer and the resulting pregnancy merely occasion a momentary lapse in her ability to exercise control over her body. Helene's pregnant body confronts her with the uncanniness of her physicality. The strange biological and dynamic operations inside of her fill her "with nausea and disgust" (126). Once the authority of law and order is imposed on her, she quickly regains the familiar control over herself: "It is almost a relief that Helene has to subject herself to the prison rules. She loves the strict, the rigid and the frugal. During the last few weeks, she has wasted her life indulging in softness. Now discipline, order and duty reenter her life" (183). The simultaneity of the reconstruction of her controllable body by this external prison world and her acceptance of her maternal role constitute Helene, the dedicated scientist, as a powerful example of the "New Mother."

Stud. chem. Helene Willfüer strongly advocates women's need to subordinate their sexual desire to the requirements of production and reproduction. Consequently, Helene's sexuality is denied, repressed, and negatively connoted throughout the narrative. A dream sequence related at the very beginning of the novel juxtaposes a positive, pure desexualized love for a father figure—a love that eventually materializes in her belated marriage to Professor Ambrosius—with a dangerous, murky desire for a man her own age, obviously Rainer: "She walks into the meadow. She senses the swaying, swampy, humid ground under her feet.... The wild orchids grow higher and higher, and finally cover her completely" (27–28). The relegation of physical desire to the realm of the subconscious supports the text's active repression of Helene's sexuality in favor of her maternal role. Her willingness to agree to sexual intercourse with Rainer is attributed to her understanding of his male sexual needs (125), not to her physical attraction towards him. "Next to this slender, immature, boyish creature," Helene does not perceive herself as his partner, but feels like a "great old and wise mother"(73).

Helene's relationship with Prof. Ambrosius is similarly desexualized, although the site of their first encounter—the highly eroticized space of the train compartment (Asendorf 46)—still implies a strong physical attraction between them. During the course of the narrative, both are purged of misleading passions that stand in the way of their love relationship. Ambrosius overcomes his sexual addiction to his unfaithful wife Yvonne, while Helene's pregnancy reorients her sexual desire towards motherhood. Their second encounter in the train compartment consequently emphasizes the mother/son relationship between them: "Ambrosius let himself fall into her arms like into his mother's. She held him firmly, strongly, like a woman" (163). Ultimately, Helene's relationship with her professor is founded on her ability to nurture and support. When he finally comes to her, he is a broken man in need of a partner who will care for him in his old age.

The text's construction of Helene as desexualized "New Mother" culminates in her representation as "modernist madonna." When Ambrosius encounters Helene in Italy many years after her professional breakthrough, he likens her image to that of Anselm Feuerbach's Nanna who modelled for the painter's madonna images.[7] Ambrosius, aware of her disenchantment with the ultimate emptiness of her laboratory work, offers her a relationship with him as a more meaningful project (295). The conflation of husband, father, and son in the figure of Ambrosius—underscored by the fact that Helene has named her child Valentin after her professor—promises her a relationship in which she can simultaneously become protected daughter, supportive wife, and caring mother. Actualizing this threefold identity, Helene assumes the characteristics of the Virgin Mary (Kristeva 169). In a relationship with Ambrosius who is not the biological father of her child, but rather a benevolent *Übervater,* Helene's motherhood gains the aura of an independent immaculate conception, which coincides with her submission to paternal authority. The platonic nature of their union is reflected in his partial loss of vision and her own misinterpretations of a key question: when asked about the existence of a man in her life, she points to her son. As Julia Kristeva has posited, the attraction of the madonna image for women in a patriarchal society is based on the fact that it allows for a reconciliation of matriarchal power with paternal agency (182). Providing her readers with the image of Helene Willfüer as "modernist madonna," Vicki Baum gratified women's need for empowerment while at the same time supporting the status quo of paternal authority.

With its cliché-like ending in marriage, its choice of protagonist—a female scientist rather than an office or sales 'girl'—and its conscious positioning within the political and moral debates of the time, *stud. chem. Helene Willfüer* appears much more closely related to turn-of-the century *Frauenliteratur* than to the "New Objectivity" of the 1920s. In its representation of single motherhood, however, the text distinguishes itself from its predecessors. Rather than a deserved punishment for a woman's loose morals, for which she has to redeem herself, single motherhood is presented as a challenging and rewarding path towards a progressive femininity. *Stud. chem. Helene Willfüer* documents an attempt to integrate the values of the First Women's Movement with the social reality and self-image of the "New Woman" of the Weimar years. The dual orientation of the text is perhaps best exposed by the 1927 film version of the novel, which transforms the light-brown haired, full bosomed, athletic Helene into a flat-chested brunette with a page-boy.

II

In choosing a typist as the protagonist of her novel *Gilgi—eine von uns*, Irmgard Keun provided readers with an even more representative portrait of the "New (working) Woman" than did Vicki Baum. As Susanne Suhr observed in her 1930 study on the female employee, "the salaried employee [*Angestellte*] is the typical working woman of the masses":[8]

> If you walk through an urban business district shortly before 8 a.m. or after the offices and stores close down at night, you will encounter an army of young girls and women rushing towards the large office buildings or coming home tired from work—they are the masses of female employees shaping our cities. They lend the metropolis its characteristic image. They appear in large numbers behind desks and counters. They have become the typical professional woman (Suhr 329-30).

The increase in the numbers of *Angestellte* from 6.5% to 12.6% between 1907 and 1925 (Peukert 101) was the consequence of two developments: the economic decline of the middle-class resulting from inflation and the accelerated rationalization in German industry after World War I (Suhr 330-31). The former released into the work force a large number of women who had not been engaged in paid labor previously. The latter displaced many from their traditional employment in households and agriculture while creating new positions in business and retail that were considered suitable for women. What made the profession of the *Angestellte* a characteristically "feminine" occupation was the high degree of mechanization, presumably well suited to woman's delicate physique, but actually detrimental to her physical and mental health (Suhr 333-38). Her high visibility behind sales counters and reception desks encouraged employers not only to exploit her labor power, but to use her youth and physical attraction as a business asset and marketing strategy for their products or services. The comparatively young age plus the relatively low pay of the *Angestellte* were further expressions of the employers' (and employees') conviction that her professional commitment would be temporary and her ultimate career goals marriage and motherhood. Reinforced by mass culture, fantasies of marrying the boss acted as surrogates for the lack of opportunities for professional advancement, and frequently merely encouraged sexual harassment in the workplace.

Despite its harsh realities, the profession of the *Angestellte* provided the basis for many women's identification with the cultural construction of the "New Woman." It offered the promise of moral and economic independence, however limited and temporary. At the outset of *Gilgi,* Irmgard Keun's protagonist wholeheartedly embraces the fashionable identity offered to her by the discourses of mass media and advertising. Constitutive for her identity as "New Woman" is her understanding of herself as a self-made working woman, an image she signals to her environment by calling herself Gilgi rather than Gisela. Determined to rely exclusively on her own professional skills—at night, she studies to be a foreign language secretary—she rejects "wife, film star and beauty queen" as unrealistic career goals. Her ability to handle unwanted male advances—by skillfully diverting their attention to a friend—is presented as proof of her business savvy and professionalism. Gilgi regards her ability to make a living as a typist as a guarantee that she will be exempted from the traditionally female life stories embodied by the women around her: her unmarried cousins who are condemned to wait for marriage or her friend Hertha, whose pregnancies and illness have irrevocably tied her to her luckless husband. Her determination to maintain complete control over her life, depending on no one, is thus at the core of her identity as "New Woman."

As in *Helene Willfüer*, Gilgi's powerful mechanism of self-control is enacted by her early morning routine:

> The ice cold water comes down hard on Gilgi's skinny shoulders, her small oval stomach, her thin muscular limbs. She grits her teeth and counts to thirty.... Don't deviate from your principles. Don't give in, not even for the slightest reason (5).

"*Maschinenmädchen,*" "*Uhrwerkmädchen*" ("machine girl," "clockwork girl") (141) are the fondly critical names Keun invents for her protagonist, whose rigorous exercise is part of her effort to "steel" her body and become a perfectly functional element in the machinery of the modern office. The perceived similarity between the human body and the machine and the ensuing cultural obsession with the former's perfectability were the foundation of Weimar body culture. The quest for everlasting youth and physical superiority had a particular impact on the lives of working women, whose employment opportunities depended on a pleasant exterior. The beauty industry did not grow tired of emphasizing the importance of beauty and youth for women's professional success. "The knowledge of your beauty and the knowledge of how to preserve it instills self-confidence. It brings success, happiness, and power," postulated a 1925 advertisement in *Uhu* for Elida Ideal soap. "Modernize your face!" urged an Elizabeth Arden ad from 1931, encouraging a woman's facial reconstruction by likening her face to an apartment in need of renovation.

The belief in the necessity and the feasibility of controlling the natural process of aging, adjusting their bodies to the cultural norm through exercise and cosmetics was thus a central part of the "New Woman's" identity. While Gilgi's foster mother, a traditional bourgeois housewife, does not need to conceal markers of either femininity or age—"She is wide and out of shape. The flesh of her arms and breasts has honorably turned flabby and tired"(9)—Gilgi has to discipline herself continuously to maintain her market value. Just as with her professional position, she considers her immaculate complexion the result of her personal achievement and thus takes particular pride in it: "Being well groomed is worth more than being pretty. It's a personal accomplishment"(6). Gilgi's internalization of the beauty industry's rhetoric of choice and determination once again underscores her belief in her own agency and independence. Admittedly, Keun's text does not uncritically adopt the mass cultural presentation of the perfectible female body, but points to the ultimate futility of Gilgi's efforts.[9] Yet, the narrative deconstructs the fantasies of control inherent in the image of the "New Woman" only to reconstruct them in a modified way in the image of the "New Mother."

As in *stud. chem. Helene Willfüer*, the sensation of love and the experience of pregnancy threaten the protagonist's ego boundaries and cause her to lose control over herself temporarily. Gilgi herself characterizes her love affair with Martin as a malfunction (*Betriebstörung*) in her machine-like life, an accident that interferes with her functionalist self-image. In her relationship with him, Gilgi loses not just her employment, but the sense of self that she derived exclusively from her ability to function in the working-world: "I always felt neat and distinct. I was sure of myself, I had my own will and I drew my own limits without ever thinking about it" (114). Her loss of control and the uneasiness related to it are once again represented on the physical level: "It's disgusting that I have no power over my own body" (129). Looking at herself in the mirror, she no longer perceives her reflection as a self-made object of her own physical discipline, but as an object dependent on the male gaze: "What I see in the mirror is someone else's image of me. I cannot be proud of it" (90). As with Helene Willfüer, the awareness of her pregnancy marks the moment of utter loss of control over her body and her future:

> The little lady Gilgi is standing next to the automobile. Helplessly, she pulls her upper lip over her pretty shiny teeth. Suddenly, she turns white under her make up. She collapses, hitting her shoulder against the windshield—soon, things will become serious, soon everything will be over...she regains her courageous little girl's face. She will make it—one way or the other—she has courage, and she won't let them get the better of her (110).

Yet, within moments of realizing her pregnancy, Gilgi regains control over herself. Her ultimate decision to leave Martin—who she feels would be reluctant to take on the role of provider—rests on her still unshaken belief in the possibility of an independent female existence in a patriarchal society.[10]

However, just like Helene Willfüer, Gilgi initially resists her female fate and seeks to abort the child. Her attempt to deny her femininity is symbolized in the androgynous fashion statement she makes by wearing a tie to the doctor's office (116).[11] And like Helene, Gilgi ultimately realizes the benefit of keeping the child: "It makes a lot of sense, the whole thing...without the child, without this strong 'must,' it would have been more difficult" (169). Once again, the successful construction of the "New Mother" depends on the redirection of sexual desire into motherhood. In her elaborations on the dissident nature of femininity, Julia Kristeva theorizes motherhood as a socially integrative force, an idea she simultaneously develops in "Stabat Mater": the subversive potential of woman's difference—embodied by her sexuality—is coopted by her commitment to and desire for continuity and reproduction. Gilgi's decision to give up Martin can be read as such a "structure stabilizing" act of female sacrifice that both preserves and revises the social norm (Kristeva 183). Through motherhood, Gilgi is able to cut the umbilical cord that connects her to the dark realm of uncontrollable sexuality and reintegrate herself into society as a functional element: "You will be part of it all again," Gilgi assures herself, "contained by duty and prefabricated machinery—you will be protected by the coercion of the working day, shielded by the willful law of your own productivity" (172).

Before Gilgi can integrate the three demands placed on the modern woman "to be a human being, woman and worker at the same time" (172) and embrace her new identity as "New Mother," she has to undergo an emotional and moral education that leads her out of the selfish isolation that characterized her as a "New Woman." Gilgi's initial perception as self-made woman is severely damaged by her adoptive parents' revelations that she is not their natural child. Confronted with the possibility that she could have been raised by a single working-class mother, Gilgi realizes that her middle-class background, which she had taken for granted, has been a prerequisite for the achievements she had attributed solely to her own efforts (39). Her quest for her mother(s) dissolves Gilgi's hardened sense of self, catapulting her out of her self-made isolation of time and space, and placing her in the context of other women. Her realization of the commonality of women's experience, initiated by the confrontation with her own history, is reinforced by the knowledge of her pregnancy. The faceless masses for whom she could feel no sympathy and from whom she wanted to differentiate herself take shape as individual fates and faces emerge: as Gilgi listens to Frau Täschler's life story, distinctive features begin to appear on the woman's wasted face. Waiting in line at the unemployment agency, Gilgi's feeling of repulsion is mixed with genuine sympathy for the women and girls around her. Rejecting her Marxist friend Pit's theory that help to an individual in an isolated situation is purposeless, she insists on exercising her humanity: the rescue action undertaken to help the impoverished Hertha and her family is sustained by the new ethics of responsibility and solidarity derived from motherhood.

As Gilgi boards the train to Berlin in search of a new future for herself and her child, she has reached the ideal combination of self-discipline and humanitarianism that might allow her to sustain the pressures of an increasingly competitive labor market.[12] As columnist Helga Schubring points out in *Uhu*, one of Gilgi's favorite reading materials:

> There is room for us in the public sphere, but only for those of us who—despite our education, our knowledge, our rationalism and our invincible seriousness—are aware that we need to enter another asset onto the balance sheet, an asset that will place us out of competition with men: it is the calming, yet supportive quality every well-groomed, nice girl should communicate to her environment (100).

Gilgi's professional egotism and her playful attitude towards sexuality clearly identified her initially as the much feared "New Woman" who sought to exploit her newly won independence by imitating male ways. Her search for her own mother and her pregnancy, however, lead her to accept and appreciate the limitations of her female role. Gilgi's development from self-centered careerist to compassionate professional thus constitutes a powerful example for the transformation from "New Woman" to "New Mother."

Vicki Baum's *stud. chem. Helene Willfüer* and Irmgard Keun's *Gilgi—eine von uns* thus support the discourse of the "New Mother" in very different ways. Yet, both document that the seemingly contradictory concepts of "spiritual motherhood" and the "New Woman" were responses to the same structural changes. Both concepts arose from women's fundamental experience of exclusion from the public sphere, from power (Brick and Woesler 66). Both represented an attempt to come to terms with the modern experience of disruption: the concept of "spiritual motherhood" posited maternal unity against the fragmentation of modernity, while the "New Woman" supported atomization and rationalization in order to prove woman's existence as individual. From those apparent opposites, the "New Mother" emerged as a logical, albeit problematic, synthesizing construct that facilitated the positive reception of fascist models of femininity.

Notes

All translations are my own unless otherwise noted.

[1] By 1932, *stud. chem. Helene Willfüer* had reached a distribution of 105,000 copies; *Gilgi* reached six editions with a total of 30,000 printed copies in 1931 alone (King 93; Krechel 106).

[2] For an extensive discussion of the concept of "spiritual motherhood" as emancipatory strategy for women see Ann Taylor Allen. Allen's reading of the lives of women activists and professionals in the educational and social movements around the turn of the century validates the "feminist" quality of "spiritual motherhood" and thus differs considerably from my own interpretation.

[3] The position on the abortion issue supported by the text is voiced by Dr. Gropius, a woman doctor, and reflects the dominant position of the women's movement on the issue at the time. The experience of motherhood should not be denied to any woman, regardless of her marital or economic status. The responsibility to provide the necessary social support and create the moral climate that would enable every woman to give birth to her child was the role of the welfare state. "The opportunity growing inside of you must not be destroyed" (137), Dr. Gropius argues to convince Helene to keep her child, reinforcing the utopian interpretation of femininity and maternity supported by the text. For a discussion on the abortion issue taken by the various political groups and parties see Grossmann (1984), Hagemann (220-69), Usborne (156-201).

[4] Stöcker's theory is contradicted by the actual life stories of women artists working in the 1920s and 1930s like Paula Modersohn-Becker, Frida Kahlo, Käthe Kollwitz, Jeanne Mammen, and Meret Oppenheimer. In her analysis of the impact pregnancy and motherhood had on these women, Jula Dech has discovered a striking correlation between motherhood and self-destructive tendencies in these artists, instead of the productive conflict postulated by Stöcker.

[5] Helene bears the hardships of single motherhood with admirable equanimity. The text emphasizes the protagonist's resourcefulness in overcoming her difficulties through a change in narrative technique. While the novel is written from the perspective of an omniscient narrator, Helene's struggle to complete her degree while raising her son is documented in her correspondence with her fatherly friend, the bookseller Kranich, and her retrospective account of her life as she relates it to Professor Ambrosius. The immediacy of this subjective perspective allows the reader to participate directly in Helene's experience and serves to represent her hardship as the memory of a past that has been overcome. Baum describes Helene's difficult situation as that of an individual under unusual circumstances that warrants an individual solution. However, as P.E. points out, in conjunction with their increase in numbers, the economic situation for female students actually worsened. She attributes this to cuts in special scholarships for women as well as the increase in housework performed by women students.

[6] As stated in her article "Erfahrungen mit der Verjüngung," Vicki Baum had informed herself on rejuvenation research before writing her novel. Lynda King interprets its publication as part of Ullstein's advertising strategy for the novel (87). King also reprints an advertisement for Greilung-Kolibri cigarettes that makes reference to Baum's novel: "For the low nicotine fabrication 'Hektor,' stud. chem. Helene Willfüer has developed a new slimming cigarette. This cigarette named 'Ford' is guaranteed to contain over one percent of minerals from the Karlsbad spa and authentic Marienbad climate. Under the combined supervision of the chemists Dr. A. and B. Piep, the desired effect has taken place twice within 24 hours" (125). This advertisement from the *Berliner*

Illustrirte Zeitung underscores the point King wishes to make about the publicity campaign that molded Vicki Baum into a celebrity. The fact that such blatant ridicule of a, if only fictional, female scientist could be used to sell a product, however, casts the emancipatory message of Baum's novel into doubt.

[7] Feuerbach's art attained great acclaim during the 1920s, culminating in a retrospective in 1929. Given the visibility of the artist, Baum must have counted on her readers' familiarity with Nanna's image and perhaps also with the story behind Feuerbach and his model. Feuerbach recalls in his journal: "One day, we were walking down the Via Tritone, the street that connects the Piazza Barbarini with his studio, when we noticed a woman standing in front of an open window with a child in her arms. Framed by the window, this image offered the most ravishing sketch for a large madonna project that any artist could have ever have come across accidentally" (168). Subsequent to this encounter, Nanna lent her features to Feuerbach's most significant works, raising herself from poverty to relative fame and fortune.

[8] I am using the German term *Angestellte* rather than its English translation, since the translated term is considerably wider and does not carry exactly the same connotations as the German. For a comparative discussion of the representation of the working women in Weimar Germany see Harrigan; see Jordan specifically on the *Angestellte*.

[9] Manfred comments on his girlfriend's vain attempts to preserve her youth and beauty: "Young, young face. And yet—here and there, under the eyes, on the forehead, around the corners of the mouth, we can detect, not lines and wrinkles, but slight hints that they will be there four, five, or ten years from now, despite facial creams, despite ointments, despite almond bran" (70).

[10] Keun's subsequent novel *Das kunstseidene Mädchen* (1932) could be read as a sequel or counter-narrative to *Gilgi*. In contrast to Gilgi, Doris no longer believes in women's social mobility in patriarchal society and instead opts for a career as kept woman and prostitute.

[11] Keun's position on the abortion issue, voiced by her protagonist, is more radical than Baum's: "Not only should women be able to obtain an abortion if their economic situation does not allow them to raise a child, but no woman should be forced to give birth to a child she doesn't want" (117).

[12] Ritta Jo Horsley bases her analysis of language in *Gilgi* on exactly this conflict between altruism and egoism inherent in the text (298–305).

Works Cited

Allen, Ann Taylor. *Feminism and Motherhood: 1800–1914*. New Brunswick: Rutgers UP: 1992.

Anselm Feuerbach: Gemälde und Zeichnungen. München: Deutscher Kunstverlag, 1976.

Asendorf, Christoph. *Batterien der Lebenskraft: Zur Geschichte der Dinge und ihrer Wahrnehmung im 19. Jahrhundert*. Giessen: Anabas, 1984.

Baum, Vicki. "Erfahrungen mit der Verjüngung." *Uhu* 3 (December 1927): 33–41.

———. *Stud. chem. Helene Willfüer*. Berlin: Ullstein, 1928.

Brick, Barbara, and Christine Woesler. "Maschinerie und Mütterlichkeit." *Beiträge zur feministischen Theorie und Praxis* 5 (1981): 61-68.

Caspar-Köslin, Adelheid. "Der Sinn des Frauenstudiums." *Die Studentin* 9 (1 March 1927): 131–33.

Dech, Jula. "Ex voto-Der Würgeengel: Leidhaftigkeit und Wahrhaftigkeit im Werk von Künstlerinnen der klassischen Moderne." *Unter anderen Umständen*. Berlin: Argon, 1993.

Dieckmann, Elfriede. "Innere Probleme des Studentinnenlebens." *Die Frau* 27 (November 1919): 33–41.

Grossmann, Atina. "Abortion and Economic Crisis: The 1931 Campaign Against Paragraph 218." *When Biology Became Destiny: Women in Weimar and Nazi Germany*. Ed. Renate Bridenthal, et al. New York: Monthly Review, 1984. 66–86.

———. "Girlkultur or Thoroughly Rationalized Female: A New Woman in Weimar Germany?" *Women in Culture and Politics: A Century of Change*. Ed. Judith Friedlander, et al. Indianapolis: Indiana UP, 1986. 62–80.

Hagemann, Karen. *Frauenalltag und Männerpolitik: Alltagsleben und gesellschaftliches Handeln von Arbeiterfrauen in der Weimarer Republik*. Bonn: Dietz, 1990.

Harrigan, Renny. "Novellistic Representations of *die Berufstätige* during the Weimar Republic." *Women in German Yearbook 4*. Ed. Marianne Burkhard and Jeanette Clausen. Lanham, MD: UP of America, 1988. 97–124.

Hollander, Walther von. "Autonomie der Frau." *Die Frau von morgen wie wir sie uns wünschen*. Ed. Friedrich Huebner. Leipzig: Seemann, 1930. 26–37.

Horsley, Ritta Jo. "'Warum habe ich keine Worte?...Kein Wort trifft zutiefst hinein.' The Problematics of Language in the Early Novels of Irmgard Keun." *Colloquia Germanica* 23 (1990): 297–313.

Jahnn, Hans Henny. "Gesund und angenehm." *Die Frau von morgen wie wir sie wünschen*. Ed. Friedrich Huebner. Leipzig: Seemann, 1930. 135–46.

Jordan, Christa. *Zwischen Zerstreuung und Berauschung: Die Angestellten in der Erzählprosa am Ende der Weimarer Republik*. Frankfurt a.M.: Lang, 1991.

Keun, Irmgard. *Gilgi—eine von uns*. München: Deutscher Taschenbuch Verlag, 1989.

King, Lynda. *Best-Sellers by Design: Vicki Baum and the House of Ullstein*. Detroit: Wayne State UP, 1988.

Knoblauch, Elisabeth. *Zur Psychologie der studierenden Frau*. Leipzig: Verlag Johann Ambrosius Barth, 1930.

Krechel, Ursula. "Irmgard Keun: die Zerstörung der kalten Ordnung; Auch ein Versuch über das Vergessen weiblicher Kulturleistungen." *Literaturmagazin* 10: 103–28.

Kristeva, Julia. "A New Type of Intellectual: The Dissident." *The Kristeva Reader*. Ed. Toril Moi. New York: Columbia UP, 1986. 292–300.

———. "Stabat Mater." *The Kristeva Reader*. Ed. Toril Moi. New York: Columbia UP, 1986. 160–86.

P.E., cand. phil. "Die wirtschaftliche Lage der Studentinnen." *Die Frau* 4 (1922): 107–15.

Peukert, Detlev. *Die Weimarer Republik*. Frankfurt a.M.: Suhrkamp, 1987.

Rabinbach, Anson. *The Human Motor: Energy, Fatigue, and the Origins of Modernity*. New York: Basic Books, 1990.

Roberts, Mary Louise. *Civilization Without Sexes: Reconstructing Gender in Postwar France, 1917–1927*. Chicago: U of Chicago P, 1994.

Rühle-Gerstel, Alice. "Zurück zur guten alten Zeit?" *Die literarische Welt* 41/42 (27 January 1933): 5–6.

Scheffler, Karl. *Die Frau und die Kunst*. Berlin: Julius Bard, 1910.

Schubring, Else. "Gut aussehen und doch was leisten! Eine Forderung an die berufstätige Frau." *Uhu* 6 (March 1931): 98–105.

Soltau, Heide. "Die Anstrengungen des Aufbruchs: Romanautorinnen und ihre Heldinnen in der Weimarer Zeit." *Deutsche Literatur von Frauen*. 2 vols. Ed. Gisela Brinker-Gabler. München: Beck, 1988. Vol. 2. 220–35.

Stöcker, Helene. "Mutterschaft und geistige Arbeit." *Die Liebe und die Frauen*. Minden: J.C.C. Bruns, 1906.

Suhr, Susanne. "Die weiblichen Angestellten." *Frauenarbeit und Beruf*. Ed. Gisela Brinker-Gabler. Frankfurt a.M.: Fischer, 1982. 328–39.

Tönniessen, H. "Die studierende Frau und das Geschlechtsproblem." *Die Frau* 11 (1927): 673–80.

Usborne, Cornelie. *The Politics of the Body in Weimar Germany*. Ann Arbor: U of Michigan P, 1992.

Weber, Marianne. "Der Typenwandel der studierenden Frau." *Die Frau* (June 1917): 23–27.

Weyrather, Irmgard. "Die Frau im Lebensraum des Mannes: Studentinnen in der Weimarer Republik." *Beiträge zur feministischen Theorie und Praxis* 5 (1981): 25–39.

Feminist Criticism and Bakhtin's Dialogic Principle: Making the Transition from Theory to Textual Analysis

Friederike Eigler

Following a brief introduction to the Russian linguist and literary critic Mikhail Bakhtin, this article reviews recent publications that combine Bakhtin's theories and feminist criticism. The article moves from a discussion of theory and "feminist dialogics" to its application in the analysis of specific literary works and then concludes with a Bakhtinian reading of two stories by Lou Andreas-Salomé. My assessment of the often uncritical appropriation of Bakhtinian notions—in particular the frequent references to "dialogue"—seeks to recover Bakhtin's "dialogic principle" as a category of critical analysis. Drawing on Bakhtin's socio-linguistic approach to literature, I maintain, can be most productive in making the often difficult transition from feminist theory to the analysis of individual texts. (FE)

The theories of the Russian linguist and literary critic Mikhail Bakhtin are of particular interest to scholars who are concerned with notions of agency and social change, notions that are often marginalized in recent critical theory. In the last decade, Bakhtin's theories have become especially attractive for a number of feminist critics who are interested in the social dimensions of language and literature.[1] On a meta-critical level, his dialogic principle has in fact fostered analyses conscious of competing "voices" within feminist criticism.[2]

Following a brief introduction to the reception of Bakhtin and to some of his central concepts, this article reviews recent publications on Bakhtin and feminist criticism, moving from a discussion of theory to its application in the analysis of specific literary works. After addressing studies that deal with feminist theories and that seek to establish a "feminist dialogics," I discuss applications of Bakhtinian concepts, such as the "dialogic," "voice," and "heteroglossia," to the analysis of literary texts within the field of feminist *Germanistik*.[3] I conclude with a Bakhtinian reading of two stories by Lou Andreas-Salomé. My assessment of the often uncritical appropriation of Bakhtinian notions in analyses of literature and culture—in particular the frequent references to "dialogue"—seeks to recover Bakhtin's "dialogic principle" as a category of critical analysis. Drawing on Bakhtin's socio-linguistic approach to literature, I maintain, can be most productive in making the often difficult transition from feminist theory to the analysis of individual texts.

I

As a result of censorship and ideological struggles in the Soviet Union, many of Bakhtin's works were published with considerable delay, appearing in the 1960s and shortly after Bakhtin's death in 1975. In the early 1980s, some of his most important essays on literature—published under the title *The Dialogic Imagination*—and his studies of Dostoevsky and Rabelais were translated into English. Since then the reception of Bakhtin's works in the USA and elsewhere has extended beyond Slavic departments to the areas of English, comparative literature, linguistics, and cultural studies.

The reception of Bakhtin's works has been complicated by at least three different factors, as Myriam Díaz-Diocaretz points out in her introduction to a special Bakhtin issue of *Critical Studies* (1989), beginning with the unresolved question of authorship. Probably due to the threat of censorship, several works often attributed to Bakhtin were published under the names of his friends, Medvedev and Vološinov. Since they were scholars in their own right, the extent to which they contributed to these works remains unclear. In addition, the terminology used in texts written by or attributed to Bakhtin is idiosyncratic and often inconsistent. Finally, translations tend to interpret Bakhtin's terminology in rather different ways and thus amplify the inconsistencies of the "original" texts.

These three factors, which shaped the dissemination of Bakhtin's works, have contributed to the appropriation of Bakhtinian ideas by adherents of very different critical schools. Among them are scholars working on intertextuality, either from a hermeneutic or from a deconstructionist vantage point (Lachmann 8), as well as critics primarily concerned with the social and political dimensions of literature and culture. Feminist approaches to Bakhtin fall, for the most part, into the latter category. Maroussia Hajdukowski-Ahmed, for example, identifies radical socio-political readings of Bakhtin whose ultimate goal is social "justice" (including Marxists and politically oriented feminists) and liberal-humanist readings of Bakhtin aiming at "liberty" (including Slavists and feminists supporting a plurality of voices) ("Éthique" 253).

Many feminist critics draw on Bakhtin's seminal essay "Dialogue in the Novel" in which he develops some of his central notions, such as the "dialogic," "voice," and "heteroglossia" (*The Dialogic Imagination*).

"Heteroglossia" conceptualizes the historical and social nature of language as a multiplicity of languages shaped by different social, professional, ideological, and age factors. The resulting sociolects and ideolects constantly intersect, coexist, contradict, and compete with each other (291). This concept of language corresponds with Bakhtin's definition of the novel (and literary prose in general) as "multi-voiced" narrative. Bakhtin's notion of "voice" is not related to "presence" (in the Derridian sense) nor identical with an individual character; instead, "voices" represent particular aspects of "heteroglossia" in narratives.

An example may help to clarify these abstract definitions. In Ingeborg Bachmann's novel *Malina,* the "I" represents the "voice" of socially constructed femininity, i.e., only *one* aspect of a more complex character that is ultimately suppressed and eliminated. While the novel *Malina* is shaped by the very tension between characters and voices, most narratives do not explicitly draw attention to the multiplicity of their "voices."

Bakhtin calls for an approach to literature that stresses and explores differences ("multiple voices") and challenges readings that harmonize differences or reduce the text to a single ("monologic") meaning. He employs the terms "dialogic" and "dialogization" to capture the specific modes in which voices are related to each other, including different degrees of tension and struggle. No voice exists in isolation but always relates to, is shaped by, and competes with other voices. The resulting "multi-voiced" narrative may challenge or undercut authoritarian language both within and outside of the text. Yet dialogized language, including its critical potential, is never entirely the product of the author's (or any speaker's) intentions but a result of the "heteroglossia," i.e., the languages that constitute the author's particular socio-historical context. This socially and historically grounded concept of language lends itself to feminist criticism that is concerned with the disruption of patriarchal language and the exploration of marginal voices within dominant discourses. As Mary O'Connor puts it in her contribution to the volume *Feminism, Bakhtin, and the Dialogic,* Bakhtin is attractive to feminist criticism because he takes into account the various determining social and historical factors of language *and* "allows for an active response on the part of the subject to these various discourses" (201).

II

A number of recent publications on feminism and Bakhtin address theoretical issues and seek to establish a "feminist dialogics." The concern for adopting a theoretical position that allows for social critique informs the 1991 volume *Feminism, Bakhtin and the Dialogic,* edited by Dale Bauer and S. Jaret McKinstry. A common thread in many of the contributions is the attempt to relate feminist criticism to pressing social issues such as apartheid, violence against women, and environmental issues.[4] In the introduction, Bauer and McKinstry provide a graphic example of gender-specific violence resulting from a "monologic" attitude that assimilates or annihilates different "voices": they mention Marc Lepine's mass murder of fourteen women (all perceived as "feminists" by Lepine) on the Montreal campus in 1989 as an extreme example of the inability to recognize the "other" within a (male) fantasy of "autonomy and power" (1).

Bauer and McKinstry provide a general framework for the articles included in this volume by defining what they term, with reference to Bakhtin, a "feminist dialogics."[5] Based on the social nature of language, "feminist dialogics" promotes the disruption and critique of dominant and oppressive ideologies (3). This includes the critique of "monolithic" views of feminism that are implicit in some feminist theories and explicit in the often stereotypical representation (and dismissal) of feminism in contemporary culture (1). Rather than merely reversing patriarchal discourse and producing a "feminist monologic voice" that makes universal claims about "woman" in a patriarchal society, "feminist dialogics" supports critical approaches based on the concept of "positionality." Thus a "feminist dialogics" includes consideration of specific contexts and conditions of women (and men) and, in regard to literature, the recognition of narratives as inherently "multivocal" (4), i.e., representing more than one (authorial) voice.

Patricia Yaeger provides a well-argued afterword to *Feminism, Bakhtin and the Dialogic*. Her comments on central Bakhtinian concepts are more succinct than the often passing references to Bakhtin in other contributions to the volume. In her concluding remarks she refers to the editors' notion of a "feminist dialogics" and summarizes its goals: first, it "re-invigorates our quarrels with patriarchy"; second, it "re-illuminates our debates with one another" (245) and often helps to raise awareness and acceptance of a "diverse feminist speech-world" (244).

Other studies that relate Bakhtin to feminist theory result in an "awareness" but not necessarily in an "acceptance" of different feminist approaches. The Canadian scholar Hajdukowski-Ahmed discusses, for instance, the reception of Bakhtin among French feminists. Following a detailed critique of what she considers "separatist feminism" (advanced by Cixous and Irigaray) and disregard for women's social reality (Kristeva), she comes to the conclusion that Françoise Collin's "feminist ethics" is the only feminist approach compatible with Bakhtinian notions of language and agency (266). Collin situates the gendered origin of an ethics of alterity in "birth"—the significance of which she sees as a *social* (not biological) event that recognizes the "other" as source of action and language. According to Hajdukowski-Ahmed, Collin's call for a feminist intervention in the "same" of patriarchy aims at a social renegotiation between the sexes, i.e., is based on a belief in "dialogue" despite existing power structures.[6]

Contrary to Hajdukowski-Ahmed's dismissal of Irigaray (and Cixous) as "separatist," Gail Schwab illustrates how a Bakhtinian approach may contribute to a more careful consideration of Irigaray. Schwab explores the "dialogic" nature of Irigaray's feminist theories and thereby challenges the wide-spread presumption that Irigaray represents essentialist notions of femaleness/woman (Moi). Like other feminist critics in recent years, Schwab reads Irigaray's references to female sexuality as a strategy that simultaneously exposes and undercuts phallocentric discourse (cf. Gallop and Fuss, among others). The Bakhtinian perspective Schwab introduces into the debate draws attention to "dialogic" versus "monologic" *readings,* i.e., our own reading strategies. She contends, for instance, that Toril Moi's "monologic" reading of Irigaray ignores the multiplicity of voices in her texts and thus reproduces a phallocentric discourse. A "dialogic" approach, by contrast, challenges a literal reading of Irigaray's "morphology of female sexuality" (65) by considering it instead as a textual strategy. Schwab's call for a dialogic reading corresponds in many ways with recent studies challenging the binarism of essentialism versus constructionism within feminist debates (cf. Fuss). By focusing on the ways feminist critics choose to read and represent other (feminist) critics, Schwab's article exemplifies how a "feminist dialogics" can assist in re-illuminating "our debates with one another" (Bauer and McKinstry).

The most recent volume relating Bakhtin to feminism is titled *A Dialogue of Voices: Feminist Literary Theory and Bakhtin* (1994), edited by Karen Hohne and Helen Wussow, who continue the discussion of a "feminist dialogics" in the introduction. Proceeding from Bakhtin's notion of language as multi-voiced, Hohne and Wussow problematize the very notion of a "female voice." If each voice contains the voice of others, then, they argue, "the singularity of the female voice is at best an illusion, at worst a silencing of the many experiences and contexts about which and within which women have spoken through the ages" (ix). Rather than working within the binary opposition of male/female, they call for a more consistent and thorough consideration of aspects of gender *and* ethnicity, race, and class. Considering the editors' convincing argument for a non-exclusive approach to issues of gender—an argument that resonates with recent developments in feminist criticism in general—it is surprising that hardly any of the articles included in this volume act on the editors' recommendation. The editors also fail to mention that the articles by Mary O'Connor and Louise Yelin in the volume *Feminism, Bakhtin and the Dialogic* (to which they refer in their critical assessment of a "feminist dialogics") integrate issues of gender and race into a Bakhtinian approach. Both O'Connor and Yelin expose the "andro- and ethnocentricity" of Bakhtin's writings and argue for a modified concept of "heteroglossia" that would include the exploration of racially marked and gendered "voices."

Myriam Díaz-Diocaretz's article "Bakhtin, Discourse, and Feminist Theories"[7] takes the discussion of differently marked "voices" even further. The Bakhtinian perspective she introduces to the contested issue of the relationship between gender and language adds a new dimension to existing feminist approaches. Bakhtin's notion of "voice" as never homogenous and autonomous but always contingent upon "other-voicedness" disrupts, she argues, any male-female dualism and, consequently, also the idea of the female voice as the "other" voice. Since a woman's voice is as "heteroglot" as any other voice, i.e., "overpopulated with other intentions and meanings," Díaz-Diocaretz suggests that strategies be developed for exploring "woman *and* the other" (including, but not limited to, issues of gender, race, and class) rather than "woman *as* the other" (136). Following the assumption that social heterogeneity is inherent in all language usage, she comes to the empowering conclusion: "the monologic, self-proclaimed authoritative word of patriarchy...is not and can never be the last word" (131).

Díaz-Diocaretz's article provides an example of a productive interaction between feminist theory and Bakhtin studies: she introduces the category of gender and thereby modifies Bakhtinian concepts, and then employs these modified notions for a critical revision of assumptions within feminist criticism.[8]

Anne Herrmann's study *The Dialogic and Difference: "An/Other Woman" in Virginia Woolf and Christa Wolf* (1989) addresses issues related to feminist theory and to its application, and thus serves as a transition to the examination of applications of Bakhtinian theory that I will undertake in the next section. Bakhtin's notion of the dialogic informs both Herrmann's textual analyses *and* the presentation of her analyses, i.e., the meta-critical dimension of her study. Her readings of Woolf and Wolf function as "metaphors for the two positions that constitute the 'double-bind' within feminist critical theory" (150): Herrmann reads Virginia Woolf's texts as deconstructing the subject and Christa Wolf's texts as advocating the construction of a distinctive female subjectivity (4). Herrmann's own "dialogue" plays Woolf's and Wolf's positions off one another.

Individual chapters of Herrmann's book are structured as a self-interview, a letter, and a fictional dialogue between Wolf and Woolf. She thus refigures Wolf's own experimentation with open narrative forms and, at the same time, she enacts Bakhtin's "dialogic" principle. These communicative forms of writing "foreground the dialogized position of the writer (including the critic, F.E.) as a reader" (8) and they allow for the presentation of differences and contradictions through the conscious inclusion of various "voices." In chapter 1, for instance, Herrmann works through Bakhtinian concepts while the mode of presentation—a self-interview—simultaneously enacts her "double-voiced position of the feminist critical theorist" (8): trying to account for agency and social change without disregarding insights of critical theory concerning the tenuous status of the subject and subjectivity.

Herrmann's creative study of Wolf and Woolf and Díaz-Diocaretz's theoretical study are different examples of a "feminist dialogics." They illustrate that a rigorous analysis and/or enactment of Bakhtin from a feminist perspective can be beneficial to Bakhtin studies as well as to feminist criticism. In light of the theoretical discussions examined in this section, I would suggest that the most productive approaches go beyond a mere "application" of Bakhtin and combine, instead, two seemingly contradictory strategies: a close adherence to Bakhtin's notions *and* a creative and critical revision of his concepts from a feminist perspective (e.g., the integration of gender and other aspects he ignored, such as race and ethnicity, into his approaches to language and literature).

III

Among the Bakhtinian notions that are most frequently appropriated for (feminist) readings of literature and culture are the concepts of "voice," "dialogic," "hybrid construction," and "heteroglossia." The widespread assimilation of Bakhtinian notions in literary and cultural criticism frequently coincides with a very broad interpretation of these terms and a lack of attention to their socio-linguistic "origin." From a pragmatic point of view, the broad application and reinterpretation of theoretical concepts may serve useful purposes within (feminist) criticism. Yet, I would contend that Bakhtinian concepts are most powerful and convincing—in terms of making the transition from (feminist) theory to the analysis of individual texts—when employed as categories grounded in a socio-linguistic approach to literature.

Suzanne Kehde's article in the volume *Feminism, Bakhtin and the Dialogic* calls for an application of Bakhtin's notion of parody that would include canonical texts (e.g., novels by Hemingway and Henry James [29]). Although feminine "voices" are often marginalized in these texts, they may nevertheless disrupt the narrative's dominant discourse, resulting in a parody of patriarchal power structures. Within the general context of parody, one of the most useful Bakhtinian concepts for literary analysis is the notion of "hybrid construction." Diane Price Herndl, in a contribution to the same volume, argues that "hybrid constructions," i.e., "another's speech in another's language" may prove helpful in conceptualizing women's position within language: while women's "voices" potentially disrupt the dominant discourse of patriarchy, we also need to acknowledge that women are "always taking part in a dialogue not entirely under our control" (18). The insight into women's double position vis-à-vis language is not new; but the linguistically grounded notion of "hybrid construction" helps to transfer this general insight to the analysis of women's multiple positions in narratives.

In my reading of Ingeborg Bachmann's collection of short stories *Simultan,* for instance, the notion of "hybrid construction" proved helpful for an analysis of the multiple voices that inhabit the female characters: they are part of the Austrian upper middle class, sharing its values and prejudices while at the same time occupying a marginal position in society. "Hybrid constructions" are present in a whole range of distancing techniques that the narrator employs in the depiction of the female protagonists (through, for instance, humorous, ironic, or satirical undertones). The dynamic of contradictory positions and distancing techniques thus indicates at least two contravening tendencies: while the female outsiders in *Simultan* represent a critical stance toward the dominant patriarchal discourse, the ironic or satirical voices that enter the narrator's discourse point to the protagonists' partial complicity with the very mechanisms that victimize them.

Many of the essays in the volumes on Bakhtin and feminism discussed above adopt the term "dialogue" in the common sense of the word—implying human interaction and conflict resolution—and apply it to various contexts mostly as an alternative to or critique of relationships based on power and dependence (Yelin, among others). This may indicate the extent to which Bakhtinian notions have been assimilated into critical discourse, but it also reflects the common tendency to identify Bakhtin's notion of the "dialogic" with "dialogue," i.e., a non-hierarchical and open exchange or relationship.[9]

Yelin, for instance, in her discussion of the representation of apartheid in Nadine Gordimer's novels points out problems and limitations inherent in a notion of dialogue that is based on the possibility of exchange and communication. The reality of apartheid (in pre-1993 South Africa), Yelin claims, called for collective protests and opposition that ultimately exceeded both the notion of dialogue and the realm of the text (220; 232).[10] Yelin rightly identifies the limits of academic discourse by referring to situations that call for political action, but her critique of the very notion of "dialogue" concerns the common usage of the term, which is not identical with Bakhtin's "dialogic principle."

"Dialogue" employed in its conventional meaning tends to tame the Bakhtinian concepts of the "dialogic" and "voice." Bakhtin does not always use these terms consistently, but neither "voice" nor "dialogic" is usually related to individual subjects in a given text. Indeed, Bakhtin distinguishes ordinary dialogue between individuals from a dialogic relationship between "voices," i.e., different aspects of heteroglossia that may overlap but are usually not identical with characters in a novel.

Dialogue constitutes only *one* possible result of a dialogic relationship and presumes the willingness of both interlocutors to communicate.[11] By contrast, the Bakhtinian notion of the dialogic includes tension or struggle between antagonistic "voices" and thus also accounts for those voices that either refuse to enter into any kind of dialogue or that are excluded from it. This definition of the terms "voice" and "dialogic" allows for an exploration of marginalized and subversive aspects within a dominant discourse. A Bakhtinian approach thus fosters textual analyses that go beyond plot and character analysis and that relate, instead, the linguistic and discursive features of a literary text to their particular historical and social contexts.

Sara Friedrichsmeyer goes beyond character analysis in her comprehensive article on Christa Wolf, one of the few feminist analyses in the field of German studies that explicitly draw on Bakhtin.[12] She discusses the changing degrees of "dialogic discourse" in Christa Wolf's works focusing primarily on narrative structure. Assuming, however, that the dialogic implies equal validity of all voices, i.e., relativism, Friedrichsmeyer maintains that none of Wolf's works (with the exception of *Störfall*) are entirely "dialogic" because they all grant some authority to the narrator. She considers *Kassandra* "not dialogic because Wolf has posited narrative authority in the self-identical protagonist" (78). Wolf's writings are of great interest to many feminists and others who call for social change, Friedrichsmeyer argues, precisely because Wolf refrains from a complete dialogization of her narratives and from a complete decentering of authorial voice.

I fully agree with Friedrichsmeyer's timely reassessment of Wolf's ouevre, but I disagree with the premise that a "pure" dialogic with its "commitment to multiple truths, leads almost inevitably to relativism or a consciously chosen position of indecision" (79). Friedrichsmeyer's reservations about relativism (because it precludes any call for social change) seem more relevant to various deconstructionist or postmodernist approaches than to Bakhtin's dialogic principle. According to Bakhtin, it is the inclusion of disruptive and dissenting voices that results in the critical potential of the multi-voiced narrative. In Wolf's text, Kassandra's voice not only participates in but also undercuts and resists the official authoritarian ("monologic") language of the "ruling class." Thus, based on this different notion of the dialogic, *Kassandra* could be considered one of the most "dialogic" of Wolf's works. Bakhtin's linguistic approach is useful for feminist criticism, I maintain, precisely because aspects of "struggle" and "tension" between different "voices" are central to his notion of the "dialogic."

IV

I want to conclude this general discussion of the application of Bakhtinian concepts to literary analysis with a closer look at two literary texts. After briefly exploring how Brigid Haines employs Bakhtinian concepts in her reading of Lou Andreas-Salomé's story "Fenitschka," I suggest a new approach to Salomé's story "Eine Ausschweifung." Both stories, "Fenitschka" and "Eine Ausschweifung," were published together in 1898 and address changing gender relations around 1900: "Fenitschka" portrays a young woman who, because of social norms and gender-specific mores in a patriarchal society, attempts unsuccessfully to combine her private and professional lives; "Eine Ausschweifung" deals with a woman artist who, despite her independent life, displays strong masochistic tendencies. Until recently, feminist critics dealing with Salomé's writings have focused on "Fenitschka," which seems to promote women's liberation, but they have hardly mentioned "Eine Ausschweifung," which does not seem to fit contemporary notions of emancipation (cf. Martin, Müller-Loreck).[13]

By contrast, Haines, in two recent articles, reads both stories against the grain and challenges any simple categorization or interpretation. By utilizing Bakhtin's concepts of the "multi-voiced narrative" for a close reading of "Fenitschka," Haines illustrates the extent to which Fenitschka has internalized the oppressive social norms she tries to resist and transgress. Haines moves beyond a content-oriented analysis of the dialogue between Fenitschka and her male companion (which makes up a large part of the story) and looks instead at the representation of Fenitschka as a "site where conflicting discourses meet, exposing...norms of gendered behavior, and refusing...any easy answers, thus drawing the reader into the problem-solving process" (423). According to a feminist reading that utilizes Bakhtinian notions, the story "Fenitschka" turns out to be a more complex and challenging text than previous readings contended.

Haines's focus on the ambivalent representation of masochism in her article on "Eine Ausschweifung" provides an innovative and historically grounded reading in its own right. She analyzes the coexisting aspects of domination and submission in the female protagonist Adine that complicate and undercut any simple (gendered) opposition of masochism/sadism. Her considerations of the socio-historical implications of feminine masochism can be further substantiated by looking at the multiplicity of feminine voices that populate "Eine Ausschweifung." Such a reading would complement Haines's and would draw on Bakhtin's concepts of heteroglossia (the multiplicity of languages in a particular historical time) and dialogism (the transformation of heteroglossia into the stratified and competing voices in a narrative). I will briefly indicate how these concepts enable us to conceptualize the shifting "voices" within the story and their relationship to the rapidly changing situation of middle-class women in Europe at the turn of the century.

The main part of the story deals with Adine's return from her life as an artist in Paris to the small town of her youth, where she relives and simultaneously distances herself from the masochistic desire for her ex-fiance Bruno. Based on Díaz-Diocaretz's notion of woman's "heterglot" voice that is "overpopulated with other intentions and meanings," one can look at the character of Adine—similar to Fenitschka—as a site where contradictory voices coexist and compete. These "internal" voices reverberate with "external" voices in the story: the various other female characters who represent merely single voices and thus appear "monologic" compared to the "dialogic" character of Adine.[14]

The female characters include women of different generations and social classes and represent a range of different experiences and views on women's role in society: Adine's mother never questions the traditional submissive role of women and disapproves of her daughter's independent life as an artist; Adine's neighbor Gabriele reverses her initial feminist stance—propagating women's equality, including the right to education, a career, and economic independence—by assuming the role of a traditional housewife; the physically deformed baroness displays submissive gratitude and erotically charged devotion toward her physician Bruno, and thus appears like a caricature of Adine's past self; Gabriele's younger sister Mutchen pursues a secret affair and is thus the only female character who does not suppress or sublimate her sexuality.

The representation of Adine within the context of the other female characters can be read as "multi-voiced" and "hybrid": the main protagonist Adine comprehends diachronically the changing views of three generations of women and synchronically the competing voices on the issue of gender relations of her time. Adine's return from her independent life to her past triggers the collision of ultimately incompatible voices. This reading also accounts for the lack of synthesis or closure in "Eine Ausschweifung." Between the two opposite representations of female sexuality—the Baroness's complete self-negation and submission and Mutchen's non-committal affair—the narrative does not indicate any other possibility and seems to preclude the realization of any love relationship for Adine. The story ends in failed communication and speechlessness between Adine and Bruno.

"Eine Ausschweifung" thus captures both the complex situation of women—facing multiple external pressures as well as internalized norms and mores—and the complicated interaction between the two sexes around 1900[15] in a manner that differs in degree but not in substance from the story "Fenitschka." The critical implications of these "multi-voiced" narratives for readers today may lie in the way they disrupt the appearance of (women's) liberation and independence by drawing attention to the ways (patriarchal) power denies *and* shapes (female) desire (Haines, "Masochism" 111).

Bakhtin provides the linguistic categories that facilitate the exploration and identification of women's multiple and often contradictory subject positions. A feminist approach drawing on Bakhtin's concepts may thus prove especially useful in the reassessment of women writers, like Lou Andreas-Salomé, who until recently were shunned or read in a selective manner because of their presumed conservative or traditional representation of women and gender relations.[16]

Notes

[1] In his article "Bakhtin and the Challenge of Feminist Criticism," originally published in 1983, Wayne Booth addressed for the first time the androcentric bent in the works of Mikhail Bakhtin. Booth criticizes the complete absence of gender in Bakhtin's explicitly socio-linguistic concept of language and challenges the masculinist bias in Bakhtin's study on Rabelais. Booth deserves credit for introducing the issue of gender into Bakhtin studies, but his article does not address Bakhtin's potential usefulness for feminist criticism.

[2] Clive Thomson presents, in a contribution to the special Bakhtin issue of *Critical Studies* (1989), a critical overview of feminist appropriations of Bakhtin prior to 1989 that serves as a helpful introduction to Bakhtin.

[3] While there are many contributions in the field of German studies that include passing references to Bakhtin, there exist few feminist studies in *Germanistik* that draw on Bakhtin more extensively: Anne Herrmann's study of Virginia Woolf and Christa Wolf, Sara Friedrichsmeyer's comprehensive article on Christa Wolf, and Brigid Haines's study of Lou Andreas-Salomé's story "Fenitschka."

[4] While the first four articles included in the volume relate feminism and Bakhtin's notion of dialogism on a more theoretical level, the remaining seven contributions discuss a range of literary texts with more or less explicit references to Bakhtinian concepts.

[5] Bauer first developed this neologism in a previous book entitled *Feminist Dialogics*.

[6] Another contribution by Hajdukowski-Ahmed is included in the special issue of *Critical Studies* (1990). Her article on "Bakhtin & Feminism: Two Solitudes?" critically reviews the Bakhtin-biography by Katherina Clark and Michael Holquist whose own stereotypical representations of women reproduce, she contends, the gender-bias in Bakhtin's life and works.

[7] While most of the contributors to the volumes discussed above are teaching in English departments at U.S. universities, the authors included in the two special issues of *Critical Studies* on Bakhtin and the special issue of *Discours social/Social Discourse* on "Bakhtin and Otherness" come from a wide

variety of national and academic backgrounds, including Eastern and Western European countries, Canada, and the USA. These special issues give ample evidence of Bakhtin's wide appeal, not only in literary and linguistic studies but also in cultural studies, philosophy, and sociology. Each of the special issues includes a few articles concerned with Bakhtin and feminism.

[8] While Díaz-Diocaretz presents the most sophisticated and convincing discussion of Bakhtin, her approach is less differentiated when it comes to the representation of feminist theories. For instance, her critique of what she sees as prevailing "deterministic" concepts of language in feminist theories (i.e., language as inherently male-dominated) largely ignores the diverse body of more recent feminist criticism that has moved beyond the binary opposition of patriarchal discourse versus feminine language.

[9] According to the latter understanding of the term, the "dialogic" dimensions in Wolf's works include dialogue between characters, the relationship between the narrator and her characters, and Wolf's dialogue with history, mythology, and other (literary) texts. This broad application of the term makes it less useful as a category of critical analysis.

[10] One may want to argue that recent developments in South Africa, namely the relatively peaceful transition from apartheid to equal racial participation in democratic elections, have proven otherwise. However, the fact that the interracial dialogue continues to be threatened by violent extremists illustrates the pertinence of Yelin's critical assessment of "dialogue" within a (post)colonial situation of severe, long-term oppression.

[11] This notion of "dialogue" is related more closely to the hermeneutic tradition of Hans-Georg Gadamer and his concept of a fusion of horizons (*Horizontverschmelzung*) and to Jürgen Habermas's utopian notion of an open communicative society (*herrschaftsfreie Kommunikationsgemeinschaft*).

[12] Feminist critics in *Germanistik,* including Anna Kuhn, Edith Waldstein, and Thomas Fox, have explored the "dialogic" and intertextual dimensions in Christa Wolf's works without always explicitly referring to Bakhtin.

[13] See the overview of research on Lou Andreas-Salomé in my entry to the *Bio-Bibliographical Handbook on German Women Writers,* ed. Elke Frederiksen. Ute Treder includes a reading of "Eine Ausschweifung" in *Von der Hexe zur Hysterikerin,* but she ignores the disconcerting aspects of Salomé's representation of masochism and projects instead contemporary notions of women's liberation onto the story.

[14] For the purpose of this brief analysis, I consider the other female characters to be "monologic" representations. Ultimately, however, language is never purely "monologic." In an in-depth reading one could further explore the extent to which the representation of each of the female characters is shaped by a number of different discourses.

[15] Nike Wagner provides a critical analysis of how "the feminine" figures in the works of male intellectuals such as Weininger, Kraus, Strindberg, and Freud

and gives a socio-historical account of the situation of middle- and lower-class women in Vienna around 1900.

[16] A Bakhtinian approach may also turn out to be helpful for the exploration of new dimensions of "heteroglossia" in the emerging fields of (post)colonial studies and cultural anthropology within *Germanistik* and German studies.

Works Cited

Andreas-Salomé, Lou. *Fenitschka. Eine Ausschweifung: Zwei Erzählungen.* Ed. Ernst Pfeiffer. Frankfurt a.M.: Ullstein, 1982.

Bakhtin, Mikhail. *The Dialogic Imagination.* Ed. Michael Holquist. Trans. Caryl Emerson and M. Holquist. Austin: U of Texas P, 1981.

Bauer, Dale. *Feminist Dialogics: A Theory of Failed Community.* Albany: State U of New York P, 1988.

Booth, Wayne. "Freedom of Interpretation: Bakhtin and the Challenge of Feminist Criticism." *Bakhtin: Essays and Dialogues on his Work.* Ed. G.S. Morson. Chicago: U of Chicago P, 1986. 145–76.

Critical Studies. Special issue on "The Bakhtin Circle Today." Ed. Myriam Díaz-Diocaretz. 1.2 (1989).

Critical Studies. Special issue on "Bakhtin and the Epistemology of Discourse." Ed. Clive Thomson. 2.1/2 (1990).

A Dialogue of Voices: Feminist Literary Theory and Bakhtin. Ed. Karen Hohne and Helen Wussow. Minneapolis: U of Minnesota P, 1994.

Díaz-Diocaretz, Myriam. "Bakhtin, Discourse, and Feminist Theories." *Critical Studies* 1.2 (1989): 121–39.

Discours social / Social Discourse. Special issue on "Bakhtin and Otherness." Ed. Robert F. Barsky and Michael Holquist. 3.1/2 (1990).

Eigler, Friederike. "Bachmann und Bachtin: Zur dialogischen Erzählstruktur von 'Simultan.'" *Modern Austrian Literature* 24.3/4 (1991): 1–16.

———. "Lou Andreas-Salomé." *Bio-Bibliographical Handbook on German Women Writers.* Ed. Elke Frederiksen. Westport, CT: Greenwood (forthcoming).

Feminism, Bakhtin, and the Dialogic. Ed. Dale M. Bauer and S. Jaret McKinstry. New York: State U of New York P, 1991.

Fox, Thomas C. "Feminist Revisions: Christa Wolf's *Störfall.*" *German Quarterly* 63 (1990): 417–77.

Friedrichsmeyer, Sara. "On Multiple Selves and Dialogics: Christa Wolf's Challenge to the 'Enlightened' Faust." *Impure Reason: Dialectic of Enlightenment in Germany.* Ed. W. Daniel Wilson and Robert C. Holub. Detroit: Wayne State UP, 1993. 65–86.

Fuss, Diana. *Essentially Speaking: Feminism, Nature and Difference.* New York: Routledge, 1989.

Gallop, Jane. "Quand nos lèvres s'écrivent: Irigaray's Body Politic." *Romanic Review* 74.1 (1983): 77–83.

Haines, Brigid. "Lou Andreas-Salomé's 'Fenitschka': A Feminist Reading." *German Life and Letters* 44.5 (1991): 416-25.

———. "Masochism and Femininity in Lou Andreas-Salomé's 'Eine Ausschweifung.'" *Women in German Yearbook 10.* Ed. Jeanette Clausen and Sara Friedrichsmeyer. Lincoln: U of Nebraska P, 1995. 97-115.

Hajdukowski-Ahmed, Maroussia. "Bakhtin and Feminism: Two Solitudes?" *Critical Studies* 2.1/2 (1990): 153-63.

———. "Ethique de l'altérité, éthique de la différence sexuelle: Bakhtine et les théories féministes." *Discours social / Social Discourse.* 251-70.

Herndl, Diane Price. "The Dilemmas of a Feminist Dialogic." *Feminism, Bakhtin, and the Dialogic.* 7-24.

Herrmann, Anne. *The Dialogic and Difference: "An/Other Woman" in Virginia Woolf and Christa Wolf.* New York: Columbia UP, 1989.

Kehde, Suzanne. "Voices from the Margin: Bag Ladies and Others." *Feminism, Bakhtin, and the Dialogic.* 25-38.

Kuhn, Anna. *Christa Wolf's Utopian Vision: From Marxism to Feminism.* Cambridge: Cambridge UP, 1988.

Lachmann, Renate, ed. *Dialogizität.* München: Fink, 1982.

Martin, Biddy. *Woman and Modernity: The Life(Styles) of Lou Andreas-Salomé.* Ithaca: Cornell UP, 1991.

Moi, Toril. *Sexual/Textual Politics: Feminist Literary Theory.* London: Methuen, 1985.

Müller-Loreck, Leonie. *Die erzählende Dichtung Lou Andreas-Salomés: Ihr Zusammenhang mit der Literatur um 1900.* Stuttgart: Heinz, 1976.

O'Connor, Mary. "Subject, Voice, and Women in Some Contemporary Black American Women's Writing." *Feminism, Bakhtin, and the Dialogic.* 199-217.

Schwab, Gail. "Irigarayan Dialogism: Play and Powerplay." *Feminism, Bakhtin, and the Dialogic.* 57-72.

Thomson, Clive. "Mikhail Bakhtin and Contemporary Anglo-American Feminist Theory." *Critical Studies* 1.2 (1989): 141-61.

Treder, Uta. *Von der Hexe zur Hysterikerin: Zur Verfestigungsgeschichte des "Ewig Weiblichen."* Bonn: Bouvier, 1984.

Wagner, Nike. *Geist und Geschlecht: Karl Kraus und die Erotik der Wiener Moderne.* Frankfurt a.M.: Suhrkamp, 1981.

Waldstein, Edith. "Christa Wolf's *Kein Ort. Nirgends*: A Dialogic Re-vision." *The Enlightenment and Its Legacy: Studies in German Literature in Honor of Helga Slessarev.* Ed. Sara Friedrichsmeyer and Barbara Becker-Cantarino. Bonn: Bouvier, 1991. 181-93.

Yaeger, Patricia. Afterword. *Feminism, Bakhtin, and the Dialogic.* 239-45.

Yelin, Louise. "Problems of Gordimer's Poetics: Dialogue in *Burger's Daughter.*" *Feminism, Bakhtin, and the Dialogic.* 219-38.

Young, Robert. "Back to Bakhtin." *Cultural Critique* 2 (1985/86): 71-92.

The Body in the Discourses of Colonial Savage and European Woman during the Enlightenment

Imke Lode

Today, issues of race, ethnicity, and racism require a new kind of attention by feminist scholarship in German Studies. The discourse of the body is proposed as a feminist model integrating these concerns. This article first examines Sigrid Weigel's essay "Die nahe Fremde" and her hypothesis that a substitution process between the Enlightenment discourses of European woman and colonial savage took place. The discourse of the body is then used to challenge this hypothesis and to argue for the need and possibility of integrating both issues, race and sexuality, on a discursive as well as on a material level. (IL)

In her essay "Die nahe Fremde—das Territorium des 'Weiblichen': Zum Verhältnis von 'Wilden' und 'Frauen' im Diskurs der Aufklärung" (1987), Sigrid Weigel traces the similarities and analogies of European Enlightenment discourses on the strange/foreign savages of the colonies (*die Wilden*) and the untamed (*wilde*) women at home. In one of her main arguments she assumes that the discourse of the savage was replaced with one of woman in the context of material practices and historical changes between 1750 and 1800, such as the end of the age of colonial discovery, the transition from explorations of foreign countries to systematic scientific field research, or the development of the humanities:

> As the age of discoveries of foreign territory approached its end, as subsequently any spatial utopias became impossible, as the exploration of foreign countries moved into the stage of systematic field research and as the history of the humanities began in Europe—during this phase and in the process of justifying one's Self by splitting off and excluding the Other, woman, or femininity, became *the substitute* for both the foreign lands and the savages: a territory of foreignness nearby (189, emphasis added).[1]

Weigel's essay is, however, less concerned with material developments than with demonstrating the structural analogy of these two discourses as she considers both of them to be based on an Enlightenment dialectic that defines one's self (*das Eigene*) in light of, in relation to, the (strange/foreign) Other (*das Fremde*) (173). Drawing upon several examples, mostly from French Enlightenment texts, Weigel convincingly demonstrates the common dialectic basis upon which male European subjectivity tried to establish and affirm itself via its constructions of Otherness. These analogical constitutions of Others are at the center of her investigation of the relation between savage and woman, and the effectiveness of her discourse analysis explains why Weigel's essay has become a core text in feminist scholarly discussions of Enlightenment constructions of woman and femininity.

Yet, Weigel's significant contribution notwithstanding, the suggested conflation of the colonized Other with the Otherness of European woman obscures vital sociohistorical moments that signify distinct elements in the histories of, for example, neo-colonialism and the Black liberation movement, as well as European gender relations and feminism. Weigel's argument that a substitution process took place thus remains problematic because it subsumes one discourse into the other, neglecting their independent, historically specific developments, which go beyond their analogical similitude. The argument seems to suggest that the Enlightenment idea of woman absorbed, and brought to an end, the previous discourse of the savage. This argumentation ignores and even conceals, however, the permanence of Enlightenment conceptions of the savage throughout the hegemonic phase of colonization and the neo-colonialist stages up to the present.

Furthermore, such a reduction of the colonial discourse of the savage does a potential disservice to feminist scholarship, which may find itself repeating what it accuses patriarchal discourses of doing: erecting an Other on terms that primarily serve one's own self-understanding and subject construction at the expense of the Other's specificity and historicity. At stake is the assumption of a replacement of one discourse with another, even when the genealogies of their analogies show obvious cross references and interdependencies. Belinda Edmundson and Leslie Adelson have convincingly argued that the conflation of historically and socially specific manifestations and discourses of racism, economic oppression, and colonialism with sexism, on the one hand, and of black aesthetics/cultures/politics with feminist aesthetics/cultures/politics, on the other, is indeed highly problematic. A female author's/feminist's claim to "blackness on behalf of female subjectivity" (Adelson 249) can be ahistorical, reductive, and, possibly, even racist.

These dangers also exist in Weigel's essay "Die nahe Fremde," although she attempts to disengage precisely this conflation within (white Western) male discourses of savage and woman. In outlining some elements of the structural logic and contestable aspects of Weigel's argument, I want to reveal its blind spots and, subsequently, to show other means of addressing analogies and distinctions elaborated by Enlightenment discourses. My aim is not to analyze the entirety of Weigel's work. Nor do I disagree with her crucial description of the patriarchal European process of conquering, mapping, defining, in short "colonizing the body" of the constructed Other, appropriating the women of European homelands and the native people of the colonies for the purpose of erecting white men's subjecthood (cf. Weigel 189–90, 192). Instead, this paper will focus on the second step of her analytical procedure, the concluding inference of a substitution process between the discourses of savage and woman. The goal is, thus, to examine a core feminist contribution to the understanding of Enlightenment discourses in order to discern where feminist scholarship in German Studies might want to direct its analytical and interpretative work today, when issues of race, ethnicity, and racism require a new kind of attention.

In order to form a more distinct picture of the contiguities as well as the differences between the two discourses of savage and woman, it seems necessary to follow the Enlightenment debate on the meaning of nature in relation to its discourse on the body, emphasizing issues of race and sexuality, on a discursive *as well as* on a material level. This procedure is based on the notion that cultural formations described independently of their socioeconomic contexts cannot but result in distorting historical analyses. In a feminist analysis of the discourses of European woman and colonial savage, the historical complexity of relations between white Western women and colonized people needs to be acknowledged, including a recognition of the multifaceted socioeconomic and ideological positions that they entail.[2] In addition, a historical account that attends to the shared grounding in the body of both discourses of woman and savage might avoid the risk of collapsing their material and discursive differences into one undifferentiated concept of supposed identification with one another. Indeed, when looked at within the framework of the body, the notion of a substitution may not only be unfounded but also unnecessary in a feminist endeavor.[3]

Weigel's ambitious essay attempts to demonstrate connections between several discourses and their historical consequences. Starting from observations of discursive analogies between Enlightenment concepts of woman and savage in terms of their relation to nature and childhood, she detects the potential of these terms for mutual exchange and sets out to deconstruct their genealogy. Her analysis is based on the thesis that woman was defined as the nearby territory of the other/stranger/foreigner (173); it assumes that the colonial movement of conquering foreign territory can be understood as a projected desire to take possession of the foreign Other in the dimension of space (181). Weigel thus sees the discursive conquest of the colonies and their native inhabitants as congruent with the construction of European woman at home: as a procedure of conquering the Other as a territory in spatial terms. This hypothesis is anchored, consequently, in several examples of visual representations of colonial land as woman, which she perceives as a process of identifying foreign territory and nature with woman's body and vice versa. Weigel argues that both nature and the female body have been subjected to territorial conquest under the Enlightenment premise that civilization requires nature's subjugation. Her focus on the discourse of conquering nature and woman in terms of space and territory rather than in terms of the body does not, however, differentiate between Enlightenment concepts of nature and the body.

This assumption of a sameness and perhaps even interchangeability of Enlightenment concepts of nature and the body must take into account that the discourse of the body involves, among others, issues of gender and sexuality *as well as* ethnicity and race, particularly in discourses of colonialism. The German terms *Wilde* or *Fremde* imply an ambiguity of connotations since they can refer to the colonies' natives or to their lands at specific moments in the colonization process and since *Fremde* can, furthermore, take on various meanings like strange/r, alien, or foreign/er. Of course, many of these distinctions were ignored, even intentionally leveled, by Enlightenment theories, and Weigel reiterates and critically accentuates what she detects in these texts, images, and concepts.

The discourse of the laws of nature in the Enlightenment interpreted social relations in terms of its postulate of the equality of all human beings, including—if only theoretically—women and men of any color, class, country, culture, or religion. If this *overt* principle were to be upheld as morally superior to any other (and worth fighting the French Revolution for), it needed to be strictly enforced. *Covert* desires for superiority in the battle for power in the private and public spheres of social relations had to be suppressed, transformed, or channeled. This process—involving both overt and covert mechanisms—was facilitated by declaring the supremacy of Enlightened reason and its achievements, especially in the natural sciences.

Accordingly, Weigel looks at the shifts in the Western concept of nature, tracing these changes in their visual representations via the body of woman:

> It is woman's body and her image which serve as the locale where a new concept of nature is brought about: nature is subjugated to man while movements have become mechanical and nature has become the object of scientific contemplation and aesthetic pleasure (178-79).

On the one hand, Weigel makes a convincing argument for the continuity of "the exchangeability of woman and nature" (190) as part of a myth that uses the female body as an allegorical or synecdochal vehicle for the representation of Nature. On the other hand, though, she also relies on a historical argument that she subsequently contradicts. At first, she anchors the Enlightenment's discursive construction of European bourgeois womanhood in its new concept of "subjugated nature." Later, however, she undermines this reasoning by drawing examples from historical periods that either precede or follow Enlightenment: as early as the Renaissance (da Vinci's *Pressure Wave after Artery Explosion,* ca. 1510) when—as she indicates—the concept of "animated nature" reigned, and as late as the Weimar Republic (Heinrich Vogeler's *War Fury,* 1919, or *Portrait of a Female Dancer,* 1918) (Weigel 178, 191). Weigel seeks to combat this contradiction:

> It is usually assumed that nature first becomes an alien outside world for man with the Enlightenment concept, which implies the domination and submission of nature. Yet, the *representational* identification of woman with earth in the concept of animated nature *actually* signifies that *nature had already been encountered by man as alien Other* (181, last emphasis added).

Two problems arise in the dissolution of Weigel's original argument about the historical specificity of the construction of European bourgeois woman in the Enlightenment via the new concept of subjugated nature: 1) The historical connection between the new European woman and the new concept of nature is obliterated when suddenly no historical differentiation in the development of the concept of nature seems necessary to locate the construct of woman as alien Other. The temporal grounding of the new type of woman, "the Innocent" (180), in the Enlightenment is thus undermined by dissolving it in an (almost) "timeless space" through examples drawn from da Vinci to Vogeler, bridging several centuries of different concepts of nature and woman. 2) The discourse of the body and the discourse of "space/territorial representation" are linked in speaking of white man's identification of woman with earth in his visual and written treatises. The question remains open, however, as to whether a "representational identification of woman with earth in the concept of an animated earth" (Weigel 181) *necessarily* implies a conception of nature as an alien Other to be mastered and subjugated.

This methodological contradiction cannot be resolved by recourse to a theoretical leap that renders superfluous the historically specific construction of woman as alien Other. Such a theoretical move seems only possible when material formations are disregarded; in fact, Weigel's own argument reflects her insistence on an exclusive discourse analysis:

> The structural analogy of savages and women on the level of discourse does not yet say anything about their real relation, inasmuch as their comparable situation in a sociohistorical sense, as, for example, in an analogy formation of race and gender relations, has been frequently

established. Such an equation ignores precisely the difference in the real that disappears when viewed from a single perspective, in the discourse of the white man, so to speak (173).

The evolution of discourses is strongly tied to material changes at specific moments in history. Therefore, to trace its genealogy without including material considerations seems an incomplete and distorting undertaking. Accordingly—although against her own presupposition—Weigel calls upon material practices like the end of the age of colonial discovery, the beginning of scientific field research, or the development of the humanities as motivating circumstances for her thesis of the Enlightenment "replacement" of the discourse of the savage with that of European woman. These historical changes are, indeed, significant in their impact on Enlightenment discourse formations and may be further illuminated by including the development from Europeans' search for new trading connections to slavery and the highly profitable triangular trade between Europe, Africa, and the Americas.[4] These socioeconomic changes generated fundamental shifts in the colonial discourses of expeditions and missionary voyages and, accordingly, in concepts of "savages" and colonized lands throughout the hegemonic and neo-colonialist phases. They cannot be neglected if we want to understand the differences and similarities between the discourses of savage and Western woman, and if we want to discern these discourses in their own material historicity.

During the first two and a half centuries of colonialism, Portugal and Spain—and from the seventeenth century on, England, France, and The Netherlands as well—considered the foreign continents they "discovered" mainly as new trading connections.[5] Hence, the discourse of the Other concentrated on the natural richness and differences of these lands, resulting in visual representations such as Adrian Collaert's *America* (cf. Weigel 196), that personified the exotic through the image of woman as simultaneously threatening and inviting.

However, over time the focus shifted from limited to expansive trade of sugar cane, coffee, cocoa, rice, tobacco, and indigo. And finally, the native people of the colonies became themselves commodities—as slaves. While this slave trade started out with the fairly unorganized "kidnapping" of small groups of people in the sixteenth century, it had expanded by the late eighteenth century into the highly efficient triangular trade of at least 15 million Africans, producing huge profits for European traders, African dukes, and American plantation owners.[6]

This slave trade caused significant shifts in material practices. The sudden accumulation of money laid the groundwork for much of the European Industrial Revolution, for even more efficient forms of capitalist production in Europe and in the North American South, for the rise of the European bourgeoisie, and for the hegemonic colonial phase and neo-colonialism. Abdul R. JanMohammed has described the changes that

British writing on Africa underwent in view of the interdependence of material developments and discursive shifts. The visiting, trading discoverer who has written on cultural differences without moral judgments becomes the resident, exploitative conqueror who needs an interpretation of the exotic Other as absolute alien Other, mirroring his new socioeconomic power (*Manichean Aesthetics* 7).

Yet, as Edward Said argues in his essay "Orientalizing the Oriental" (1978), it is not the domestication of the exotic—or the fixation of colonial Other upon the image of the savage (cf. JanMohammed, "Economy" 62)—as such that is controversial or reprehensible. Rather, the objectionable practice lies in the "limited vocabulary and imagery that impose themselves as a consequence" (264-65) within a mental operation of repeated and continuous "incarnat[ion] of the infinite in a finite shape" for narcissistic Western purposes (267). Thus, a constantly reiterated, dogmatic image of the colonies' natives and their cultures made the latter effectively disappear behind the walls of their colonial, discursive prison. The reasons for this European mental operation of a "monologically structured colonial discourse" (cf. Streese 10) are obvious, for its theoretical justifications (e.g., Christianizing the "heathen barbarians" or introducing the "savages" to Western civilization) clashed with the actual "missionary" practice of slave trade. An inherent contradiction (or dialectic?) is exposed: The material erection of European Enlightenment's high moral values of *égalité, fraternité, liberté* occurred at the expense of other human beings to whom these same values were denied (cf. Gürth 4).

Western (colonialist) literature,[7] religion, philosophy, and anthropology of the time reflect discursive attempts to come to terms with this contradiction, which frequently crystallized around two basic stereotypes of the colonized Other: the noble and the ignoble savage, *der edle Wilde* and *der rohe Wilde*. Thinkers who were tired of civilization indulged in the dream of noble savages who embodied a "lost paradise" of simple, (sexually) free, "natural" life inhabited by "instinctively good" (Harris-Schenz 59), naive "eternal children" lacking any instrumental reason or concepts of a future and whose social structures "naturally" derived from nature.[8] On the basis of the anthropological belief in a monogenetic origin of man from one (Biblical) set of parents (cf. Blumenbach, Kant, Sömmering, Camper, Herder),[9] "the noble savage" was (to varying degrees) considered a human being equal to the European.

Nevertheless, the idea of one origin of wo/man, and thus the equality of all human beings, did not prevent some theorists from insisting on (biological) difference in other ways.[10] While, for example, Herder and Kant remained monogenetic anthropologists, believing in one human race, they correlated the hot African climate not only with the natives' physiognomy but also with the Black as "lazy, feeble and dallying" (Kant, "Racen" 99) and "by nature restricted to a more sensual realm of life"

(Herder, "Organisation" 236). Thus, they drew conclusions about moral behavior and ethical nature from selective physiological observations, subsequently representing "the noble savage" in terms of hierarchical difference(s) rather than equality.

What at first appears to be a liberal and progressive discourse of the equal, noble savage turns out to be barely distinguishable from the discourse of the ignoble savage/devil, the cross between animal and human being. The epistemological contradiction within the monogenetic conception becomes obvious when perceived within the framework of the body, the site used to create discursive difference. For example, the monogenist Samuel Thomas Sömmering believed Blacks to be as "good as us"—the white Europeans. Yet, in his book *Über die körperlichen Verschiedenheiten des Negers vom Europäer* (1785), he insists that the Black is physiologically more closely related to the ape than to the European (xiv). Sömmering's opinions might have been influenced by his friend Georg Forster, one of the most renowned spokesmen for polygenesis, who resolved the issues of race and different skin colors by classifying Blacks and Whites as varieties of the same species—i.e., having (two) different originating parents.

Forster was quite aware that his polygenetic theory of two races could make Blacks more vulnerable to white European cruelty and contempt (154). As an abolitionist he contends: "Let me ask, rather, whether the thought that Blacks are our brothers [reference to monogenetic philosophy, IL] has anywhere even once caused the whip of the slave-master to be lowered?" (154). While Forster does not claim "racial superiority" for the white Westerner, his arguments against slavery are, nonetheless, firmly rooted in a patriarchal, moral superiority that explicitly regards the native Others as children in need of European paternal guidance (155). It was polygenetic theory, after all, that facilitated the concept of the ignoble savage—a creature with both animal and human features, embodying the myths of the Dark Continent, cannibalism and excessive sexuality. It was subsequently employed to justify the ideology of racial superiority and slavery.

The Enlightenment discussion of slavery and of its abolishment represents the epitome of its inherently dialectic contradictions. On the one hand, the concept of the noble savage provided the ground upon which abolitionists were fighting for the equality and freedom of all people. On the other hand, the emerging myth of the Dark Continent inherently counteracted these supposed liberation efforts.

As Patrick Brantlinger demonstrates, with the weakening of their global economic power in the dominant colonial phase, countries like Britain could afford to call for the abolition of slavery in the name of civilization during the approaching Victorian era. They even promoted themselves as "potential saviors of the African" (173) in order to fight on moral grounds against the gain of economic strength and independence through the continuous practice of slavery in the United States (173). Against this backdrop, it becomes clear that

> the myth of the Dark Continent was thus a Victorian invention. As part of a larger discourse about empire, it was shaped by political and economic pressures and also by a psychology of blaming the victim through which Europeans projected many of their own darkest impulses onto Africans. The product of the transition—or transvaluation—from abolitionism to imperialism, the myth of the Dark Continent defined slavery as the offspring of tribal savagery and portrayed white explorers and missionaries as the leaders of a Christian crusade that would vanquish the forces of darkness (Brantlinger 198).

Brantlinger perceives the "myth of the Dark Continent" as a re-definition of the already discovered and conquered 'dark' colony. Weigel, on the other hand, draws on Marion Schmid when she transfers this axiom to female sexuality: "Female sexuality *only* emerges as 'Dark Continent' when the female body has been completely described [*be-schrieben*] and covered with interpretations" (175–76, emphasis added). Weigel thus invokes a potential end to the procedure of defining Woman as soon as all the "white spots" have been "discovered" and marked, i.e., "darkened." Subsequently, though, she makes the contradictory observation that the formation of legends around the "riddle Woman" has actually not ceased but rather persevered until today (176).

Brantlinger, in contrast to Weigel in her first proposition, describes the myth of the Dark Continent as an incessant, tautological Western construct, embodying an endless—psychological—need for affirmation through more and more (scientific) discourse,[11] thereby echoing Said's assessment of Orientalism (266–67).

It is precisely within the discourse of positive Western knowledge, philosophical anthropology, natural sciences, and, at its focal point, the body, that the supposed differences between the concepts of noble savage and ignoble savage/devil dissolve into one single ideological construct of difference, of the bodily Other. Hence, the contiguity of savage and woman becomes visible in their grounding through the body. Thomas Laqueur asserts: "Bodies...are not the sign of but the foundation for civil society" (157), noting that "there are important parallels between post-eighteenth-century discussions of sexual and racial differences, since both seek to produce a biological foundation for social arrangements" (282).

As Weigel has made clear, both constructs of savage and woman embody an ambivalent utopian desire for a paradisiacal nature as well as a fear of its destructive potential (cf. 180). The emotive[12] roots of this dialectic can be traced to the Enlightenment crisis of male European subjectivity, projected onto both European woman and foreign colonized

Other. This crisis can be deciphered in the cognitive discourse of the body, as the natural sciences exemplify.

As a result of the secularization process that occurred during the Enlightenment, the simultaneously expanding sciences did not merely enhance other discursive practices but served to replace former transcendental justifications for existing social orders. Science had to identify, interpret, and build wo/man's connection to "reality," for "the genuine form in which truth exists, can only be its scientific system" (Hegel 14). Laqueur considers this epistemic shift to be one of two major explanations for the discursive changes from what he calls the one-sex-model to the two-sex-model. Laqueur argues that, from Aristotle to the eighteenth century, the dominant concept of gender was connected to a one-sex-model that assumed that: 1) Women and men had the same basic sexual organs, either turned "inside out" or "outside in," measured by the standard of the male body. Any distinctive name for "vagina" or "ovary" was, accordingly, lacking until around 1700 and even later (4, 61, 159). 2) Both women and men were capable of, and indeed experienced, the sexual pleasure believed imperative for reproduction (48–49). 3) Woman was "a lesser being than man" (151). This was perceived as an *a priori* truth, since in "generation the male was the efficient and the female the material cause" (152). 4) Consequently, gender or woman's role in the world was "natural" and beyond any doubt or need for ("scientific") explanation (29, 152), because the social system was a microcosmic representation of the higher cosmic order (10–11).

While the vertical one-sex-model with its hierarchical power structure survived, the horizontally ordered opposition of the two-sex-model, with its insistence on biological (and subsequently social) differences between the sexes, emerged and gained dominance:

> One sex...did not die. But it met a powerful alternative: a biology of incommensurability in which the relationship between men and women was not inherently one of equality or inequality but rather of difference that required interpretation. Sex, in other words, replaced what we might call gender as a primary foundational category. Indeed, the framework in which the natural and the social could be clearly distinguished came into being (Laqueur 154).

Consequently, the unstable female body was created as an "empty category" (Laqueur 22), "the signifier without the signified" (Laqueur 150), defined by the new scientific proposition that women do not need to have orgasms or even be conscious in order to conceive: "The purported independence of generation from pleasure created the space in which women's sexual nature could be redefined, debated, denied, or qualified" (Laqueur 3). This body, opened up for reinterpretation and reconstruction, was subsequently locked into the social construct of the passive, passionless innocent (cf. Weigel 180).

However, as Weigel succinctly emphasizes, the discourse of "the innocent whose white gown...threatens to tear apart at any moment" (180) is signified by extreme artificiality and dangerous fragility in its attempt to dam up and exclude the assumed underlying, barely controllable female sexuality. By reducing the gender of woman to the discourse of a (potentially dangerous) sexualized female body, this dialectic episteme can reproduce itself tautologically, as does the continuous call for woman's self-control and/or her suppression by male social arrangements. The door slammed shut on the prison of bourgeois womanhood, leaving woman only the discursive alternatives of idealized innocent or pathologized prostitute.

What shines through is the contiguity between the dialectic systems of noble-ignoble savage and noble-ignoble woman. Both woman and savage were perceived either as noble, signifying the utopia of "instinctively good" and "naive eternal children" from "the lost paradise," or as ignoble, personifying a threatening excessive sexuality and a cross identity, partly animal, partly human. The contiguity of both discourses becomes particularly apparent where they merge into one single discourse of the body, as analyzed by Sander Gilman in "The Hottentot and the Prostitute." Gilman points out that the genitalia of female blacks—mostly slaves and/or "objects of scientific study" from the colonies—were of much greater concern to Enlightenment scientists than black male sexual organs (89). Due to epistemic desires for establishing the colonized Other as more primitive than the European in general and the male European in particular, rather grotesque equations were created: "The primitive is the black, and the qualities of blackness, or at least of the black female, are those of the prostitute" (99). At the conclusion of his examination of Zola's *Nana,* Gilman remarks:

> The Other's pathology is revealed in her anatomy, and the black and the prostitute are both bearers of the stigmata of sexual difference and thus pathology. Zola sees in the sexual corruption of the male the source of political impotence and provides a projection of what is basically a personal fear, the fear of loss of power, onto the world. The "white man's burden," his sexuality and its control, is displaced into the need to control the sexuality of the Other, the Other as sexualized female. For the colonial mentality that sees "natives" as needing control easily shifts that concern to the woman, in particular the prostitute caste (107).

Gilman attests to the white man's colonial mentality of control, which easily shifts from the natives of the colonies to (European) women. He does not, however, evoke a substitution process of woman for the Black/savage but, rather, suggests that both discourses developed more or less simultaneously, parallel to each other, rooted in the same colonial mentality (107).

Enlightenment philosophers like Rousseau acknowledged the existence of incommensurable differences between various races and cultures while ignoring those between women and men: "The savage and the civilized man differ so much in the bottom of their hearts and in their inclinations, that what constitutes the supreme happiness of one would reduce the other to despair" (270). Weigel elaborates on the paradoxical dimension of this claim in the context of woman:

> The discourse on woman remains always caught in the gaze of one gender upon the other...dealing with the nearby Other apparently does not permit the concession of difference...woman is always considered as dependent on man.... She establishes herself as function in the reflection of man about himself (187).

The problem with this otherwise astute observation lies in Weigel's conclusion of her reading Rousseau's *Discourse on the Origin of Inequality* (1755), that, if only a "concession of difference to the nearby Other" *were* made, man would refrain from mapping woman's body, from establishing her as Other using himself as yardstick. But it is precisely Otherness that Western man around 1800 *did* attribute to woman over and over again, imprisoning her in biological and social difference. Woman as a passionless, or, rather, sexually better controlled human being had "naturally" to complement man's contrasting, uncontrolled sexual desires and to advance civilization through her female "delicacy and sensibility."[13] This philosophical and fictional construct was mirrored by the social one of "gender characters," which "naturally" matched the separation of public and private spheres, thus constituting the dissociation of employment and family life not only as necessary but ideal (cf. Hausen 378).

The division of society into man's alienating outside world and woman's protective home is a reflection of the power struggle between the sexes over the public and private spheres. This power struggle represents in Laqueur's eyes the second and crucial, the political, explanation for the development of the two-sex-model (193). While the Christian image of *Hausmutter* defined women's social function since the Reformation (cf. Becker-Cantario 342), Enlightenment proponents went a step further and constructed a tautology of discourses.[14]

Enlightenment's more secularized world view exposes its own limits by grounding the construction of gender on the more "rational" discourse of biology and its conception of female sexuality. Enlightenment faith in a supposedly value-free, objective science allowed white Western man to project his desires onto the body of woman (and of the [female] savage).

Only by deconstructing Western man's discursive marginalization of Others, by revealing the emotive motivations beneath his cognitive vindications, can women intervene in the patriarchal making of histories and knowledges, can they reclaim their bodies, their discourses, and an identity as "provisional subjects." Particularily important in this endeavor is the need to differentiate the specific discursive and material positionalities of various Others. As Nancy Hartsock has strikingly put it:

> ...I believe we need to sort out who we really are. Put differently, we need to dissolve the false "we" ... into its real multiplicity and variety and, out of this concrete multiplicity, build an account of the world as seen from the margins, an account which transforms these margins into centers (34-35).

At stake is the construction of an oppositional agency engaged in the transformation of the patriarchal order.

Notes

I am especially grateful to Helmut Peitsch for his generous support, critical readings, and persistent belief in this project. For their encouragement, insightful comments, and helpful material my thanks further go to Martin Black, Patricia Doykos Duquette, Jan-Erik Gürth, Ruth-Ellen B. Joeres, Andrew Krivine, Anne Moss, Hector Rodriguez, Ina Ruthenberg, Heidrun Suhr, and the editors of the *Women in German Yearbook*. Marjorie Gelus and the anonymous reviewers provided useful suggestions.

[1] All English translations of German quotations are by this author. Weigel writes in the original text: "In einer Phase, da das Zeitalter der Entdeckungen fremder Gebiete seinem Ende entgegengeht, da mit diesem Ende auch die Utopien im Raume unmöglich werden, da die Erforschung der fremden Länder in das Stadium systematischer Feldforschung übergeleitet wird und in Europa die Geschichte der Humanwissenschaften beginnt—in dieser Phase wird die Frau bzw. Weiblichkeit *zum Substitut* für die Fremde bzw. Wilden im Prozess der Begründung des Eigenen über die Abspaltung und Ausgrenzung des Anderen: ein Territorium der nahen Fremde" (189, emphasis added).

[2] Within this context, one should keep in mind that Western bourgeois women were a strong economic force as consumers of new and "fashionable" imported products from the colonies. One could even claim that they, thereby, in/directly promoted the slave trade. Their construction as capitalist consumers, however, is strongly intertwined with their domestication and definition as bourgeois woman by white Western men: bourgeois and aristocratic women were confined to the home, hosting social events and, sometimes, literary salons (consumption of coffee, tea, chocolate, sugar). Also, they were "constituted" as aesthetic (sexualized) objects through fashion (need for cotton, silk, indigo). Women from lower social classes were employed in spinning and weaving cotton

and silk, and other aspects of textile manufacturing, using raw materials from the colonies.

Thus, Western women's complex two-sided positionality as both "oppressed" and "oppressors" becomes quite obvious. A further complication rests in the fact that most of the African slaves were women, although, within the European export market, male slaves were purchased by a margin of at least two to one (cf. Robertson/Klein 3, 4). In addition, female slave owners, users and traders were also engaged in the African slave trade (Robertson/Klein 12). Clearly, one has to look very carefully at women's individual positionality in matters of nationality, race, socioeconomic situation, age, religion, etc., before one jumps to any general conclusions about how and where they were specifically involved and located in these discursive and material issues.

[3] I am aware of Gisela Brinker-Gabler's critical assessment of Leslie Adelson's concept of an "agential female body" (Brinker-Gabler 241), which I adapt here. And at this point I am, admittedly, not able to answer Brinker-Gabler's justified questions concerning the relation between the "female body" and "woman," and the process of how a "female body come[s] into being" (241–42). I hope, nonetheless, to provide some clues about the usefulness of a theoretical/methodological approach that assumes the "possibility of agency" (Brinker-Gabler 242) of the (female) body. The two-sided positionality of women as simultaneously included and excluded from dominant orders extends to their bodies (of various colors, sexual orientations, etc.) as "resistant or in opposition to the dominant system...and, at the same time,...[as] a cultural construct through and on which that system is inscribed" (Adelson 239; see also Valie Export 4, 23). While such an assumption of a two-sided positionality eliminates the (absolute) Otherness and Outside of logocentric discourses, it provides, by the same token, potential spaces and moments of resistances to the dominant order (see here also Biddy Martin 15). This notion of resistance and the possibility of agency are the motivating factors in my examination of specific moments in the discourse of the body.

[4] At no point do I want to suggest that all colonized native people shared an identical history of material practices, nor that their discursive treatments as savages or others entailed one single image. Rather, I want to emphasize the complexity of socioeconomic implications and issues of race within the discourse of the savage. Examining some aspects of the history of African colonialism and of the triangular slave trade seems especially helpful for such an undertaking. The triangular trade was based on the European sale of kidnapped Africans to American plantation owners (mostly from the North American South) who exploited these Africans as slaves in, e.g., their cotton and tobacco production. The resulting harvests were, in turn, shipped to and sold in Europe, thus closing the profitable circuit of trade.

[5] While I will concentrate on some elements of the colonial history of the African continent, Tzvetan Todorov describes very similiar discursive and material developments with regard to the course of colonialism in the Americas.

⁶ See Jean Meyer, *Sklavenhandel*. Jan-Erik Gürth speaks of 40 million Africans having been deported from their homelands, of whom half reached their destinations alive (3).

⁷ Note JanMohammed's interpretation of the functions of colonialist fiction: 1) Colonialist literature forms imperial ideology in a process of symbiosis "by articulating and justifying the position and aims of the colonialist." 2) It tries to mask the contradiction between "the theoretical justification of exploitation and the barbarity of its actual practice...by obsessively portraying the supposed inferiority and barbarity of the racial Other, thereby insisting on the profound moral difference between self and Other" ("Economy" 83-84).

⁸ See here Weigel's discussion (174, 177, 181-85) of Charles-Marie de La Condamine's and Louis-Antoine de Bougainville's accounts of their colonial excursions and Rousseau's *Discourse on the Origin of Inequality* (1755), Harris-Schenz's chapters three and five as well as her conclusion, and Gürth's elaborations (5, 7) on the "noble savage" and "the paradise on earth" in reference to texts by Montaigne (*Of Cannibals,* 1578-80, *Of Coaches,* 1585-88), Rousseau (*Discourse on the Moral Effect of the Arts and Sciences,* 1750), and Montesquieu (*Esprit des Lois,* 1748).

⁹ Peter Camper caused an uproar with his claim that all men are inherently black, having different degrees of blackness according to climatic differences. For a detailed discussion see Harris-Schenz's first chapter, "Anthropological Treatises."

¹⁰ See, for example, Rousseau's hierarchical construction of *homme savage, homme civil,* and *homme sauvage* in his *Discourse on the Origins of Inequality* (1755).

¹¹ See Brantlinger (198-99), referring in part to Chinua Achebe's similar conclusions (2, 12).

¹² In reference to the concept of "emotive" and "cognitive" discourses of a text, I follow Terry Eagleton's definitions. Ideological propositions (in contrast to referential enunciations) may be "decoded" into an "emotive" (subject-oriented) discourse or an emotive "intentionality" underlying their "cognitive structures" (64).

¹³ Cf. Laqueur (200-01); Cranston (190), especially on Rousseau's concept of *femme savante*; and Hausen (378).

¹⁴ This imprisonment through male Enlightenment "knowledges" was an attempt to arrest white Western bourgeois women in their social place (gender) through reference to their supposedly natural place (sex) and vice versa. Since these "knowledges"—like "Orientalism" (cf. Said) or "sex and gender models" (cf. Laqueur)—can be viewed in Foucauldian terms as simultaneously "limitless" and "poverty-stricken" (30), they reveal a contiguity with the colonial myth of the Dark Continent: the endless need to be redefined over and over again.

Works Cited

Achebe, Chinua. "An Image of Africa." *Research in African Literatures* 9.1 (Spring 1978): 1–18.

Adelson, Leslie A. "Racism and Feminist Aesthetics: The Provocation of Anne Duden's *Opening of the Mouth*." *Signs* 13.2 (Winter 1988): 234–52.

Becker-Cantario, Barbara. *Der lange Weg zur Mündigkeit*. Stuttgart: Metzler, 1987.

Blumenbach, Johann Friedrich. *Über die natürlichen Verschiedenheiten im Menschengeschlechte*. Leipzig: Breitkopf & Härtel, 1798.

Brantlinger, Patrick. "Victorians and Africans: The Genealogy of the Myth of the Dark Continent." *Critical Inquiry* 12.1 (Autumn 1985): 166–203.

Brinker-Gabler, Gisela. "Alterity—Marginality—Difference: On Inventing Places for Women." Trans. Elizabeth Naylor Endres. *Women in German Yearbook 8*. Ed. Jeanette Clausen and Sara Friedrichsmeyer. Lincoln: U of Nebraska P, 1992. 235–45.

Camper, Peter. "Rede über den Ursprung und Farbe der Schwarzen gehalten in Gröningen auf der anatomischen Schaubühne den 14. November 1764." *Kleinere Schriften die Arzneykunst und fürnehmlich die Naturgeschichte betreffend*. Volume 1. Leipzig: Crusius, 1782.

Cranston, Maurice. *The Noble Savage: J.J. Rousseau 1754–1762*. Chicago: U of Chicago P, 1991.

Eagleton, Terry. "Ideology, Fiction, Narrative." *Social Text* 1.2 (1979): 62–80.

Edmondson, Belinda. "Black Aesthetics, Feminist Aesthetics, and the Problems of Oppositional Discourse." *Cultural Critique* 22 (Fall 1992): 75–98.

Export, Valie. "The Real and Its Double: The Body." *Discourse* 11.1 (Fall-Winter 1988–89): 3–27.

Forster, Georg. "Noch etwas über die Menschenraßen." *Georg Forsters Werke: Kleine Schriften zu Philosophie und Zeitgeschichte*. Ed. Akademie der Wissenschaften Berlin. Berlin: Akademie-Verlag, 1991. 2nd ed. 130–56.

Foucault, Michel. *The Order of Things*. New York: Vintage Books, 1973.

Gilman, Sander L. "The Hottentot and the Prostitute: Toward an Iconography of Female Sexuality." *Difference and Pathology: Stereotypes of Sexuality, Race, and Madness*. Ithaca: Cornell UP, 1985. 76–108.

Gürth, Jan-Erik. "Black Images in Eighteenth-Century German Literature." Unpublished paper, New York University, 1992.

Harris-Schenz, Beverly. *Black Images in Eighteenth-Century German Literature*. Stuttgart: Akademischer Verlag Hans-Dieter Heinz, 1981.

Hartsock, Nancy. "Rethinking Modernism: Minority vs. Majority Theory." *The Nature and Context of Minority Discourse*. Ed. Abdul R. JanMohamed and David Lloyd. Oxford: Oxford UP, 1990. 17–36.

Hausen, Karin. "Die Polarisierung der 'Geschlechtscharaktere'—Eine Spiegelung der Dissoziation von Erwerbs- und Familienleben." *Sozialgeschichte der*

Familie in der Neuzeit Europas. Ed. Werner Conze. Stuttgart: Klett, 1976. 363–93.

Hegel, Georg Wilhelm Friedrich. *Phänomenologie des Geistes.* Frankfurt a.M.: Suhrkamp, 1986.

Herder, Johann Gottfried von. "Organisation der afrikanischen Völker." *Sämliche Werke.* Volume 27, "Ideen zur Philosophie der Geschichte der Menschheit," part 2, book 6, section IV. Stuttgart: Cotta, 1853. 229–37.

JanMohamed, Abdul R.. "The Economy of Manichean Allegory: The Function of Racial Difference in Colonialist Literature." *Critical Inquiry* 12.1 (Autumn 1985): 59–87.

———. *Manichean Aesthetics: The Politics of Literature in Colonial Africa.* Amherst: U of Massachusetts P, 1983.

Kant, Immanuel. "Bestimmung des Begriffes einer Menschenrace. 1785." *Immanuel Kant's Sämtliche Werke.* Volume 6, "Immanuel Kant's Schriften zur Physischen Geographie." Ed. Friedrich Wilhelm Schubert. Leipzig: Voss, 1839. 333–54.

———. "Ueber die verschiedenen Racen der Menschen." (1775) *Immanuel Kant's sämtliche Werke.* Ed. J.H. von Kirchmann. Berlin: L. Heimann's, 1873. 85–107.

Laqueur, Thomas. *Making Sex: Body and Gender from the Greeks to Freud.* Cambridge: Harvard UP, 1992.

Martin, Biddy. "Feminism, Criticism, and Foucault." *New German Critique* 27 (Fall 1982): 3–30.

Meyer, Jean. *Sklavenhandel.* Ravensburg: Maier, 1990.

Robertson, Claire C., and Martin A. Klein, eds. *Women and Slavery in Africa.* Madison: U of Wisconsin P, 1983.

Rousseau, Jean Jacques. *The Social Contract and Discourses.* Trans. G.D.H. Cole. New York: Dutton, 1950.

Said, Edward. "Orientalizing the Oriental." 1978. *Contemporary Critical Theory.* Ed. Dan Latimer. San Diego: Harcourt, 1989. 254–77.

Schmid, Marion. "Der weiße Fleck auf der Landkarte." *Mythen der Neuen Welt: Zur Entdeckungsgeschichte Lateinamerikas.* Ed. K.-H. Kohl. Berlin: Frölich, 1982. 264–71.

Sömmering, Samuel Thomas. *Über die körperlichen Verschiedenheiten des Negers vom Europäer.* Frankfurt a.M.: Varrentrapp & Wenner, 1785.

Streese, Konstanze. *"Cric?"—"Crac!" Vier literarische Versuche, mit dem Kolonialismus umzugehen.* Bern: Lang, 1991.

Todorov, Tzvetan. *Die Eroberung Amerikas: Das Problem des Anderen.* Trans. Wilfried Böhringer. Frankfurt a.M.: Suhrkamp, 1985.

Weigel, Sigrid. "Die nahe Fremde—das Territorium des 'Weiblichen': Zum Verhältnis von 'Wilden' und 'Frauen' im Diskurs der Aufklärung." *Die andere Welt: Studien zum Exotismus.* Ed. Thomas Koebner and Gerhardt Pickerodt. Frankfurt a.M.: Athenäum, 1987. 171–99.

The Generational Compact: Graduate Students and Germanics

Sara Friedrichsmeyer and Patricia Herminghouse

Perhaps the major component of our professional lives is the preparation of those who will come after us. Hardly a controversial statement. The controversy begins, however, when the discussion becomes more specific: just exactly how is it that we can best fulfill this portion of our role? The ensuing debate takes place not just within departments and universities, but within the professional organizations that support our discipline as well.

It is tempting to say that academic life used to be simpler. When Women in German was founded two decades ago, many of us who now find ourselves with titles and tenure were living our lives as graduate students or junior faculty. In general, we were taught by academics who defined their job—if indeed it were thought to warrant definition—as providing us with a body of knowledge that they in turn had absorbed from teachers before them. In retrospect, that tacit agreement between generations seemed to revolve around the maintenance of continuity. Given everything that has happened at universities within the past few decades, including the much-discussed "graying" of the professoriate and the more recently remarked upon "feminization" of the profession (Nollendorfs), it is not surprising that this pattern too has changed. Responsible professionals today see their roles not just as imparting knowledge. They also find themselves engaged in preparing students to teach language *and* literature *and* film *and* culture, to prepare materials for publication, to manage the stresses of conferences, and, perhaps most importantly, to interview. In short, how to get a job and keep it.

The generational compact of the 1990s then is more complex than its predecessors. And as with most compacts, this one is not being shaped by easy consensus. One of the touchiest issues to emerge recently revolves around graduate student participation at conferences and their submissions to professional journals. Increased student participation, it is argued—and the argument is based on there being a finite number of annual journal articles and conference sessions—limits the opportunities for professorial participation. In addition, so goes this line of reasoning, the prestige value of conferences and journals when graduate students share space with faculty is diminished. Strangely, this discussion, as far as we can tell, is not one preoccupying colleagues in other disciplines. Perhaps there are more major conferences and possibilities for publication in other disciplines, perhaps job openings are especially tight in Germanics, or perhaps the expectations of those doing the hiring in other fields do not include conference presentations and/or publications. Disciplinary differences certainly exist. We, however, are less interested in the reasons for those contrasts than in how we deal with this potentially damaging issue within our own discipline—in our departments, at our conferences, within our organizations, and in our professional journals and yearbooks.

There are those who view the graduate years as best devoted to the kind of acquisition of knowledge that students will presumably need in their own academic careers, which, they point out, will quite naturally include publishing and conference presentations, but all in due time. They have a point, especially when one considers the almost exponential expansion of what today can be included as a topic of study within a German department. Writers are being discovered and rediscovered, the emergence of theory and theoretical debates presents on-going challenges to old paradigms, film studies and culture studies are being added to the curriculum, and bibliographies grow longer every year. The counter to this position comes from those who believe that the best possible training is the "hands-on" kind; according to this logic, graduate students should be learning by doing, ergo, they should be publishing and presenting papers. This too is hard to refute, as long as student participation offers exposure and training and is not understood as a proving grounds.

Both these positions then have obvious merit; they can also be carried by theoretical arguments untainted by the vagaries of Germanics or the mission of the academy in the USA; advocates of both can base their arguments on the shibboleth of "quality education." But their contentions are swept aside by the pragmatists among us. The realities of the job market in Germanics, they insist, is such that without publications and at least some conference activity, a candidate will not be taken seriously when applying for a job.

As most would agree, this predicament is part of a complex of problems extending far beyond the kind of activities engaged in by graduate students. It is a consequence of the current general crisis of the humanities in this country and is intertwined with the alarming fact that while increasing numbers of students who do not find employment after their undergraduate years are studying for graduate degrees, the number of jobs for which they can apply is decreasing (cf. Holub, Huber, Magner, Nelson and Bérubé). Within the past few years, the ante has been raised so that graduate students who do not want their applications to be discarded immediately know the merits—indeed necessity—of having published work and conference presentations listed on their vitae. Even those professors who are dubious about graduate student *participation* at conferences acknowledge the importance of graduate student *attendance*. But most departments have funding contingencies based on participation. Thus if the already exploited graduate student wants financial support, she or he needs to participate. Some national conferences structure graduate sessions into their programs, and within larger departments we have seen recently the creation of graduate student journals and even the founding of entire graduate student conferences to enhance the possibilities for student participation. But whether we view such steps as attempts to ghettoize and marginalize graduate students or as important ways to facilitate networking among them, we need to acknowledge that they do not alleviate the increased pressures under which graduate students are being forced to labor.

Although the stakes are far less dramatic, professors too are working under increasing pressures; that fabled ivory tower has all but disappeared. All but the most obtuse are daily aware of the pressures of the job market and the precariousness of our discipline. And just at the point where women students are becoming the majority in our field, ethical constraints require us not to encourage graduate study and to point out clearly and emphatically to those who come to us the realities of a job market where many of them face a future as underpaid part-time and temporary workers—the segment of our profession where women have long predominated. And the preparation for the job market of those who do persevere is fraught with its own contradictions. It is possible, but extremely difficult, to buck the trend when hiring and consider for our job openings candidates with fewer lines on their vitae. But to minimize the urgency of these activities for our own graduate students would be criminally negligent. This conundrum will not resolve itself quickly or easily. We seem to have created our own academic Catch 22.

So what about Women in German? Do we have a "position"? If so, how does it relate to our discipline and the profession as a whole? In part as a response to the intensity with which the issue has been discussed elsewhere, Women in German has raised and deliberated the matter of graduate student participation in several forums: in its Steering Committee, in the *Yearbook*'s Editorial Board, at our annual conference, and most publicly, in the electronic media—on our Women in German-List.

In Women in German, the development of graduate students into professional peers has been and continues to be an integral, even conscious, component in the structuring and governance of the organization. In over two decades of its existence, in two decades of conferences, and one decade of the yearbook, graduate students have always been a valued constituency. And that for many reasons, including the indispensable role of graduate students at its very inception. It was students and faculty together who, largely because feminist concerns were elsewhere being ignored, recognized a need for the formation of Women in German and worked to make it a reality. Even in the 1990s, those same needs impel many graduate students to join Women in German.

Women in German members have worked hard to make newcomers to the organization feel welcome. But perhaps there is more to it. If graduate students and professors in various stages of their careers feel comfortable together, perhaps it is also because the inclusion of graduate students has never been dealt with hierarchically. There is no sense that the dominant reason for our togetherness is so that "we" can help to train "them," or that "senior" professors should be accorded special attention. On the contrary, there has been a general accord within the membership that faculty of all ranks can learn from graduate students too—that the sharing of information, techniques, and perspectives as well as new ideas and ways of dealing with literature, culture, and language is not dependent on rank or status. The benefits, it is clear to most, can be mutual. Additionally, it is presumptuous in any large organization such as ours to assume that most people attending a conference or perusing a professional journal teach in a graduate department. This will, in fact, be ever less the case. Even having a faculty position can mean vastly disparate things. Contact with graduate students from around the country can be one way for all of us to share the satisfactions of preparing the next generation and staying in touch with cutting-edge trends.

Although there is nowhere an articulated policy, the ramifications are clear: at Women in German conferences, graduate students do present; in the *Yearbook,* they are usually represented. We have heard stories about professors encouraging entire seminar sections to submit their papers to designated journals. Highly questionable professorial advice, to be sure, and fortunately, this has not happened to us. But if we were to be suddenly inundated, we would read the manuscripts as we do all papers sent to us; we would determine whether they merited being sent out to the two anonymous readers our guidelines require and proceed as we would for other submissions. We are aware that, by remaining open to graduate student participation, we too can be seen as helping to create the problem of increased expectations. Nevertheless, some graduate students are ready to present their ideas publicly and, given the present situation, we feel obliged to offer them space to do so. For our part—we are interested in quality and originality. And if the graduate students we are educating are so good that blind evaluations do not detect the origins of their papers, their articles, or their conference proposals, then perhaps we should acknowledge that as a good sign, as something that can reflect positively on us all.

There is, of course, no "solution" to what some view as the "graduate student" problem. But we can hope that a public discussion of the issue forces us to recognize that *we* have created the problem and that only *we* can begin to change the rules under which graduate students function. Doubtless, attempting to deal conscientiously with the predicament will continue to entail enormous amounts of work for job search committees, conference organizers, and—yes—journal editors and the referees upon whom we rely. To fault students or penalize them for a situation that we have all helped to create misses the point. Rather than attempting short cuts such as setting quotas, we should be pressuring our institutions to accord commensurate recognition to those working on these issues, instead of, as we have heard it expressed, evaluating that service about as highly as membership on a parking committee.

As we look back on the recent history of our discipline, it is clear that many of the issues to which we and our various organizations have responded have taken on a different complexion over time. There is every reason to believe that the next decades will bring even more substantial changes. For the moment, the responsibility for our discipline, indeed for our profession, rests with the faculty. As we ponder the issues before us, we would do well to remember that, regardless of our individual positions on the appropriate spectrum for graduate student activities, responsibility for their future belongs to us all. Through our public discussions we can help prepare them to participate in the debates with which they will be confronted in their professional lives. They will have their own issues to resolve; they will surely have their own generational compact with their own graduate students to forge. We must transmit this generational obligation to the graduate students of today. The future of our profession demands it.

Works Cited

Holub, Robert C. "Professional Responsibility: On Graduate Educations and Hiring Practices." *Profession 94.* New York: MLA, 1994. 79–86.

Huber, Bettina J. "The Changing Job Market." *Profession 92.* New York: MLA, 1992. 59–73.

———. "The MLA's 1991–92 Survey on PhD Placement: The Latest Foreign Language Findings and Trends through Time." *ADFL* Bulletin 26.1 (1994): 34–48.

Magner, Denise K. "Job-Market Blues." *Chronicle of Higher Education* 27 April 1994: A17–A20.

Nelson, Cary, and Michael Bérubé. "Graduate Education is Losing its Moral Base." *Chronicle of Higher Education* 23 March 1994: B1–B3.

Nollendorfs, Valters. "Out of Germanistik: Thoughts on the Shape of Things to Come." *Die Unterrichtspraxis* 27.1 (Spring 1994): 1–10.

ABOUT THE AUTHORS

Barbara Becker-Cantarino, Research Professor at Ohio State University, has also taught at Indiana University, at the University of Texas (Austin), and as a visiting professor at the Free University of Berlin. Her teaching and research interests center on German literature of the seventeenth and eighteenth centuries, literary theory, and contemporary Germany, especially as pertaining to women. Her publications include editions of Sophie LaRoche and A.O. Hoyers, an edited volume *Frauen Freundschaft—Männer Freundschaft: Literarische Diskurse im achtzehnten Jahrhundert* (1991), and the books *Die Frau von der Reformation zur Romantik* (3d ed., 1987) and *Der lange Weg zur Mündigkeit: Frau und Literatur 1500-1800* (1987 and 1989). She is currently completing a study titled "Friendship, Love, and Patriarchy: Gender and German Romanticism."

Jutta Brückner is a filmmaker and professor for film and video at the Hochschule der Künste in Berlin. She studied political science and wrote her dissertation on German statesmanship in the eighteenth century. Subsequently she did radio plays and wrote essays and filmscripts for directors such as Volker Schlöndorff. As an author of screenplays, director, and producer she has made eight films of her own, including *Years of Hunger* (*Hungerjahre*), *One Look and It's Love* (*Ein Blick und die Liebe bricht aus*), and *Colossal Love* (*Kolossale Liebe*). She is currently preparing a documentary film essay on Bertolt Brecht, a feature film about Brecht and the women in his life, and a documentary film essay on Ingeborg Bachmann.

Lewis Call is a PhD candidate in History at the University of California, Irvine. In his dissertation, "Friedrich Nietzsche as Critic and Captive of Enlightenment," he explores Nietzsche's often virulent critique of the Enlightenment tradition, focusing on Nietzsche's attacks on Descartes, Rousseau, and Kant. He also examines the ways in which Nietzsche critiques such scions of nineteenth-century enlightened thought as John Stuart Mill, Charles Darwin, and Herbert Spencer. He concludes with a look at how, despite all efforts to escape the influence of Enlightenment, Nietzsche retains important elements of Enlightenment thought, notably the utopianism exemplified by his *Übermensch*.

Friederike Eigler received her PhD from Washington University in St. Louis and is Associate Professor of German at Georgetown University. She is the author of a monograph on Elias Canetti (1987) and coeditor of *Cultural Transformation in the New Germany: American and German Perspectives* (1993). She has published articles on nineteenth- and twentieth-century women authors including Lou Andreas-Salomé, Ingeborg Bachmann, Sarah Kirsch, and Elke Erb. Currently, she is working on *The Feminist Encyclopedia of German Literature* (forthcoming 1996), which she is coediting with Susanne Kord.

Sara Friedrichsmeyer is Professor of German and Acting Head of the Department of Germanic Languages and Literatures at the University of Cincinnati. Her publications include *The Androgyne in Early German Romanticism* (1983) and the coedited volume *The Enlightenment and Its Legacy* (1991). She has published articles on German Romanticism, feminist theory, and various nineteenth- and twentieth-century German women, among them Caroline Schlegel-Schelling, Annette von Droste-Hülshoff, Paula Modersohn-Becker, Käthe Kollwitz, and Christa Wolf. She is working on the representation of "Gypsies" in German literature and coediting a volume titled *The Imperialist Imagination*. She has been coeditor of the *Women in German Yearbook* since 1990.

Alyth F. Grant is Senior Lecturer in German at the University of Otago, Dunedin, New Zealand, where she teaches courses in language and literature, specializing in German women's writing. She has published articles on Helga Schubert, Christa Wolf, Louise Aston, and Christoph Meckel, and is at present working on the reception by women writers of the *Jahrhundertwende* of the ideology of femininity current at that time.

Patricia Herminghouse is Karl F. and Bertha A. Fuchs Professor of German Studies at the University of Rochester. Her research has focused on nineteenth- and twentieth-century literature, particularly on the literature of the GDR and the social contexts of women's writing. Editor of the textbook anthology, *Frauen im Mittelpunkt* (1987), she was also coeditor of *Literatur und Literaturtheorie in der DDR* (1976) and *DDR-Literatur der 70er Jahre* (1983). In addition to on-going work on a book with the tentative title *History, Literature and the Political Agenda in the GDR*, she is currently finishing a volume of short prose works by Ingeborg Bachmann and Christa Wolf for the German Library series. She became coeditor of the *Women in German Yearbook* in 1994.

Lynda J. King (PhD, University of Southern California) is Associate Professor of German at Oregon State University, where she teaches language, literature, and culture courses. She has published in the fields of German and Austrian literature and culture between the world wars, popular culture, and international education. She has also worked in university administration and headed the Oregon/Baden-Württemberg exchange program 1990-92.

Imke Lode is a PhD candidate in German Studies at New York University, where she also received an MA in Cinema Studies. She has taught at New York University and Columbia University and is currently completing her dissertation on the motifs of the eyes/vision and insanity in two case studies centered on E.T.A. Hoffmann and Fritz Lang. Previous articles have included studies on Selma Meerbaum-Eisinger and Rainer Werner Fassbinder's *The Third Generation*. She co-edited *Proceedings and Commentary: German Graduate Students Association Conference at New York University* (1994) with Patricia Doykos Duquette and Matthew Griffin.

Margaret McCarthy completed her PhD at the University of Rochester and is presently an assistant professor of German at Davidson College in North Carolina. Her dissertation, "Bodies, Beautiful Souls, and *Bildung*: Reconstituting the First-Person Singular 'I,'" reassesses the concept of *Bildung* primarily in autobiographical texts written by German women during the 1980s. Her research interests include German film, feminist and literary theory, and post-World War II German literature by women. She has received both Fulbright and DAAD research grants. Currently she is working on a publication on Ingeborg Bachmann's *Malina*.

Renate Möhrmann, Member of Parliament in North-Rhine/Westphalia, 1990-95, is Professor of Theater and Film Studies at the University of Cologne and, since 1989, visiting professor at the University of Vienna. She has also held visiting professorships at the Centro Universitario de Estudios Cinematographicas in Mexico City, the University of Bari (Italy), University of Texas-Austin, University of Cincinnati, University of Toronto, and University of California at Davis. Holder of the Canada-Germany Research Award in 1994, she is on the supervisory Board of German Public Television and the Film Foundation of North-Rhine/Westphalia. Author and editor of nine books on topics ranging from women in pre-1848 Germany to a cultural history of female performers, Möhrmann is particularly well known for *Die Frau mit der Kamera: Filmemacherinnen in der Bundesrepublik Deutschland* (1980) and *Frauen—Literatur—Geschichte: Schreibende Frauen vom Mittelalter bis zur Gegenwart* (edited with Hiltrud Gnüg, 1988).

Janice Mouton is Associate Professor in the Department of Modern Languages and Literatures at Loyola University Chicago. Her main fields of interest are twentieth-century literature and culture, women's studies, and film studies. Her publications include essays on Bernardo Bertolucci, R.W. Fassbinder, Günter Grass, Werner Herzog, and Jeanine Meerapfel. She is currently at work on a book about literary and cinematic texts of the city.

Katharina von Ankum has published on GDR women writers as well as social issues affecting women in East Germany. More recently, she has explored the specifically female experiences of modernity. She is the editor of a forthcoming collection of essays entitled *Women in the Metropolis: Gendered Urban Discourses of Modernity*. Her current project is a book length study on gender and modernist utopias. She is presently a Charles Phelps Taft fellow at the University of Cincinnati.

Dagmar von Hoff teaches at the University of Hamburg, Germany. She is also responsible for its feminist research center, the "Arbeitsstelle fur Feministische Literaturwissenschaft," and is co-editor of *Frauen in der Literaturwissenschaft*. She is the author of *Dramen des Weiblichen: Deutsche Dramatikerinnen um 1800* (1989) and has published articles on Elfriede Jelinek, Marguerite Duras, Aby Warburg, and J.M.R. Lenz, as well as on film and theater.

Jenifer K. Ward is Assistant Professor of German at Gustavus Adolphus College in St. Peter, Minnesota. Her 1992 Vanderbilt University dissertation dealt with the films of Margarethe von Trotta. Most recently, she has worked on the film adaptation of Jurek Becker's *Bronsteins Kinder*, and she is currently working on a larger collaborative project on gender, authority, and the construction of national culture in postwar German cinema.

NOTICE TO CONTRIBUTORS

The *Women in German Yearbook* is a refereed journal. Its publication is supported by the Coalition of Women in German.

Contributions to the *Women in German Yearbook* are welcome at any time. The editors are interested in feminist approaches to all aspects of German literary, cultural, and language studies, including teaching.

Prepare manuscripts for anonymous review. The editors prefer that manuscripts not exceed 25 pages (typed, double-spaced), including notes. Follow the fourth edition (1995) of the *MLA Handbook* (separate notes from works cited). Send one copy of the manuscript to each coeditor:

Sara Friedrichsmeyer ***and*** Patricia Herminghouse
Department of Germanic Department of Modern
Languages and Literatures Languages and Culture
University of Cincinnati University of Rochester
Cincinnati, OH 45221 Rochester, NY 14627
Phone: 513-556-2751 Phone: 716-275-4252
Fax: 513-556-1991 Fax: 716-273-1097
E-mail: sara.friedrichsmeyer@uc.edu E-mail: pahe@troi.cc.rochester.edu

For membership/subscription information, contact Jeanette Clausen (Department of Modern Foreign Languages, Indiana University–Purdue University, Fort Wayne, IN 46805).

CONTENTS OF PREVIOUS VOLUMES

Volume 10

Richard W. McCormick, Private Anxieties/Public Projections: "New Objectivity," Male Subjectivity, and Weimar Cinema; **Elizabeth Mittman,** Locating a Public Sphere: Some Reflections on Writers and *Öffentlichkeit* in the GDR; **Ruth-Ellen B. Joeres,** "We are adjacent to human society": German Women Writers, the Homosocial Experience, and a Challenge to the Public/Domestic Dichotomy; **Marjorie Gelus,** Patriarchy's Fragile Boundaries under Siege: Three Stories of Heinrich von Kleist; **Gail K. Hart,** *Anmut*'s Gender: The "Marionettentheater" and Kleist's Revision of "Anmut und Würde"; **Brigid Haines,** Masochism and Femininity in Lou Andreas-Salomé's *Eine Ausschweifung*; **Silke von der Emde,** Irmtraud Morgner's Postmodern Feminism: A Question of Politics; **Susan C. Anderson,** Creativity and Nonconformity in Monika Maron's *Die Überläuferin*; **Ruth Klüger,** Dankrede zum Grimmelshausen-Preis; **Karen Remmler,** Gender Identities and the Remembrance of the Holocaust; **Suzanne Shipley,** From the Prater to Central Park: Finding a Self in Exile; **Sigrid Lange,** Dokument und Fiktion: Marie-Thérèse Kerschbaumers *Der weibliche Name des Widerstands*; **Miriam Frank,** Lesbian Life and Literature: A Survey of Recent German-Language Publications; **Luise F. Pusch,** Ein Streit um Worte? Eine Lesbe macht Skandal im Deutschen Bundestag; **Jeanette Clausen and Sara Friedrichsmeyer,** WIG 2000: Feminism and the Future of *Germanistik*.

Volume 9

Ann Taylor Allen, Women's Studies as Cultural Movement and Academic Discipline in the United States and West Germany: The Early Phase, 1966-1982; **Susan Signe Morrison,** Women Writers and Women Rulers: Rhetorical and Political Empowerment in the Fifteenth Century; **Christl Griesshaber-Weninger,** Harsdörffers *Frauenzimmer Gesprächspiele* als geschlechtsspecifische Verhaltensfibel: Ein Vergleich mit heutigen Kommunikationsstrukturen; **Gertrud Bauer Pickar,** The Battering and Meta-Battering of Droste's Margreth: Covert Misogyny in *Die Judenbuche*'s Critical Reception; **Kirsten Belgum,** Domesticating the Reader: Women and *Die Gartenlaube*; **Katrin Sieg,** Equality Decreed: Dramatizing Gender in East Germany; **Katharina von Ankum,** Political Bodies: Women and Re/Production in the GDR; **Friederike Eigler,** At the Margins of East Berlin's "Counter-Culture": Elke Erb's *Winkelzüge* and Gabriele Kachold's *zügel los*; **Karin Eysel**; Christa Wolf's *Kassandra*: Refashioning National Imagination Beyond the Nation; **Petra**

Waschescio, Auseinandersetzung mit dem Abendlanddenken: Gisela von Wysockis *Abendlandleben*; **Dagmar C.G. Lorenz,** Memory and Criticism: Ruth Klüger's *weiter leben*; **Sara Lennox,** Antiracist Feminism in Germany: Introduction to Dagmar Schultz and Ika Hügel; **Ika Hügel,** Wir kämpfen seit es uns gibt; **Dagmar Schultz,** Racism in the New Germany and the Reaction of White Women; **Sara Friedrichsmeyer and Jeanette Clausen,** What's Missing in New Historicism or the "Poetics" of Feminist Literary Criticism.

Volume 8

Marjorie Gelus, Birth as Metaphor in Kleist's *Das Erdbeben in Chili*: A Comparison of Critical Methodologies; **Vanessa Van Ornam,** No Time for Mothers: Courasche's Infertility as Grimmelshausen's Criticism of War; **M.R. Sperberg-McQueen,** Whose Body Is It? Chaste Strategies and the Reinforcement of Patriarchy in Three Plays by Hrotswitha von Gandersheim; **Sara Lennox,** The Feminist Reception of Ingeborg Bachmann; **Maria-Regina Kecht,** Auflehnung gegen die Ordnung von Sprache und Vernunft: Die weibliche Wirklichkeitsgestaltung bei Waltraud Anna Mitgutsch; **Maria-Regina Kecht,** Gespräch mit Waltraud Anna Mitgutsch; **Susanne Kord,** "Und drinnen waltet die züchtige Hausfrau"? Carolina Pichler's Fictional Auto/Biographies; **Susan L. Cocalis,** "Around 1800": Reassessing the Role of German Women Writers in Literary Production of the Late Eighteenth and Early Nineteenth Centuries (Review Essay); **Konstanze Streese und Kerry Shea,** Who's Looking? Who's Laughing? Of Multicultural Mothers and Men in Percy Adlon's *Bagdad Cafe*; **Deborah Lefkowitz,** Editing from Life; **Walfriede Schmitt,** Mund-Artiges... (Gedicht); **Barbara Becker-Cantarino,** Feministische Germanistik in Deutschland: Rückblick und sechs Thesen; **Gisela Brinker-Gabler,** Alterity—Marginality—Difference: On Inventing Places for Women; **Ruth-Ellen B. Joeres,** "Language is Also a Place of Struggle": The Language of Feminism and the Language of American *Germanistik*.

Volume 7

Myra Love, "A Little Susceptible to the Supernatural?": On Christa Wolf; **Monika Shafi,** Die überforderte Generation: Mutterfiguren in Romanen von Ingeborg Drewitz; **Ute Brandes,** Baroque Women Writers and the Public Sphere; **Katherine R. Goodman,** "The Butterfly and the Kiss": A Letter from Bettina von Arnim; **Ricarda Schmidt,** Theoretische Orientierungen in feministischer Literaturwissenschaft und Sozialphilosophie (Review Essay); **Sara Lennox,** Some Proposals for Feminist Literary Criticism; **Helga Königsdorf,** Ein Pferd ohne Beine (Essay); **Angela Krauß,** Wieder in Leipzig (Erzählung); **Waldtraut Lewin,** Lange Fluchten (Erzählung); **Eva Kaufmann,** DDR-Schriftstellerinnen, die Widersprüche und die Utopie; **Irene Dölling,** Alte und neue Dilemmata: Frauen in der ehemaligen DDR; **Dinah Dodds,** "Die Mauer stand bei mir im Garten": Interview mit Helga Schütz; **Gisela E. Bahr,** Dabeigewesen: Tagebuchnotizen vom Winter 1989/90; **Dorothy J. Rosenberg,** Learning to Say "I" instead of "We": Recent Works on Women in the Former

GDR (Review Essay); **Sara Friedrichsmeyer and Jeanette Clausen,** What's Feminism Got to Do with It? A Postscript from the Editors.

Volume 6

Dagmar C.G. Lorenz, "Hoffentlich werde ich taugen." Zu Situation und Kontext von Brigitte Schwaiger/Eva Deutsch *Die Galizianerin*; **Sabine Wilke,** "Rückhaltlose Subjektivität." Subjektwerdung, Gesellschafts- und Geschlechtsbewußtsein bei Christa Wolf; **Elaine Martin,** Patriarchy, Memory, and the Third Reich in the Autobiographical Novels of Eva Zeller; **Tineke Ritmeester,** Heterosexism, Misogyny, and Mother-Hatred in Rilke Scholarship: The Case of Sophie Rilke-Entz (1851–1931); **Richard W. McCormick,** Productive Tensions: Teaching Films by German Women and Feminist Film Theory; **Hildegard M. Nickel,** Women in the GDR: Will Renewal Pass Them By?; **Helen Cafferty and Jeanette Clausen,** Feministik *Germanistik* after Unification: A Postscript from the Editors.

Volume 5

Angelika Bammer, Nackte Kaiser und bärtige Frauen: Überlegungen zu Macht, Autorität, und akademischem Diskurs; **Sabine Hake,** Focusing the Gaze: The Critical Project of *Frauen und Film*; **Dorothy Rosenberg,** Rethinking Progress: Women Writers and the Environmental Dialogue in the GDR; **Susanne Kord,** Fading Out: Invisible Women in Marieluise Fleißer's Early Dramas; **Lorely French,** "Meine beiden Ichs": Confrontations with Language and Self in Letters by Early Nineteenth-Century Women; **Sarah Westphal-Wihl,** Pronoun Semantics and the Representation of Power in the Middle High German *Märe* "Die halbe Decke"; **Susanne Zantop and Jeannine Blackwell,** Select Bibliography on German Social History and Women Writers; **Helen Cafferty and Jeanette Clausen,** Who's Afraid of Feminist Theory? A Postscript from the Editors.

Volume 4

Luise F. Pusch, Totale Feminisierung: Überlegungen zum unfassenden Femininum; **Luise F. Pusch,** Die Kätzin, die Rättin, und die Feminismaus; **Luise F. Pusch,** Carl Maria, die Männe; **Luise F. Pusch,** Sind Herren herrlich und Damen dämlich?; **Ricarda Schmidt,** E.T.A. Hoffman's "Der Sandmann": An Early Example of *Écriture Féminine*? A Critique of Trends in Feminist Literary Criticism; **Renate Fischetti,** *Écriture Féminine* in the New German Cinema: Ulrike Ottinger's *Portrait of a Woman Drinker*; **Jan Mouton,** The Absent Mother Makes an Appearance in the Films of West German Women Directors; **Charlotte Armster,** Katharina Blum: Violence and the Exploitation of Sexuality; **Renny Harrigan,** Novellistic Representation of *die Berufstätige* during the Weimar Republic; **Lynda J. King,** From the Crown to the Hammer and Sickle: The Life and Works of Austrian Interwar Writer Hermynia zur Mühlen; **Linda Kraus Worley,** The "Odd" Woman as Heroine in the Fiction of Louise von François; **Helga Madland,** Three Late Eighteenth-Century Women's Journals:

Their Role in Shaping Women's Lives; **Sigrid Brauner,** Hexenjagd in Gelehrtenköpfen; **Susan Wendt-Hildebrandt,** Gespräch mit Herrad Schenk; **Dorothy Rosenberg,** GDR Women Writers: The Post-War Generation. An Updated Bibliography of Narrative Prose, June 1987.

Volume 3

Ritta Jo Horsley and Richard A. Horsley, On the Trail of the "Witches": Wise Women, Midwives and the European Witch Hunts; **Barbara Mabee,** Die Kindesmörderin in den Fesseln der bürgerlichen Moral: Wagners Evchen und Goethes Gretchen; **Judith P. Aikin,** Who Learns a Lesson? The Function of Sex Role Reversal in Lessing's *Minna von Barnhelm*; **Sara Friedrichsmeyer,** The Subversive Androgyne; **Shawn C. Jarvis,** Spare the Rod and Spoil the Child? Bettine's *Das Leben der Hochgräfin Gritta von Rattenzuhausbeiuns*; **Edith Waldstein,** Romantic Revolution and Female Collectivity: Bettine and Gisela von Arnim's *Gritta*; **Ruth-Ellen Boetcher Joeres,** "Ein Nebel schließt uns ein." Social Comment in the Novels of German Women Writers, 1850–1870; **Thomas C. Fox,** Louise von François: A Feminist Reintroduction; **Gesine Worm,** Das erste Jahr: Women in German im Goethe Haus New York.

Volume 2

Barbara Frischmuth, Am hellen Tag: Erzählung; **Barbara Frischmuth,** Eine Souveräne Posaune Gottes: Gedanken zu Hildegard von Bingen und ihrem Werk; **Dagmar C.G. Lorenz,** Ein Interview: Barbara Frischmuth; **Dagmar C.G. Lorenz,** Creativity and Imagination in the Work of Barbara Frischmuth; **Margaret E. Ward,** *Ehe* and *Entsagung*: Fanny Lewald's Early Novels and Goethe's Literary Paternity; **Regula Venske,** "Männlich im Sinne des Butt" or "Am Ende angekommen?": Images of Men in Contemporary German-Language Literature by Women; **Angelika Bammer,** Testing the Limits: Christa Reinig's Radical Vision; **H-B. Moeller,** The Films of Margarethe von Trotta: Domination, Violence, Solidarity, and Social Criticism.

Volume 1

Jeanette Clausen, The Coalition of Women in German: An Interpretive History and Celebration; **Sigrid Weigel,** Das Schreiben des Mangels als Produktion von Utopie; **Jeannine Blackwell,** Anonym, verschollen, trivial: Methodological Hindrances in Researching German Women's Literature; **Martha Wallach,** Ideal and Idealized Victims: The Lost Honor of the Marquise von O., Effi Briest and Katharina Blum in Prose and Film; **Anna Kuhn,** Margarethe von Trotta's *Sisters*: Interiority or Engagement?; **Barbara D. Wright,** The Feminist Transformation of Foreign Language Teaching; **Jeanette Clausen,** Broken but not Silent: Language as Experience in Vera Kamenko's *Unter uns war Krieg*; **Richard L. Johnson,** The New West German Peace Movement: Male Dominance or Feminist Nonviolence.